MONTECITO BOY

With best wishes to Ric Parker

Montecito Boy

from Kendel's Father,

An Irreverent Memoir
1923–1940

Nevill Cramer

NEVILL CRAMER

FITHIAN PRESS, SANTA BARBARA, 1997

Published by Fithian Press
A division of Daniel and Daniel, Publishers, Inc.
Post Office Box 1525
Santa Barbara, CA 93102

Cover design by David Bazemore
Constantia photo by Wayne McCall
Book design by Eric Larson

LIBRARY OF CONGRESS CATALOGING-IN-PUBLICATION DATA
Cramer, Nevill, 1922–
    Montecito boy : an irreverent memoir, 1923–1940 / by Nevill Cramer.
      p.   cm.
    ISBN 1-56474-208-3 (pbk : alk. paper)
    1. Cramer, Nevill, 1922–   —Childhood and youth. 2. Montecito (Calif.)—
  Biography. 3. Chicago (Ill.)—Biography. I. Title.
CT275.C8655A3   1997
979.4'91—dc21   96-45025
[B]   CIP

To my daughter,
Kendal Bazemore,
with love

A chiel's amang you takin' notes,
And faith, he'll print it.
                —ROBERT BURNS

I must speak freely of people behind their backs. It
is better than Godwin's way of telling a man he is a
fool to his face.
                —CHARLES LAMB

Every man knows something worse of himself than
he is sure of in others.
                —SAMUEL JOHNSON

You must laugh before you are happy for fear of
dying without having laughed.
                —LA BRUYERE

Contents

Introduction

There are very few things—besides dying—that should be put off until one is old. One of these is the writing of memoirs of one's early years because by then most of the people a person wants to write about are dead, and that is a very good thing from the memoirist's point of view.

I am neither a historian nor a sociologist, so you mustn't expect a history or a treatise; and I lack the patience to do research. In any case, research would be at odds with my purpose in writing this book. I sat down a couple of years ago before a clean computer screen to confront my memories of the far-off past in the marvelous community where I grew up and still live today. It was a simple matter to bring them to the surface of my mind; the problem was, as it is in all writing, what to leave out. This is not a short book, but it could have been a much longer one, because I like to think I have forgotten nothing and no one from my childhood and youth. (Events and facts referred to that were outside my own experience were told me over the years by loose-lipped elders of the tribe.)

Montecito Boy is no confessional, though I have portrayed aspects of my youthful character that I am not proud of (but am on the whole amused by). I have left out the agonies of adolescence. Everyone undergoes them to a degree, but who today has the stomach for reading about one more "sensitive" boy's struggles to find himself in "a world he never made"? It was my intent to write a lighthearted, entertaining story that would be both an account of a privileged childhood in one of the most delightful places on earth and at the same time a series of vignettes of my family members and others who were too special to be forgotten.

While aware, as who is not, of the fundamentally tragic nature of our finite lives, I have never needed to watch or read comedies by way of compensation because I have been hugely entertained by the human comedy acted out in real life before my eyes. I think my greatest source of amusement has been the observation of people's follies and foibles (my own included). For better or for worse, these follies and foibles have been meat and drink to me all my life, and as this book will make clear, my capacity for amusement at others' expense started at an early age. Many memoirs, especially those by one-book authors, tend to err on the sentimental, Pollyanna side. Not this one. The word "irreverent" in the subtitle belongs there. Some may think the word "indiscreet" does, too.

Thomas Hardy, in a characteristically gnarled poem called "The To-Be Forgotten," bemoans each person's fate in having to die "a second death" when the last person who remembered him or her alive has died in turn. For the many people whom I loved (and even those I didn't) in my early days and who are gone now, perhaps by writing this account I have put off for a little their final disappearance.

This book has been read aloud, chapter by chapter as each was completed, to a group of a dozen or so good friends, book lovers all. (It was their idea, not mine!) Their enthusiastic reactions have encouraged me to think that a wider public than my family and close friends might enjoy it, too.... I would like to express my gratitude to Professor Donald Pearce and his wife, Dorothy, for their extraordinary interest and encouragement from beginning to end.

NEVILL CRAMER
JULY 1995
MONTECITO, SANTA BARBARA, CALIFORNIA

P.S. Now that I think back on it, some of my audience became occasionally confused about the Meeker family's relationships and suggested I provide a family tree. Instead, I hope the following will clarify matters.

My maternal grandparents, Arthur (1866–1945) and Grace Murray Meeker (1867–1947), figure prominently in this memoir.

They had four children: Katharine Meeker Gray, 1894–1985; Grace Meeker (Cramer) Lloyd, 1895–1983; Arthur Meeker, Jr., 1902–1971; and Mary Meeker Cramer, 1904–1996. All of the above were born in Chicago.

In the next generation, Katharine Gray had three children, Horace, Arthur, and Joan Gray; Joan died in 1990, and Horace in 1996. Grace Lloyd was mother to Ambrose and Nevill Cramer and Nancy Lloyd Kittle; all her children survive. Arthur Meeker, Jr., and Mary Cramer died without issue.

MONTECITO BOY

BOOK I

The Years

🦋 How It All Began

THE REASON I GREW UP IN MONTECITO is that my father injudiciously fell in love with Mary Meeker, my mother's fifteen-year-old sister, while the latter was visiting the young married couple and their little son Brosie in Paris. (Poor Father; I never knew anyone who had more regard for the proprieties or the esteem of his fellows, who yet contrived throughout his seventy-nine years to flout the one and jeopardize the other.)

I neither know, nor would care to reveal if I did, the exact sequence of events. I have the impression that I was born as the result of a misguided effort on the part of Grace, my mother, to hold her man, Ambrose Coghill Cramer. Has this ruse ever worked? It did not work for Mother. On September 6, 1922, I was born at the American Hospital in Neuilly-sur-Seine, a suburb of Paris, where Father was studying architecture at the Ecole des Beaux-Arts. Father was repelled by babies, so how could he possibly be drawn to this one, born for him at the very worst of times? He delayed as long as he legally could in facing up to naming it, and then at the very last minute came up with Josselin, the name of a chateau he admired. The name was duly recorded, to Mother's dismay, but soon replaced (whether legally or not I don't know) by Nevill, after Nevill Coghill, an Anglo-Irish cousin who later became a celebrated English professor and scholar at Oxford; as a middle name I was given Murray, my maternal grandmother's maiden name. At the age of eighteen, when I was going through a period of virulent Anglophilia, I decided two middle names were the thing to have, and popped in Joscelyn, a name I had found growing on the family tree, a fortuitous and elegant reminder of my original naming. I thought, and still think, Nevill Murray Joscelyn Cramer has a portentous sound to it, the name of someone I'd like to know, or even be.

Nine months after I was born, Mother gave up trying to hold on to her husband, and fled for the States on the steamer *Paris* with her two sons, one five and the other less than a year, besides a governess and a nurse. We all spent the summer in Nahant on Boston's North Shore, where her sister Katharine with her three children was summering, having married a Proper Bostonian, Horace Gray, M.D. But the cheerless simplicities of life in a summer colony of "cold roast" Bostonians were no solace to a Midwestern plutocrat's daughter who had just lost her husband. Where to go? What sort of new life to make for herself and her boys? Chicago, where her own family and her husband's had been entrenched for as many generations as there had been a Chicago, was out of the question. Far too many wagging tongues. There would be scandal, and she certainly didn't want to be an object of pity. It was time to make a new life in a new place. But where?

I'm sure she hardly hesitated. Her mind whirled back to a place she associated with some of her happiest childhood memories. Santa Barbara, way out in California, had long been popular with rich Chicagoans as an escape from the numbing severity of Midwestern winters. In the early years of the century, Katharine and Grace had been sent away with governesses to ride out a siege of influenza under palm trees and blue skies. After the first interlude, the girls saw to it that every winter produced its own threatening flu and bronchitis or whatever, no matter how much it might to others resemble an ordinary cold. For several years, after the excitement of Christmas, the two girls could be found with their governess in a Pullman drawing room, chugging and puffing towards Montecito with the same unerring regularity and sense of direction as the swallows homing in on San Juan Capistrano.

They stayed in Montecito Park, a group of "California bungalows" clustered under the palms where now the Biltmore Hotel sits so gracefully and elegantly. As far as I know, there was no true hotel yet in Montecito. The Miramar, I believe, was still a seaside farm belonging to the Doulton family of English "Royal Doulton" fame. (The Miramar Hotel will figure soon enough in my tale.) I don't know what the girls did with themselves exactly, but it was delightful enough for Santa Barbara to remain a lodestar by which all other places were judged throughout their long, long lives. One supposes from historical accounts of how winter tourists amused themselves in the early 1900s that there were picnics and beach walks and horses to ride. Horses (and other farm animals) they had learned a good deal about because their father, Arthur Meeker, in addition to his grand establishment in Chicago, had built and developed a handsome country seat in Lake Forest called Arcady Farms, which he ran as a model farm. As a result, Mother grew up loving all aspects of farm and ranch life except the murder of animals and for many years had her own small horse farm on Refugio Road in the Santa Ynez Valley. (Her horses lived in clover and expired gently in the veterinarian's arms.) Her sister Katharine's equal exposure to elegant rusticity had a precisely opposite effect, for she indulged herself in an unshakable, lifelong detestation of all quadrupeds, including "man's best friend."

So at the close of that interminable summer on the charmless shore in Nahant, Mother, aged twenty-eight, and her entourage headed west to start a new life in the dreamland of her childhood, full of urgent hope that it would delight her now, responsible mistress of a household and mother of two, as it had in those so different days of *dolce far niente* twenty years before.

And delight her it did, right from the start, up to her death at eighty-eight in 1983, sixty years down the road. It turned out to have everything she valued: physical beauty, climate, attractive and hospitable people of her own kind, endless chances for gardening and riding, and even a broad range of charities that could, and soon did, give a sense of purpose to her life beyond the satisfactions of motherhood or mere socializing.

The Miramar Hotel was our first address. I wonder if someone stood by the tracks in September of 1923 and waved the red flag that I remember so well to stop the train at the tiny little Miramar station (reconstructed today), or perhaps Mother pulled a cord within the train to bring it to a screeching stop. Soon we moved in to a series of rented houses in Montecito of which I remember only one, an English cottage on lower Santa Rosa Lane that should by rights have had a thatched roof; the artist Douglas Parshall later lived in it for many years. The memory that brings that house to mind is of losing a beloved canary that flew off into the woods across the street, where we pursued it fruitlessly. Mother always referred to them as the Knott woods, probably for good reason. She knew the name of every geographical or topographical entity, no matter how small, within her extensive sphere that covered a great deal of California and western Nevada. (When she "found" two peaks in the Sierra Nevada that were unnamed on whatever map she was consulting, she promptly christened them, and frequently referred to them as, Mt. Grace and Mt. Emmy, the latter in honor of her beloved German maid, friend, and fellow mountain-lover, Emma Krick.) Today those woods are preserved as a part of the handsome development called Ennisbrook. On the day in question, they provided a natural escape for our bird, similar to another escape that Chicago provided a good many years later for a pet canary of my grandparents, while they were boarding a train for California. This later event, unlike our humble Montecito one, made the *New Yorker* because of a classified ad that the Meekers had foolishly placed in the *Tribune* for the vanished darling: "Lost, in La Salle St. Station, tame canary; answers to name of Pipi Balbo." What do you suppose his little answer would have been, even supposing someone had had the nerve to shout such a name into those incredibly lofty rafters? Balbo, by the way, was the name of a then-celebrated Fascist air marshal who had been put up in their Chicago apartment by the Meekers after a highly publicized mass flight by the Italian air force across the Atlantic. The marshal turned out to be very presentable, and the Meekers had wined and dined him mightily before bestowing his name upon the bird.

I have already played fast and loose with my narrative, so I don't think any harm will be done if I relate a third and final canary story, this one too from Chicago. One of Grandfather's canaries that he was especially fond of was allowed to hop freely about the informal sitting room where he and Grandmother were apt to sit of an evening in their old age; alas, the little bird invariably profited from his freedom by relieving himself copiously, especially on lampshades, but Grandfather would disparage any criticism by saying, "Nonsense, it's just a little bit of wax." One day the bird disappeared. The servants scoured the large flat, peering under tables and chairs. Grandfather clucked and crooned from his big leather chair. At last he rose to leave the room, heaving his massive bulk from the chair. And now, lo, the mystery was revealed; there was the little favorite, in very low relief, plastered to the seat of his master's trousers.... One last association with the Knott woods. I remember that dirty-minded ten-year-old classmates of mine from the nearby Crane School used to patrol the woods looking not for lost birdies, but for condoms, which they referred to generically as "merry widows" and found there in bountiful supply. (I much prefer the joyful cry of discovery of Piero Fenci, my young stepson aged four or so, as he looked down into the turbid water from the planks of Fisherman's Wharf in Monterey: "Oh, look at the little elf's cap!")

THE MIRAMAR is the focal point of my earliest Montecito memories, and I look back on it lovingly. We stayed in it more than once, probably between rentals, and, what is even more important, it was a playground, a destination for strolls with my French nurse, Maminette, or, later, my American governess, Miss Davis. It was not the brightly painted Miramar of today with its dazzling blue roofs intended to catch the eye of weekenders from Los Angeles. The main building, a two-storeyed Victorian near the railroad tracks, and all the cozy cottages scattered around the spacious grounds, were of brown shingles. The effect was mellow. Grass, with winding paths bordered by shrubs and gay, multi-hued flowers, provided a background that wouldn't have been out of place in a Victorian children's story book. Each cottage bore its name on a sign attached to the building. It pleases me to see that many of these signs are still in place today. (One cottage, though far and away the smallest, yet had its own front porch right under a sign proclaiming it to be "Doll" cottage; its regular occupant, the doll herself who must have rented it by the year, was an enormous woman, whose huge, sausage-like arms overspread the supporting arms of the wicker chair she lolled in as she endlessly fanned herself.)

A Miramar resident we regularly met was "the peppermint man," as we called him. White-locked, with a neatly trimmed matching beard, he never passed us by without offering me a peppermint or two. I see him now, smiling and courtly, with a Norfolk jacket and plus-fours, a 1920s holdover from the turn of the century. Inspired by him, I daresay, Mother taught us the famous "beaver game," which we played regularly on our jaunts to town. It was scored like tennis. One bearded man was the basic beaver, worth 15 points. A bald bearded man was a beaver egg, good for 30 points, which I believe was also the score for a royal beaver, i.e., a red beard. The ultimate, which ended the game for the day, was a royal beaver egg. As you can imagine, such a treasure was not often sighted. The game was supposed to keep Brosie and Nevie from squirming and whining or worse in the back seat of the car.

On the beach side of the tracks, and to the left as one descended, was the dining-room structure, quite separate from the main building. Of course we patronized it three times a day when we were living at the hotel and so came to know it very well indeed. We were always greeted by the staid hostess, Miss Eyehorn(!), who would guide us to a table by the windows that overlooked the beach, the famous pier, long since demolished, and the sea and distant Channel Islands. At anchor near the pier rocked the hotel's sport fishing boat, the *Miramar*. My chief memory, perhaps my only specific one, of the no-doubt delicious meals was the melba toast served along with radishes and celery while one was waiting for the real food to arrive. I suspect the melba toast was simply so delicious when slathered over with butter that I hadn't the stomach to enjoy the staple fare that followed. On one's way to these adult glories, there was a dark slice of a room just before the entrance to the main dining room: the children's dining room, and a horrid comedown it was when one had to patronize it. I think it was obligatory when a child was accompanied by a nurse without a parent, for what hostess in her right mind would dream of wasting a good table with a view on the likes of them?

After lunch or dinner, one might stroll out onto the delightful pier. People would stand next to their fishing lines dangling in the water; seagulls flapped and crapped at very close quarters; and from the pier's tip there was a marvelous view back to the wooded shore of Montecito with its magnificent great mountains as a backdrop, capped in summertime with vast, bulging cumulus clouds.

I am harking back, of course, to the 1920s, before Maximilian Fleischmann's breakwater changed the littoral drift of the sand down the coast, destroying Edgecliffe (of which more later) and Sandyland beaches. Miramar beach was invitingly wide. Most of today's wooden cottages perched on stilts were in existence at the time I refer to. They were more rustic-looking then because they were intended for day use or perhaps family living for a matter of weeks in summer. Their owners in those days had substantial residences elsewhere in Montecito. As recently as the 1930s and '40s, real people wouldn't dream of living there the year round; if the cottages were let at all in the non-summer months, they were let to weirdos such as local college boys for practically no rent. Fancy wanting to live on the beach between October and June!

I remember a few substantial stucco houses on the beach downshore from Miramar, but not many. The larger houses on Fernald Point date mostly from the 1930s and later. I must pay brief tribute to the Indian pueblo-styled cottage with two independent wings built in the '20s by our cousins, the Bernhard Hoffmanns, the couple who more than anyone else were the driving force behind Santa Barbara's rebuilding in the Spanish Colonial mode after the calamitous earthquake in 1925. The cottage was an odd but pleasing bit of old Santa Fe set down not very appropriately in Chumash country. It plays a part in my life story because my first wife and I and my stepson rented the cottage during our Monterey period in 1951 to get away from northern fogs; in those days it belonged to Frank and Kitty Bishop of Goleta's Bishop Ranch. Each of the two independent wings had a living room and master bedroom facing the beach. It was in our bedroom that my only child and daughter Kendal was conceived. The other unit was lived in by a melancholy spinster who later committed suicide. Soon after we left the cottage, our bedroom sagged noticeably in the sand and continued its list to port for many years before it was torn down to make way for an English-style villa built for an architecturally conservative (I cannot speak for his morals) rock star. What do you suppose the sagging bedroom meant? I like to think it was the result of the passion that I brought to the creation of my darling daughter. Let it be noted that the bedroom of the depressed spinster, who had no gentleman callers, remained rock-steady and level.

I've one more recollection of the Miramar Beach scene. The boardwalk, though narrower then, was similar to today's, except that instead of today's motel units, it had damp and sour-smelling wooden dressing rooms presided over by an elderly Chinaman named Chickie. I remember a lot of eucalyptus litter in the area of the little train station and the boardwalk: messy trees with a distinctive and somewhat disagreeable fragrance.

BEFORE LONG, as it seems to me, Mother decided to build a house on La Vereda Road. Today it stands much too close to Highway 101, but in the mid-'20s the Coast Highway had only a trickle of trucks and cars. She found two acres of level ground with fine live oaks upon which she built a handsome Italianate villa christened La Villetta. It was sizable enough not to deserve the diminutive "etta," since it had to house besides its mistress her two little boys, nurse, governess, and cook. It really was just about everything a house should be, graceful and commodious without being intimidating. The grounds provided a big lawn ideal for playing, a huge tree that made a perfect home for a tree house, and a large flower garden for those who cared for that sort of thing. The forecourt consisted of a gravel drive that circled around a fishpond. The designer of the house was Mother's friend Mary Craig, the recently widowed wife of Osborne Craig, Scottish-born architect of the El Paseo complex owned by our cousins the Hoffmanns, mentioned earlier. When Mr. Craig died in his thirties, his enterprising widow, devoid of any architectural training but blessed with a shrewd and tasteful eye for balance and proportion and subtly attractive details, carried on his practice. Fortunately she inherited and made good use of her husband's chief draughtsman, a licensed architect named Ralph Armitage, who translated her esthetic whims into solidly engineered structures. (Almost thirty years later, the pair designed a charming house for my first wife and me on El Cielito Road above the Sheffield reservoir.) Soon after La Villetta was built, Mr. Armitage's engineering was put to the test by the famous earthquake of 1925, which did considerable damage and claimed twelve lives in relatively congested Santa Barbara, but caused very little destruction in rural Montecito.

I remember distinctly being carried downstairs in the arms of my French nurse. For several days we camped out on our lawn in a tent. (Where on earth would Mother have found or bought a tent in those days? Or, come to think of it, at any other time? Tents were not her sort of thing.) I was three, or maybe even two, depending on which month the quake struck—not worth researching.

I haven't yet mentioned that at this time in my life I spoke French exclusively. The nurse, Maminette, knew no English, and Mother enjoyed the opportunity to keep her own French alive. Besides, it was chic to have a little tot mouthing what I like to think was perfect idiomatic French. A few years later I learned to run for my life when I saw adults approaching who wanted to try out their own imperfect and unidiomatic French on the *petit poussin blond* (little blond chick), a name I was, alas, commonly known by at that time. There was one particularly offensive old lady, a veritable witch, who used to lurk in the shrubbery on San Leandro Lane and leap out to confront me with cooings and gurglings when I was out walking with my nurse. "How's my little baybay today?... Oh, the little precious!" Can a three-year-old glare? If he can, I did.

It apparently does one no "good" to learn a language in infancy. My French lasted only as long as Maminette did. When she returned to France after my fourth birthday, my French went with her because her replacement, Miss Gertrude Audrey Davis, a young South Dakotan with cultural pretensions and a diploma from a convent in her native state, could barely conjugate a French verb or two in spite of the nuns' ministrations. And I daresay by then Mother was tired of speaking nothing but French to her little darling; for one thing, it's hard to lose your temper in a foreign tongue. Instead she helped to found a *Cercle Français* whose ladies heard and entertained visiting Frenchmen of modest distinction. I have virtually no recollection of my then-fluent French. I remember that I had two standard prayers in my evening repertoire, invoking blessings upon all my relatives and other dear ones; these I repeated in a rapid, mechanical French for years and years until the words became so slurred that they made no sense even to me. One began by invoking "Petit Jésus," but what followed became with the years a hopeless jumble. At least the prayers spared me from having to recite the sappy "Now I lay me down to sleep..." that most American children were saddled with.

Two other French words from that period are fixed in my memory. One was *baleine,* the generic name for a greatly admired whale that often shared my bathwater. It had a windup motor and was able to dive when certain things were done to it. Can it have had a horizontal stabilizer in its tail? Another word, one that still makes me feel resentful, is *phénomène*. I was promised one if I looked up at the moon after dark; it was held out to me as something extremely rare and special that would give me great pleasure. Somehow I got the idea that there was going to be a giant in the sky revealed to me. It was my first big letdown, and possibly the most deeply felt. At midnight: *Voilà, bébé!* But it was nothing, just an eclipse. I still feel cheated, and have cared nothing for eclipses to this day.

I am trying to sort out early memories that I associate with La Villetta. We had a cat that I named "Grape Nuts Butter"; obviously I was not yet fully in command of my new language. And there was a huge cream-colored Great Dane, Gerda. A noble-looking animal, certainly, and well disposed towards children, but every time she came near me and wanted to display her good intentions, she knocked me down. I learned to admire her from a distance, but it was frustrating not to be able to hug her. We had other, smaller dogs, too, that were better suited to my size: a cocker spaniel that I recall only because there's a photograph of me in our driveway, squatting while holding on to the dog's outstretched forepaws; and Sammy Kinks, a Boston bulldog, said by Mother to be "high strung," who spent most of his time at the vet's. These early exposures to dogs touched something in my otherwise not very touchable nature, and I have been a helpless dog-lover ever since.

And from this period, too, dates my other passion—for automobiles. At a remarkably early age I was celebrated within the family for my ability to make out a car's identity from an incredible distance, and this at a time when there must have been ten American makes for every one we know today, and a surprisingly high number of truly exotic European cars beloved of Montecito millionaires, conservative tycoons and rakish playboys alike. I can remember but two cars of ours at this period, and they were both wretchedly dull, as Mother's continued to be (but not mine!) for the rest of her life. My first memory is of a spacious but ugly Dodge "touring car" about which the nicest thing one could say was that it held the whole family, household staff included. A touring car was a long convertible with four doors and no fixed windows. In lieu of windows it had portable, stowable windows made of canvas and isinglass, unwieldy monsters vastly larger than their miniature offspring that came with the earlier models of MGs. Of course one erected these constructions only in fierce winter storms; the rest of the time one shivered. Picture us in a rainstorm, with curtains up and steaming to the point of opacity from our collective breaths, with Mlle Perrier, my brother's irritable French governess, operating the hand-powered windshield wipers while Mother urged her on ever faster. We were a menace!

The other car, called a club coupé or Victoria, was a gift from Grandfather. An olive-green Studebaker, it suddenly appeared one afternoon at our front door. I got in as soon as I could—and no one could get me out again. On the extreme left of the back seat there was a snug built-in compartment for parcels, with a lid on it. I sat down on that lid, knees cramped up against my chin, and there I my took my stand, or rather seat. When people grew tired of cajoling me and left, I was free to stretch out and explore other delicious parts of the interior. It was as deeply satisfying an afternoon as I think I have ever spent.... But some of the pride of ownership melted away the following year when Aunt Katharine Gray, inflamed with sisterly envy, wheedled a much smarter-looking new model, also a Studebaker, out of Grandfather; hers was a very chic midnight blue with crisper styling that made ours look dumpy and dowdy. Score one for Aunt Kay. In the years to come, she scored often because she knew best how to handle Darling Daddy.

There were other very special ways to spend the afternoon in those far-off days. One was to go to Featherhill, the estate of Christian Holmes, playboy nephew of Max Fleischmann, to visit his private menagerie of wild animals. I especially remember the antics of the orangutans, which amused me no end. Today I realize that if I had been more astute in my observations, many of the mysteries of sexuality would have been made plain to me there and then at the age of four. If that was a test of my precocity, I failed it. Later, in other ways, perhaps I redeemed myself, as I shall try to explain in the chapter "The Grays."

Another expedition I greatly enjoyed was a visit to what was known as "the Ward place." It has been for many years the home of the John Bacon family. It consisted then of a foundation with no building upon it, but deeply excavated open cellars that were most alluring. The foundations were upon that beautifully situated ridge shared with half a dozen or so other establishments, including my grandparents', that runs between and parallel to upper Santa Rosa Lane to the south and Valley Road to the north. The ridge offers notable views of both the channel and the mountains, especially Montecito Peak. Besides the mysterious foundations, there was the exotic magic of three large reflection ponds rich in water lilies and gold fish descending towards the north, each on its own grassy terrace on the mountain side of the property. Here was a glorious preserve inhabited by no one, yet immaculately maintained. It seemed a secret garden, a dream garden, for anyone who chose to claim it.

I was introduced to horseback riding during these years. Horses were to play a very large part in my life from my earliest years through the age of seventeen, and although I soon became and remain proficient as a horseman, I will say here and now that I consider horses immoderately stupid brutes whose chief purpose in life, beyond fouling the environment with their droppings, is to step on one's foot—and stay there. Be that as it may, my first riding experiences came during this period, at McDonald's livery stable in back of the Miramar, near the Miramar Garage, which housed something far more interesting than a horse—viz., a full-sized electric runabout, high enough for a grownup to stand up in, which was permanently plugged in while waiting to be sent for by its mistress, an elderly Montecito lady. Because of their cleanliness and quietness (and slowness), I believe electric cars were relegated to women; but this was the only one I knew of in the 1920s. I think most of my riding at this time in my life was of the training variety, done in a ring. I do remember being in an egg-and-spoon race with my lifelong friend Dave Park (his life long, that is; he died untimely in the 1950s when he was 30-something, not long after marrying Alice Keck, famous for her later munificence to the Museum of Art and the Alice Keck Park Memorial Garden). This equine high drama took place on the old Bartlett polo field, whose clubhouse still stands at 184 Middle Road. I think I won; and Dave is in no position to contradict me.

I have a memory from this period of being told by someone in the house that Mother was having a nervous breakdown and not to bother her. I don't remember any eccentric behavior on her part. Probably it was connected with her having to return to Chicago with Brosie to testify in her divorce hearing, which must have been a very distressing prospect, worthy of some degree of collapse. I was left at home with the staff, and retain a vivid memory of Christmas Day without any family members, but presided over by Mother's close friend Fanny Brown-Browne. (What an extraordinary name! She must have liked things to be doubled because when she greeted one she always called out breezily, "Hellohello!" I was very fond of her and think now with shame, though with less shame than I should, of the nasty tricks Cousin Joan Gray and I played on her at a later date in her little shop. More of this in the chapter entitled "The Grays.") I have a clear memory on this day of a large Christmas tree of which the chief decorations were raw wieners, put there for the delectation of Gerda, the giant dog. Some adult later told me that Father had, according to this person, behaved disgracefully by not acknowledging my existence with a present. Well, "Daddy didn't want you, Daddy didn't want you," as my brother used to chant to me in later years. It seems to me like explicable behavior if one believes that I was Mother's idea exclusively; think of the good money he saved that he would much rather have spent on presents for his adored but forbidden sister-in-law! Since I had no memory of my father at that time, I didn't feel in the least left out; besides, Mrs. Brown-Browne was excellent company, and not many other small children in Montecito in the mid-1920s were so fortunate as to have a Christmas tree decorated with wieners.

WHEN I WAS FOUR, we did something very exciting in the summertime. We took the train to a dude ranch in Wyoming, near Sheridan. I remember a bad attack of the heaves in a hotel in Sheridan, but that was the only black mark against the trip. The rest was pure pleasure. I have no recollection of Brosie on the trip, but he must have been with us. I clearly remember Mother and Davie, my new governess. I see rolling green hills, with splendid mountains behind them, much pleasanter for riding than the dusty corrals and trails of Montecito. Not far away was an encampment of

Indians, Blackfoot I think, whose revered chieftain was named, of all things, "White Man Runs Him." That was something to be proud of? Why wasn't he subject to recall or impeachment? Well, I was too young to formulate that question, but not too young to smoke my first cigarette, a Camel, offered to me behind the barn by one of the cowboys. I loved everything about it. That first cigarette planted a seed in me that sprouted during vacation times at the age of fourteen or so, achieved a full and luxuriant year-round maturity at seventeen when I became a free man subject to no rules but my own, and lived on, full-blown and untrammelled, till at the age of fifty-six I lopped off its alluring head just before I retired.

I could blame it all upon that Satan, the Wyoming cowboy, but it would be unjust. If anyone could ever be said to be lying in wait to discover the thrill of nicotine (not to mention alcohol), I would be the one. When we attained to our early teens, Mother offered her two sons each in turn $1,000 (in Depression dollars, enough for instance to buy a small Buick convertible, white with red leather, that I picked up at the factory in Flint, Michigan, when I had just turned nineteen) to abstain from smoking and drinking till twenty-one. Neither one of us toyed with the idea for longer than three seconds. Thus did we show our mettle and our honesty, too.

Few other memories from that four-year-old's summer remain in this seventy-year-old head. Brosie and I both were soon outfitted with handmade Indian costumes—pants, vest, and headdress, all of deerskin embellished with colored beadwork. We kept the costumes for years; and who was so foolish as to dispose of them? And I distinctly remember a delicious blue berry called a June berry that we often came across and picked off the bushes while riding. I can smell it today, and taste its distinctive, pungent juiciness. It is not to be confused with the juniper berry, responsible for that abomination, gin, which flattened me at my very first cocktail party. More of that later.

Having mentioned Gertude Davis twice now, in passing, I think the time has come to elaborate upon her. As I said earlier, she succeeded my beloved French peasant nurse, whom I cannot remember anecdotally except for two things: rescuing me from our quivering house during the Great Earthquake, as I have mentioned; and referring to my yet-to-be-beloved cousin, Joan Gray, as *Cette*

Joanie! Why *cette?* Because, nine months older than the infant Nevill, she had *mordu mon bébé!* "That Joanie! She bit my baby!" A monster therefore; and so she remained to Maminette. I remember that I loved the latter dearly and cried for a long time when I was told she was to return to France (to take care of an illegitimate daughter, I learned much later). But Davie was a worthy replacement. She came to us when I was four, and remained till I went to school at six. Then she left, but returned to take care of my half-sister, Nancy Lloyd, when she was three or so. I think that Nancy was fifteen and off to boarding school at Katherine Branson's in Marin County before Davie was dropped that second and final time from our bed and board. And even that departure wasn't really final, as she kept popping in and out of Mother's life until she died in her 90s around 1980.

I see Davie as she was in a picture I have of her in Wyoming dating from that summer, bareback astride an Indian pinto pony, with a kerchief around her hair and a great deal of gold in her smile. She was for the most part a happy and cheerful person who knew how to give a child a good time, and she had a strong inclination toward such laudable things as classical music, Indian culture, and the inexhaustible world of nature. What does it signify that she was unable to instill the slightest interest in these areas in her little blond charge? Or that they "took" beautifully some years later with Nancy Lloyd? I have few specific memories that date from this first exposure to Davie. I do remember that she talked furtively and thrillingly about a 1920s kidnapping and murder case featuring a monster named Hickman and a little boy of about my age. I think he dismembered the child. Ostensibly she was putting me on my guard against kidnappers, but she dwelled with unwholesome relish on the gruesome details. Of course this was far more riveting than tales of the disappointingly friendly Sioux in her South Dakota childhood. She also talked endlessly, as governesses are reputed to do, about other families that she had worked for before coming to us. Even today I could recount some of the incidents that gave color to her employment with the Mixsell family of Los Angeles; could, but won't. Except that there was frequent reminiscing about hairbrush "paddlings," as she called them, on bare Mixsell bottoms. She tore into those anecdotes with real gusto, and her eyes glowed.

I feel pretty sure she was the victim of a spanking fetish, and I've often meant to ask sister Nancy if she has similarly lurid memories. Of course Davie may have worked her way out of that particular obsession by the time she came to us a second time, so that she was able to entice and capture Nancy with her better self, the one that cared about fossils and arrowheads and wild flowers. Or perhaps she simply knew, with a performer's intuition, how to play to her audience, both times.

When she did leave us that first time, she dropped from sight for a while before returning to pay a call during which she shared the gripping but improbable news that she had up-and-married someone, but that it was all over now and she was Miss Gertrude Davis again, thank goodness, because it had been a very unpleasant experience. She had married a man named Mr. Curran (she never referred to him in any other way, then or later), a reporter on the local paper. Like all self-respecting reporters in those days, and as Davie might have surmised, he was a drunk. I strongly suspect the marriage was never consummated. In fact, it turned her against men for the rest of her life—which was a far longer and happier one than most.

Davie left when I turned six and went to school as a first grader. The Crane Country Day School had just opened its doors but started with the third grade, so I had to go up San Ysidro Road a quarter-mile to the little Howard School, which tolerated boys in the first grade only. And there I remained for one year, the only year in my entire education when I found myself in a classroom with girls, except for a few months spent at UCLA in my junior year waiting for my call into the Army Air Force in World War II. I have skimpy but entirely happy memories of the year at Howard. I remember being mildly scared my first day, but the feeling wore off within an hour or two. Old Mrs. Howard was still a presence, though a background one: a sort of Canadian bush-league Queen Victoria. Her two daughters, Miss Isabelle and Miss Esther, were everywhere and seemed to teach everything. Miss Isabelle was slightly alarming, though I don't remember why, but Miss Esther was a sweetheart, firm and affectionate at the same time. Class time was devoted exclusively, it seems to me now, to learning to read and write. And to what better purpose could it possibly have been put? (Though I do remember a tiresome Christmas pageant complete with the three wise men, only they were big, lubberly girls from the upper grades with burned-cork moustaches.) I remember primers with engaging tales about Little Half Chick and others of that ilk, and Aesop's *Fables*. It was to a later generation that Dick and Jane and Spot came along to poison the springs of reading pleasure. In those days the system was phonics pure and simple and it worked very well for me; I turned out to be a natural speller, a blessing that has eased my way through life. I remember the school as providing a warm and caring environment for any little boy or girl cast adrift from the snug security of home.

I have a very faint memory of Mother's having tried to teach me to read some years before I went to school. (In those days of governesses there were no such things as nursery schools and kindergartens for the *bon ton* of Montecito.) I remember also, but again faintly, that our joint effort was very disappointing to Mother. Years later, when I was middle-aged, Mother reminded whoever was present at the time that she had found me flatly unteachable on this far-off occasion and had worried then about the grave problems I might face in my years of schooling. I was sorely tempted to reply that since my academic career during the first twelve years was one of almost unbroken excellence, my earlier failure just might have been due to the ineptitude of the teacher rather than of the one taught. I was tempted, I say; I did not succumb.

This first and on the whole paradisaical period of my life came to an end with the abrupt and fateful words, spoken by Mother to Brosie, that were to change my life profoundly: "Dear, we're going to join forces with the Lloyds." He says his heart sank when he heard them, even though he wasn't quite sure what they meant.

CHAPTER TWO

🌀 Joining Forces

AND WHO WERE THESE LLOYDS that we were supposed to join forces with? By way of background, let me quote from Cleveland Amory's *Who killed Society?*, published in 1960:

> William Penn was easily one of America's greatest men. His descendants, however, contrasted unfavorably with him, and though he had given Philadelphia its name as the "Quaker City," it was Thomas Lloyd who, says Frederick B. Tolles, historian of Quaker merchants, "was in a real sense the patriarch and progenitor of the Philadelphia Quaker aristocracy." One of the few genuine patricians to be converted to Quakerism, the descendant of an ancient Welsh family, he came to Penn's colony in 1682, bringing a "Family Coat of Arms with fifteen quarterings."

Francis Vernon Lloyd and his son, FVL, Jr., were direct descendants of Thomas Lloyd, and products of Philadelphia's Main Line, the string of fashionable suburbs that have housed the local elite for generations. Let us think of them for the moment as Frank (as Mother and his friends called him) and "Pick" or "Pickie," standing for the many pickles that the boy had allegedly got himself into when younger. I stress "allegedly," because he was the straightest arrow that ever flew towards his target. I doubt that he *ever* breathed a naughty or rebellious breath. Frank and the boy's Boston Lowell mother had gotten divorced (she later married the Earl of Berkeley), and Frank had received custody of his son, whose heart had been seriously damaged through a childhood illness. (As I write, the latter has just died, aged eighty-five or so, in Massachusetts.) In search of a mild climate, the two had migrated from Philly, as Frank called it, to San Diego, and then up the coast to Santa Barbara, where Pick attended the Deane School in Montecito, predecessor of today's Westmont College, years older than his classmates because his heart disease had kept him out of school for long periods. He was also seven or eight years older than Brosie and twelve or thirteen years older than I; join forces indeed—he could have been my uncle. And he stood six-foot-four.

Frank was a couple of inches less tall, but still forbiddingly large to a runty Cramer. Incredibly old-looking, too, we thought. He was probably in his late forties when he lumbered into our ken. Bald, with grey hair encircling the large dome. Big nose, big jaw, big voice. What had he to do with us, this ancient and unamiable giant?

Plenty, it seemed. He was to be our stepfather, and Pickie our brother. Unfairly soon, it seemed to us, the knot was being tied on the lawn at La Villetta. (A Montecito aside: the minister was an old and worldly friend who later cast off the cloth and built himself a handsome Lutah Riggs-designed house on the ridge next to the Valley Club, where he committed suicide after disastrous speculations on the commodities market. And who should own and live in it now but my former wife?)

I have only the most indistinct recollections of the wedding, but for years we had a short film of it that was highly entertaining. Everyone of course was in 1920s fashions, with flat bosoms (to the extent possible, and not including Grandmother Meeker) and *cloche* hats. This was the very lawn we had camped on just a few years before during the earthquake. One bit from the film featured Aunt Katharine Gray looking into the camera just as someone's cigarette smoke drifted almost palpably across her face. Immediately her chin went up and her nose thrust into the clear ozone above the smoke as she smiled with satisfaction over a job well done. We had the wedding "breakfast" (silly word for lunch) seated at round tables under umbrellas. Charming, I daresay; but for Brosie and me, it was the beginning of seven lean years of bondage.

From now on we had to refer to this unwelcome stranger as "Pop," of all things. Our lucky Gray cousins got to call him Uncle Frank, which we could have lived with, but Pop—an outrage! Only Perry Winkle's father in the comics bore this foolish name, and the latter's only appeal for us was that his particular kind of baldness, with a large concavity in the top of the skull, made him look exactly like Hewitt "Hewie" Reynolds, headmaster of the Deane School. "Pop" implies intimacy and affection tinged with humor and self-deprecation on the part of the one bearing the name, and these were not characteristics of the developing relationship with our tyrannical new boss.

They went east on their honeymoon in Pop's new bright-yellow Buick roadster, so that he could show off his new brideto his relatives in Philly. There she met and was duly received by his many brothers and sisters as well as other Main Liners; she evidently passed muster and remained on the friendliest possible terms with her Lloyd in-laws for the rest of her life or theirs. Her husband made a special point of taking her to his farm in St. David's, where he had lived for a while with his son while carrying out his proud duties as MFH (Master of Foxhounds) of the nearby Radnor pack.

This happiest of honeymoons (away from his new stepchildren!) was shattered by the news that Brosie had been injured in an automobile accident and hospitalized with a broken pelvis. Mother knew that she had to return at once to Santa Barbara; it would not be fair to surmise what her husband's feelings may have been. Back they drove across the continent in Pop's roadster.

This is what I remember of the accident, which happened offstage as far as I was concerned. Brosie was in Santa Barbara in a car driven by one Noel Messimer, who was hired by the Grays and Mother during vacations to keep their brattish sons, Horace and Arthur Gray and Brosie out of mischief and out of their respective homes to allow their parents a modicum of peace. They did things like camping out in the remote Carrizo Plains, somewhere near Santa Maria, and shooting scores of jackrabbits, whose long ears they brought back pinned to the car's radiator. But Brosie was alone with Noel when the crash took place. What I remember most significantly was that I was scheduled that day to see a perfectly marvelous new World War I film called *Wings*, whose subject matter can well be imagined (Spads and Fokkers chasing each other through the skies, closeups of helmeted pilots with oil streaming across their goggles as they fired off their rounds, grinning with the thrill of the chase as the various Red Barons went spiraling down, trailing plumes of smoke, into fiery crashes in the fields of poor, brave little Belgium). But the accident took place just hours before the movie was to start, and I was bitterly disappointed. And for quite a while Brosie was the center of attention, and that wasn't so good, either.

Many years later, on the occasion of my brother's fortieth birthday, while he was summering with his wife and two children on the coast of Maine, he was taken aback to receive the following telegram, read out over the telephone in the homey, Down East accent of a native Western Union woman: "Happy birthday, fat and forty! If I'd known what you were going to turn into, I'd have broken every bone in your body!...(signed) Noel Messimer." That must have rocked him back on his heels, but he was a good enough sport to *say* that he found it vastly amusing. I like to think the incident paid him back for making me miss that movie. And as we hadn't either of us thought of Noel Messimer for thirty years, my telegram helped to freshen Noel's memory and keep it green.

One of the joys of writing a personal and non-commercial narrative is that one can break the thread whenever one damned well wants to. I would like at this point to relate a second incident in which I scored side-splittingly (i.e., *my* sides split) off my brother. Since it happened in the 1950s, long after the self-imposed cutoff point of this book, it has no relevance except the one I have just mentioned. And I am sure that you, dear reader, are willing to wait a moment for the resumption of the story of my early life, with Mother and Pop home again from their happy, though aborted, honeymoon.

This new trick required premeditation and the careful baiting of a trap, whereas the telegram had been the work of a sudden, gratuitously outrageous inspiration, so bluntly shocking that it had to be laughed at by the recipient.... Somewhere around 1950, when I was living in Monterey with my first wife, Louise, and her little boy Piero Fenci, we were house guests in Mother's house on San Ysidro Lane. Rummaging around in an idle moment, I found in a guestroom drawer some memorabilia that pertained to Brosie's life as a youth and young man. Among them was a slightly faded card from an old girl of his. I remembered her well. She was strikingly pretty, gently born, warm and charming to talk with, and—what really mattered—a nymphomaniac. I had been too young to sample her favors, but that was not the case with Brosie or his friends, five years older than I. And the thought came over me, back in 1950, could I not put this card to some good use?

On a piece of writing paper I practiced copying the signature and then formed other words of harmonious appearance. When I was comfortable with my forgery, I wrote these words on the original card: "I'm back. Come see me!" Then I sealed and stamped the envelope and in my adopted feminine hand with circles dotting the *i*'s addressed it to his home. On the upper-left corner I wrote a return address: a street in Santa Barbara on the wrong side of the tracks with a number such as 1634½. It was all meant to suggest a decline in fortunes that well suited the faded envelope and the fly-blown old card. The impression of course was one of ready, almost instant availability.

I knew my victim well. Only a few days after I had posted the envelope, Brosie came to dinner at Mother's with his then wife (the first of four, and mother of his two children). I led the conversation around in a natural way to girlfriends we had had in youth. That was all it took. The fish, it seemed, had snapped at the bait within twenty-four hours of receiving the card. Not only that, but he had brought a close friend of his into it, promising who knows what salacious treats at the end of the brief journey to town. But the two of them couldn't find the imaginary street number that I had given even though they had driven round and round the block and ultimately had got out of the car and looked in windows. Total failure, and he couldn't understand it! By then, I was nearly dead from laughing, as were Louise, who was in on the plot, and Brosie's wife Lee, who knew her husband's propensities only too well and no doubt thought he had been well served. The victim went along with the joke, though he was clearly rueful; it had been such an appetising dream while it lasted, and it was painful to give it up. I pointed out that it would have been even more frustrating to go on believing the woman was in there somewhere—but where? So I had actually done him a kindness by exposing the hoax (though not, I suppose, by inventing it).

AND SO MOTHER AND POP returned to Montecito. La Villetta

was considered too small for the joined forces, so they rented a more spacious house at the end of the cul-de-sac known as Green Lane, which juts off San Leandro Lane just before the latter makes its last right-angle bend towards the Crane School.

The house was attractive to look at and pleasant to live in; we called it simply Green Lane. I think we were there for only a couple of years before buying a bigger house on La Vereda Road near our old La Villetta, but I'll try to sort out my memories as they pertain to Green Lane and to my life during the period we lived there.

First, the house. The lane ended, after a curving rise, in our gravel turnaround. On the left was a multi-car garage with an apartment attached, where the maids lived. (But I remember a ping-pong table in its living room; how can that have been? It must have been thought more fitting that the young should have a play-room than that the servants should have a comfortable sitting room. Also, we made toy soldiers in that room. I remember the molds into which we poured the molten lead, and how very careful we were as we did so because a boy we knew had been blinded in one eye while carrying out that same procedure carelessly.)

And on the right was the house itself, the usual two-storey Montecito white stucco with a tiled roof, but it differed in that it had dormer windows upstairs. On the ground floor, off by itself and up a few steps, was a master bedroom suite for the bridal couple; near it was a living room that gave onto a flagstone terrace and ample lawn bordered by brightly colored plants that would thrive in the shade under massive oaks. Almost hidden by the oaks was a tall water tower with a forbidden but extremely tempting ladder attached. (I climbed it surreptitiously many times with no ill effects.) On the less desirable north side of the house were the dining room and kitchen. I have but two special memories of the dining room: one day I had a friend over for lunch, and we were served lima beans, among other things. My friend had no fondness for limas and made no bones about it, so I pretended to share his distaste, and to show my hospitable mastery of the situation scraped all my beans into the bouquet that formed the centerpiece of the dining table; he delightedly followed suit.... Poor Mabel Impey; she was the staid little English waitress who must have had to tidy

41

things up later. Mabel was a colorless soul, unlike most of our succession of servants over the years. Once, I suppose because she was so imperturbable and dull, Brosie persuaded me to sing a little jingle at her that went like this (she wore glasses with very thick lenses): "Four-eyes Impey, bolly-jolly cockney!" She recoiled slightly but kept her composure, so I sang it again. Nothing but frost. I'd say now that she won, and good for her.

My other dining room recollection concerns a mynah bird that had been given to Pop by a friend. I was thrilled to be told that mynahs could be taught to speak, and far better than parrots. This was a magical creature that was going to make me celebrated among my playmates; with this in mind, I spent hours in front of the wretched bird, repeating words and phrases, trying with escalating frustration to hit upon something that would catch his fancy. It was time wasted. He learned nothing from me, whereas I learned from him, time and time again, that a sharp beak can easily puncture the skin of a finger.

At night he slept in a paper bag, from which his head would emerge jauntily when the first family member arrived for breakfast, and he would look round the room with jerky head motions. The whole family was highly disgruntled by now because he couldn't or wouldn't perform. Nobody liked him well enough even to give him a name; he was just "the mynah." And then one day, emerging from the paper bag, he broke his silence: cocking his head at an angle, he squawked out, "Morning, Pop!"

And that was all he ever did learn to say, though he repeated it *ad nauseam*. Presently he was given away.

This was the only house we ever lived in that had two staircases, one in the front hall and the other in the kitchen wing. Both rose of course to opposite ends of the second floor, where our bedrooms were. There was a long hall running the length of the house, from which all the bedrooms and baths branched off. The ceiling sloped in farmhouse style, and, as I mentioned earlier, the second-floor rooms had picturesque dormer windows. Once a month Brosie and I were herded (a small herd, admittedly) into one of the bathrooms that contained a scale for our weighing-in ceremony. Like most young boys, we were very skinny, so Mother offered us a dollar for each pound of weight gain. Therefore there was some tension, some sense of drama as the day for the ceremony drew near each month. I never seemed to gain an ounce, whereas Brosie added several pounds with remarkable regularity. The trouble was, as even guileless Mother noticed, he was just as skinny as ever, whereas his very expensive (or profitable, depending on one's point of view) weight gains indicated he should have been obese by now. And then one day, finally suspicious that she was being taken advantage of, Mother scrutinized Brosie during the procedure. The truth came out with shocking clarity. As he stood on the scale, his head made very deliberate and forcible contact with the sloping "provincial" ceiling; he could *press* onto the scale however many pounds he desired. There were more weighings-in after that day, but no more payouts. Let me add, so as not to seem sanctimonious, that I would have done exactly the same thing if I had thought of it. I was still too young to have criminal intent. That would come later.

I HAD IN THOSE DAYS a very close affinity with maids, and I still look back with affection upon each and every one of the many that shared our daily lives when I was a child. It seems to me that they were all characters in varying degrees (at least I like to think so), and some were positively lovable. They played very important roles in my life, and on the whole, I preferred them to my friends. They were more trustworthy and loyal; they never turned on one, or if they did, it was because I had goaded them beyond endurance. Some of them had fascinating stories to tell of their earlier lives in the British Isles and elsewhere in Europe, which is where they almost all came from in those days.

Ann Mackie was the cook that I remember best from the Green Lane days. She was a buxom, strapping middle-aged woman, Scottish I think, very much in control of her kitchen domain. She would brook no nonsense from brats, so I treated her circumspectly. The thing that made her precious to me was the eggnogs she fashioned when she was in a good mood. (Readers, note well: This retired English teacher asks you to observe that I have used the singular verb *was* as governed by its subject *thing*. So many misguided professional writers today would write a plural *were* to agree with *eggnogs,* the subject complement, not the subject. Wrong, wrong,

wrong. *O tempora, o mores!*) The eggnogs were unbelievably rich and thick and eggy, and heavily sprinkled with nutmeg, a new flavor to me, and of course unpolluted with bourbon or whatever. I have never met their like since; in fact, years ago I gave up eggnogs altogether because they were such wretched travesties of Ann's product. She also made lovely ice cream in the old-fashioned way, in a barrel-like device crammed with salted ice. I was often ordered to crank the handle till my arms ached while only the purity of my passion kept me at it, but my reward came when I got to lick the dipper after Ann had ladled out the soft ice cream. Thus did I learn that the world has luscious rewards for those willing to work hard for them. Ann was very apt to preface her instructions with the phrase "Now then..." which interested this embryo language student mightily: Why would one say those two words together? Surely it should be one or the other. But it was Ann's phrase, and it sounded right in her mouth. I don't think I learned anything about her life; in fact, she stuck firmly to business, and doubtless was a better cook for doing so.

Suddenly I see before me her successor, Dora Petersen, a heavy-set woman from Missoura, as she pronounced it. She moved around her kitchen in ponderous, brooding fashion. I've an idea she was part Indian; she wore her hair in braided loops, black turning gray, coiled over her ears. She has just seeped quietly into my brain from decades spent resting in my unconscious. I am pleased to have retrieved her for a brief public appearance, but I don't know how to make her interesting. Yes, suddenly I do. I see her now in my mind's eye opening the back door for the iceman, who bears a huge chunk of brilliantly clear ice on his shoulder, balanced with the help of great tongs on a piece of protective burlap. With a groan and a sigh he offloads it into the icebox, where Dora will soon be chipping away at it with an icepick, that lethal tool that ended, I'm sure, many a domestic quarrel in those days. How beautiful those chipped-off chunks were, unpredictably suggestive as to shape, each one a delight to observe and to handle! We were later than most of my friends' families in switching to electric refrigerators (and acquiring a radio, too, for that matter), I suppose because of the innate conservatism of the senior Lloyd, ponderous and infinitely slow-moving, rather than for esthetic reasons, as I'd prefer to think. Brosie put it neatly thus: "Philadelphia born, Philadelphia bred; / Stout of arm and thick of head." (The faulty scansion of that bit of doggerel makes me think that another city was originally the butt; "Boston" would scan, but then Bostonians were not reputed to be thick of head. Well, I give Brosie full marks for a sensitive application of an old rhyme.) Ah: and one more tidbit about ice. The trucks that delivered it throughout Montecito had painted on them the company's improbable slogan, "Be perspicacious. Use Mission ice!" And so I added another sesquipedalian word to my vocabulary, which could almost be mistaken for Samuel Johnson's by the time I was a teenager.

So the ghost of forgotten Dora Petersen had a reason for returning after all—she gave me a chance to reminisce about ice. Real ice.

And the next cook that comes to my mind was Mary Mulloy. Irish, obviously, short, and white-haired. By pushing hard with my tongue against the part of my face that comes between lower lip and chin, I found I could mimic very effectively the strange protuberance that made the lower part of her face so memorable. (By now I had become a pretty fair mimic, specialising in physical frailties and deformities, especially limps, in which category I developed a substantial repertoire from a plentiful supply of local models in Montecito and downtown. Before long my mimicry extended to oral imitations; that was when the fun really began and my reputation spread. More later on that subject. My talents in this direction could be said to have flowered in my teens at boarding school.)

Mary's feet, like those of many servants, gave her no end of trouble, and she usually padded about the kitchen in carpet slippers. And even they were not enough to give her true relief. She cut out holes in the slippers to give more freedom to her two smallest toes, and only thus could she get through the day, poor soul. Bunions and corns, those were the servants' everlasting complaints, whether they were in their sixties or their twenties. Why? Was it from standing up a great deal? From ill-fitting shoes? Did they stand up more than other workers? Were they through some strange occupational disability simply unable to select shoes of the right size? This remains for me an unsolved problem, but I have not lost any sleep over it, I must confess.

Now I see myself with old Mary, seated together on stools around a central table in the spacious kitchen, shelling peas. Very soothing and satisfying it was once one got the hang of it, rhythmical and restorative. It took quite a while to shell enough to feed a large household. I don't remember that she ever opened up about herself, but she was agreeable company. There was a steady demand in the family for cookies, and when I came home each afternoon from school my sense of smell would be titillated with the aroma of fresh batches baking in the oven. (What a treat! In World War II, when I was in training in the Army Air Force, in the barracks we used to receive food packages from home. Lots of chocolate chip cookies came my way, lovingly prepared by that most wonderful of women, Mother's German Emmy Krick. When we all passed our goodies around to share, I remember a fellow cadet once asking, "Mmm! Did your mom make these?" I answered at once before trying one, "God, I hope not!" Montecito mothers in those days did not cook, and Mother was the most inept woman in a kitchen I ever knew, except for *her* mother.)

I have one final tidbit connected with Mary. Ten years or so later I read a brief obituary in *Time* about one Mary Mulloy, incredibly ancient, who had been identified at long last as the notorious "Typhoid Mary" who had unwittingly infected hundreds, perhaps even thousands, of the people she had worked for and with over a long period of time. She was, in fact, the most notable typhoid "carrier" of her day. Brosie was at Yale then, and I took delight in sending him the clipping. It amused us to pretend that it was our Mary that had in this way achieved immortal status in her apparently humble life.

I HAD BEEN PROFOUNDLY ATTRACTED by the mystique of cigarette smoking ever since those first forbidden puffs at the age of four behind a barn in Wyoming. In the drawing room in Green Lane, and in our next house too, there was a double-decker tortoiseshell cigarette box whose lid swung forward cleverly to reveal not only the first level's contents, but those of the lower level as well, a fragrant treat of the most exotic sort to my inquisitive nose. The cigarettes were for parties, but the Lloyds entertained infrequently, and I had free, if secret, run of the box between parties. Probably they were Old Golds, the brand Pop favored, whose widely disseminated slogan in those days was "Not a Cough in a Carload!" This amused my brother and me no end because every morning we were harshly awakened in our upstairs bedrooms by Pop coughing his head off in his room under our windows, clearing out gobs of tobacco-induced mucus that had collected while he slept. (He also hocked huge lungers out of his big roadster. Now I ask you, was this fitting behavior for one whose ancestor boasted not four, but fifteen quarterings on his coat of arms?) At any rate, at a very early age I learned once and for all that truth was not to be sought or found in advertising copy.

My cousin and closest friend, Joan Gray, a year older than I, was just as much under the spell of cigarettes as I was, and we would raid the tortoiseshell box together, then go slouching down Green Lane with ciggies in our mouths or fingers. One day we were caught on the lane *in flagrante* by our "John the Gardener," as he was known. We were terrified he might report us, but I doubt the thought ever occurred to him or that his English would have been up to it if it had. I suspect Italian children started smoking young, too. This nice man, John Vizzolini by name, kept a huge red kerchief in his hip pocket with which he mopped his brow and did a hundred other useful things. I envied him that splendid kerchief. But one day he was gone and our secret with him, to be succeeded by Mr. Petersen, a Dane. We couldn't communicate well with him, either, Joanie and I, because he was very deaf. One day we decided it would be interesting to mouth meaningless words at him, making no sound but looking as though we were trying to say something important. He just looked at us in a gently puzzled way and then went on with his raking. We felt small and were extra nice to him from then on.

Davie had taught me some card games before she left, notably poker and hearts, and I had many very satisfactory games with my two teddy bears; I say satisfactory because I always won as I had control over the bears' hands. Fortunately for me, they didn't know one card from another. Holdovers from my French-speaking days, Monsieur et Madame Philibert (pronounced Feeleebair) were special favorites of mine for many years. M. Philibert's arms and legs were rotatable, but his best position was sitting down, appropriate for an aging male, whereas because Madame's limbs did not articulate, the tireless creature was always on all fours, poised to run errands for her mate. That is the way things were in those halcyon days.

In an old photograph album, snapshots from the Green Lane period show me in a variety of costumes: in a flowered black kimono holding a parasol over my tow-headed bangs, far from suitable for a young Japanese gentleman; in cowboy regalia, including ten-gallon (more likely, ten-ounce) Stetson, sheriff's badge and chaps of a strange amber-colored curly wool, with rifle-shaped capgun in hand and a menacing scowl; in a white sailor's outfit with the traditional gob's cap but without the traditional thirteen-button fly (which I never could have handled because in those days the desire to pee used to come over me with almost irresistible suddenness, and no wonder, since x-rays many years later proved what I had always suspected, that I was cursed with a small bladder that prevented me from ever sitting through movies and sporting events or indeed anything); and in a dark-blue policeman's uniform, complete with cap and badge. I remember too a picture of me in rather dramatic profile wearing Indian regalia including feathered headdress, standing outside my tepee.... Where did all those silly costumes come from? The answer to that is simple: from F.A.O. Schwarz in New York. Surely nothing in the mail since that time (not even my monthly *Road & Track* that I have looked forward to so ardently for decades) has caused me so much dreamy joy as the Schwarz Christmas catalog. Quite simply, I wanted everything in it. What spoiled, red-blooded child wouldn't? Page after page of Lionel trains and costumes and wonderfully imaginative games and big bicycles with little engines, and God knows what all—all of it rich fare not to be sampled in Santa Barbara's modest little downtown toy stores, and all of it to be had, one hoped, at the easy stroke of a maternal pen. Such juicy descriptions under each desirable piece of frippery! How could one not want them all? How could one ever be happy with one's thin little slice of the whole? But one was. One settled for the attainable reality and was told to think of all the little poor children who would receive nothing at all. (Pop never tired of telling of the time one Christmas in Philly when his brothers had removed all the goodies from his stocking and replaced them after bedtime with chunks of coal. Mother would get teary when she thought of this cruel injustice, but I saw nothing odd about it. Presumably the brothers felt about him just as Brosie and I did.)

For quite a while I had had bouts of tonsillitis, so the doctor decided when I was six or so to remove my tonsils, standard procedure in those days. I remember with great embarrassment now my really shameful fear of this prospect. The idea of someone's reaching down into my throat and yanking out a piece of it was unspeakably alarming. I could think of nothing else for days. I remember vividly now the horrors of the Night Before. Poor Mother; I badgered her time and again with questions about the operation and what it would feel like. Over and over and over, until she finally lost her temper, but even that failed to stop the churning of my mind. Of course the operation, which might have been a guillotining as far as I was concerned, came off as scheduled, and I really remember very little of the experience except the obsessive worry that preceded it. In later years, in a spirit of contempt for my childhood cowardice, I learned by simple will-power to still my pre-surgical fears. I've had an awful lot of operations, major and minor, in the sixty-four years since that first one and have trained myself to ride out each surgical invasion with stoic equanimity. It is a comfort to me to think that now and then one can rise above childhood fears, however fundamental they might seem to be. Not in all things, but in some. I still have an abnormal dread of drowning.

(My second operation was actually enjoyable. It took place when I was about twenty, and was performed by Dr. Henry Profant, the same surgeon who had extracted my six-year-old tonsils and adenoids. This time, by order of the Army Air Force, it was to straighten my crooked septum, the cartilege that splits one's nose into two halves, before I could become an aviator in World War II. Dr. Profant used a local anesthetic, and I sat upright in a chair like a barber's. I remember that the shot affected me just like a stiff cocktail, say a double martini, and I chattered ceaselessly as I gave away family secret after secret, mostly about my beloved Aunt Katharine Gray, whom the doctor knew well. He told me later that he was laughing so hard at my sallies that he could hardly carry on with the business at hand. He must have made notations in the Cottage Hospital's archives because every other surgeon since Dr. Profant has seen fit to knock me out completely before rolling up his sleeves.)

GREEN LANE was a cul-de-sac, as I mentioned earlier, that circled up a rise and ended in our forecourt. There was another substantial house along the lane before one came to ours, also in the prevalent Montecito Spanish idiom, that housed a family whose parents were friends of our parents, and whose children of course became friends of ours. The Timmons family (a pseudonym): poor souls, everything that could go wrong with a family went wrong with them. When I think back and realize that most of the events covered by this memoir took place in the years of the Great Depression, I am astonished at what little effect it had upon our family and our friends' families. But it destroyed the Timmonses.

They were from Boston, I'm pretty sure, and must have been moneyed or they wouldn't have built their big two-storeyed house with its wide expanse of sloping lawn. It was spacious enough to house the three children as well as two grandmothers-in-residence, Bo-ma and Muzzy. Bill and Ruth Timmons, contemporaries of Mother's, had three children, John and Sam, closer in age to Brosie than to me, and a daughter, Mary Helen, younger than I. The four of us boys roamed the neighborhood together. We went to the same church and belonged to the beach and country clubs. Then Bill Timmons and a friend who lived next door decided to build the Montecito Inn. Not Charlie Chaplin, as current lucrative mythology would have it, but Bill Timmons. It never took off. The Depression set in and Bill lost his shirt. The family's shirt, actually. And more than their shirt. The second son and the daughter one after the other became victims of what was called dementia precox, known today as schizophrenia, and had to be sent off to a state hospital for the insane, which was the approved "treatment" for the mentally ill in those benighted days. Their house was foreclosed on and the family dropped from sight. From time to time in the years to come the parents would appear in Santa Barbara, Bill to promote one foolish venture or product after another, sweet gentle Ruth to line, with infinite pains, the closet shelves of people such as our parents whose dinner companions they had been in happier times. Bill was asked by the vestry not to present himself any longer at the local church because he used the social hour after services to try to promote his latest product. I remember in particular an evil concoction called Kevo, rich in seaweed, that pretty much guaranteed its users eternal health (if only one could force it down one's throat without gagging). There were other Kevos over the years, and old friends became less and less willing to remember the days when the Timmonses had been members of the scene. People looked away when they came back to town, and in time they stopped coming. I am still touched and moved when I think of the pathos of their fall from grace, and saddened when I realize that nobody did anything of consequence to help them. Ruth's kind, suffering, patient face haunts me today as I call the family to mind.... But a remarkable thing is that so few people that we knew suffered in any cataclysmic way from the Depression.

Footnote to the above: The other day I asked my seventy-five-year-old brother without warning whether he remembered the Timmons boys' words for the bodily functions (I used coarser language). He went into a sort of trance for a few moments, then dredged up this response: "Sudsy...and—and—moomy!" Bravo, Brose! Who says the human brain loses its mnemonic powers with aging? At least it remembers the important things.

BICYCLES PLAYED A LARGE PART in children's lives then, probably a larger part than they do now because, since traffic was light in Montecito, one could safely ride anywhere. Anywhere, that is, where one-speed bikes could take one. I remember my first bike vividly. I think I was six when it was given to me. It was small, muddy maroon in color, and bore no manufacturer's label; definitely a "stripper." Could it have been stolen, a "hot" bike? It was clearly a used model but had been nicely reconditioned by the bike shop man, Hap Hazard, whose premises I remember well. They were on the first block of West Canon Perdido, on the north side, nearer to Chapala than to State. I think it was the only bike store in Santa Barbara at that time. Hap was something of a local character.

He had built an open car that had the ability to rear back on its hind legs like a bronco with Hap in the saddle, as it were. It was a fixture in every local parade and never ceased to give pleasure to young and old. Not only that, but he owned and raced real, live speedboats in our harbor and in the channel waters outside it. A dashing sport he was, a far cry from the effete polo players that Montecito spawned.... I wonder why I was given a used bike. When I was a little older, that would have bothered me horribly, but at six I suppose I didn't care, though it's plain that I have never forgotten its "usedness." Since the Depression hadn't struck yet, it must have been simply an example of wise parental thrift, given that I would outgrow it very soon. And that is exactly what happened. When at seven I entered the Crane School a mile from home, I was given a big, heavy *new* Columbia bike with balloon tires to handle the commute. No more little kid stuff. This was Mr. Hazard's finest. I was to be a boy among boys.

ABOUT THIS TIME Mother presented us with a seven-pound half-sister, Nancy Lloyd. "Joining forces" with the two Lloyds was one thing, and quite enough. Nobody had ever suggested that there might be yet *another* Lloyd. Now we'd have to move again, to an even bigger house.

CHAPTER THREE

La Vereda and the Crane School

POP AND MOTHER bought a large Mediterranean house on La Vereda Road, the very road that La Villetta had Graced (that was Mother's name). La Vereda, meaning "path," did a lot of winding, and there were so many hedges and properties between the two establishments that they might have been miles apart. The house presented a clean, almost classical facade to the street. Under the pedimented front and over the imposing double front doors there was a motto chiseled into a large stone plaque: CLARIOR HINC HONOS. Honor brighter here? The trouble is that *hinc* means "hence, from here." Does that make sense? Maybe. Whose fancy was it? That of the highly regarded Los Angeles architect, Carleton Winslow? The original family's? And if so, what made them think their honor was so special? It was imposing, certainly, and perhaps a little daunting, but I never felt that it committed me to fighting duels, or anything like that. The exterior was buff, restful, or dull depending on one's mood, and the trim was a conservative blue. The roof was of course tiled.

The present owners have done extraordinary things to its sober exterior so that it presents quite a different face to the world today. The short, semi-elliptic driveway is framed by enormous peacock gates, and balustrades that were never part of the original concept sprout pompously from the main structure. I believe the owners are newcomers, relatively speaking, and almost certainly from Los Angeles. Perhaps the new motto for the house should be DE GUSTIBUS NON EST DISPUTADUM. Someone over the years has paved the drive; in our day it was gravel, dangerous for bike-riding. Poor sister Nancy skidded on the drive when she was nine or ten, and had to

53

be ambulanced to the hospital with a concussion. There was no permanent effect as far as I know, though she has always been on the pleasantly eccentric side. My other driveway memory involves Pop. He took a dim view of women's driving abilities at best and especially resented the aggressive confidence that Aunt Katharine, his sister-in-law, brought to her seat behind the wheel. When she would leave our house after a social call, the gravel would fly, and he would bark at Mother, "That damned sister of yours! She drives out of here like a bat out of hell!" Wheel tracks in the gravel; unendurable! No true lady would drive like that.

Now I'll take you on a tour of the house as we pass under CLARIOR HINC HONOS. This, after all, though it was supposed to be just a temporary dwelling for the Lloyds until they could build their dream house on their Park Lane acres in upper Montecito, turned out to be Mother's home for the next seventeen years, and, as it happened, Pop's ultimate home, for he died here in his bed a mere six years later, in 1935.

First we enter a large, square front hall floored with dark-red tiles. Near the front door is a table with a silver salver for visiting cards. The most interesting of the rather sparse furnishings is a large Swiss cuckoo clock sent us by Grandmother. It was a delight to me, though there were those who found its loud, relentless chirping of the hours an irritant. I related it to a favorite Victorian story, "The Cuckoo Clock" by Mrs. Molesworth, that Mother read to me. Near the clock, on the right, is a narrow hallway that leads to the master bedroom suite and a cozy paneled room with bookshelves and fireplace known as the study, where the family gathered of an evening.

If we proceed straight ahead through the hall, we pass through a sort of solarium with informal wicker furniture and a half-dozen or so tall windows side by side looking out onto a formal garden, and enter a large drawing room with high ceilings and an air of spaciousness and modest elegance. French doors on three sides look out onto brick terraces shaded by awnings.

Returning to the center of the entrance hall, we find a door just to the left of the solarium that opens into the dining room, a large, airy, high-ceilinged room that could seat a great many people if the need arose. The long table is expansible thanks to enormous wooden leaves. This room looks out upon a large lawn, modestly landscaped and intended for the use of us children. Across it stands a wooden playhouse where I spent a great deal of time, as I will explain later.

From the left wall of the front hall rises a broad staircase, whose landing halfway up can just be seen before the stairs angle out of sight. And further to the left is a door leading first to the servants' cozy dining room with its red-painted wooden table and chairs (where I greatly enjoyed supping with the help when Mother and Pop were out for dinner), the kitchen wing, and the servants' quarters. One more door remains, on the same wall as the front door(s)—the guest lavatory. This useful but commonplace little convenience would ordinarily not be worth mentioning; however, it was to this room that Pop would repair after dinner to break wind systematically. Brosie and I have always been fond, perhaps excessively so, of bathroom humor, and when we discovered that it was Pop's habit to make use of this facility, so accessible from the dining room, as a vital part of the digestive process, we would follow him there on tiptoes and, just barely outside the door and bent double with silent laughter, enjoy the rich sound effects. *Sic semper tyrannus!* There aren't many ways that the small and helpless can get even with all-powerful tyrants. Our best, our only, weapon was ridicule. Over the years we honed our skills.

Upstairs are five bedrooms. To one side of the staircase, and flanked by a smaller room, is one that is larger and brighter than the others, so of course that went to baby Nancy, the new Lloyd, and the small room just outside its entrance was reserved for her nurse. The other three, across the staircase, were assigned to Pickie, Brosie, and me, though Pickie's room was usually empty because by now he was enrolled at Stanford, where he was indulging in orgies of wholesome extraversion, a veritable Joe College. My room had only one exposure, onto a large expanse of tiled roof with a row of pines beyond. My bedroom was freshly papered, and the walls gave off a delicious scent. Mother chose furniture for Brosie and me from a store in town that carried unpainted furniture. Mine was stained "walnut," which I thought modest and elegant: spool bed, slant-top desk, and dresser; Brosie's stain was said to be "maple," a vile orange hue that never dulled down over the years. By now we have completed our tour.

MOTHER HAD PRODUCED NANCY; there was no question of that; but she certainly wasn't going to look after her. Whatever of Shakespeare's "mewling and puking" there was to be would take place "in the nurse's arms," not Mother's. So a nurse moved in as soon as the mother and child returned from the hospital. Margaretta Mangels: I can see her so plainly, even though she played a very small part in my life: a perfectly round face with apple cheeks and braided hair and a Mittel-European accent. She didn't stay very long because she specialized in very young babies and apparently lost interest as soon as they began to seem human. The reason I mention her at all is that her name gives me the excuse I need to relate the most marvelous putdown I have come across, from a book of memoirs by Sir Edward Marsh. Lady Somebody was being chauffeured in her Rolls-Royce to do a round of errands in her feudal village. She stopped by a new store to try out its wares; the sign read, "Mangel and Wurzel, Ironmongers." One of the partners rushed out to make his obeisance. She looked him over coolly from head to toe and then spoke these few but devastating words: "If you're Mangel, send me Wurzel. If you're Wurzel, send me Mangel."

Miss Mangels was succeeded as Nancy's nurse by one of the truly angelic people I have known, Anna "Mimi" Koselka. Mimi was Czech-born and very proud of it. I adored her. She was lighthearted, infinitely patient, unflappable, kindly, and wise. I wish I could bring her to life in these memoirs, but that is a difficult thing to do with people who are truly good. She gave me a beautiful Oxford dictionary upon my graduation from Cate many years later. This dear woman died while driving her car along with a friend on the Casitas Pass. Mother was told the steering failed and the car plunged over a cliff.

And now I want to describe briefly other members of the staff because they played such substantial and interesting roles in my prepubertal days. After all, we lived together day after day, month after month. We had two Scottish girls in their early twenties just off the boat from "Abairdeen," as they called it, "the Grrranite City."

One of them, Chrissie King, a scrappy redhead, had an aunt who had emigrated before her to Santa Barbara and by now was married happily to a Montecito chauffeur. This gave the girls an entree to the local world and a wise counselor as well. The other girl was my special pet, Annie Cruickshank. Annie had dark hair and storybook-pink cheeks. I named her "Cruika" and loved to tease her, imitating her delightful but to me very comical Scots accent, at which I became as proficient as a native. I love to recite even today for anyone interested in that dialect a jingle she taught me that was presumably a Caledonian version of our "Eenie, meenie, miney, mo...." It went as follows:

Eenerty, feenerty, fickerty, fay,
Ell, dell, dominay;
Irkie, birkie, stolen rock;
Ann, tan, to her jock!

The girls worked hard, Annie as chambermaid and Chrissie as our waitress, for $60 a month plus room and board in those grim Depression days. They had no intention of making a career of domestic service; they were just supporting themselves until the right man, preferably a Scot, proposed and swept them into the great American middle class, where there would be no limit to their aspirations. I would think they were in their very early twenties, but already their (one would have supposed) sturdy Scotch bodies were starting to crack up. When off duty both padded about in slippers, like their much older predecessors at Green Lane, complaining constantly of corns and bunions. Annie could hardly shake a mop without grimacing and crying out, "Oooo, ma bahck!" And both of them, as they prepared for bed in their quarters, would, to my fascinated horror, proceed to remove their teeth.

There were other Scottish girls in service in the neighborhood, with whom Annie and Chrissie exchanged frequent visits during their time off. Chrissie would suggest, "C'mon, Ahnee, lesgorta Brooooks'!" And down the road they would scamper to visit their Scottish pals who worked for Mother's friends the Brookses. And one evening a week they would repair to the downtown Caledonian Club, which was the social hub of their lives. Probably there they would run into our dour old gardener, Mr. Webster, a dead ringer for Peter Rabbit's Mr. McGregor or Old Macdonald, if you prefer, with his straw hat and bib overalls. Annie gave me a decorated autograph book and, inscribing it to me, wrote, "In the garden of my heart many fragrant flowers grow / But the names of loving friends are the sweetest ones I know!" I knew or thought I knew at the age of seven that that was sentimental claptrap. (I don't remember collecting any autographs but hers, though I kept the book for many years.) In a similar vein, I remember receiving a book from its author, elderly Cousin Julia Schwartz, living out her days in a rose-covered cottage in La Jolla, who churned out books for children in the '20s and '30s; she had inscribed it, "To Nevill, little friend of all the world." I knew very well even then that she had me all wrong. I may just possibly have been "little friend of all those at 31 La Vereda Road," but of all the world? Who could be? Indeed, who would want to be? It wasn't till years later that I came across the source of the quotation; and now I can't remember where it came from. Like "best beloved," it has a mawkish Kipling ring to it, but I can't be bothered to track it down. Cousin Julia's book was called *From Then till Now* and consisted of chapters in the lives of children from the dawn of civilization to the present day. And very readable it was.

READING BECAME A JOY to me early in life; it has been and remains today my greatest single pleasure. Mother read aloud very appealingly, usually when one was sick in bed, but mostly, of course, I read on my own. One day she bought from a door-to-door salesman a whole set of books entitled *My Book House,* edited by one Olive Beaupré Miller, an anthology of juvenile literature in both prose and verse, chosen with discrimination. I fed on it for years—alas, literally as well as figuratively because I early formed the habit of tearing off the corners of pages and chewing them cud-fashion. (Different books on my shelves had distinctive flavors depending on their paper but were all of them delicious.) And when, like pieces of gum, they had lost their savor, I spat them out onto a nearby wall, whence I retrieved them later, dried hard, with the side against the wall smooth as the wall itself and the rest of it looking like a miniature papier-mâché mountain. Highly satisfying.

The bloodthirsty but mystical and idealistic Arthurian legends held me in their thrall for many a year. And another favorite, pure magic to me, was the Oz books, many of which Mother read aloud to me. My literary tastes since the age of fifteen have been highbrow, but if backed to the wall today I would have to admit that I would trade all of Henry James for the original sixteen or so Oz books, i.e., those by L. Frank Baum, not his inept successors. In recent years, as one of my retirement projects, I have read aloud all sixteen twice over to a group of very frail, very old people at Montecito's Friendship Senior Day Care Center. All knew the Judy Garland movie but had no idea there was anything beyond that story, which was of course merely the series' first volume, *The Wonderful Wizard of Oz*. For me, none of their magic had fled. And it was great fun inventing voices and accents for all the characters, and growling and barking and cluck-clucking at odd moments whenever the text inspired me to do so.

Except for a few years in my teens when I became a passionate supporter of the Irish independence movement, I have been a literary Anglophile, to a large degree because of the reading I did in my early years. Such works (introduced to me by Mother) as *The Wind in the Willows,* E. Nesbit's novels about the Bastable children, and A.A. Milne's books for children in both prose and verse, all provided me with a sort of acculturation into English ways of thinking and behaving that would remain a source of enjoyment throughout my life. Reading gave me intense pleasure then; and it gives me intense pleasure now to recall that earlier pleasure.

But were books my only escape (or stimulus)? Of course not. Radio was just as beguiling then as television is to today's children. Perhaps more so, because one had to engage one's imagination. I think I can remember the look, the tone, the "personality" of almost every set we owned in those days. Now-forgotten names such as Atwater Kent, Majestic, Philco, and Emerson ruled the market and found happy homes with us.

My sharpest and most emotional memories are attached to a huge Philco set with an enormous circular dial. Its bulk was tucked away, more or less, behind the Steinway in the drawing room. It might just as well have been my own. I don't remember anyone else's turning it on because, as I've indicated, the drawing room was

used only for sporadic entertaining, and of course it was mute during such gatherings. I remember one especially appealing knob that
provided swift but coarse tuning capabilities when extended but allowed slow, precise tuning when pushed home. (Another set had a
baleful green eye that expanded and contracted as one tried to find
the perfect setting.) To this big Philco I would repair when I came
home from school, either hunched up on the carpet or stretched
out at my ease. And then I would give myself up to a succession of
children's programs that filled the airwaves in the late afternoon
hours while pale daylight faded into dusk and dusk slid into darkness. How hard one tried to use and enjoy the often distasteful
products artfully pitched at small consumers! I hope Little Orphan
Annie appreciated all the mugs of steaming Ovaltine I gagged over
for her sake or Bing Crosby the malodorous Palmolive soap with
which I cleansed my grubby hands for a couple of weeks. In fact, I
was so susceptible to radio commercials that once I entered a con-
test sponsored by King's Kredit Klothiers in Los Angeles in which I
was challenged to come up with a catchy final line for a limerick
touting the excellence of King's fall line of haberdashery. What can
have possessed me to enter it? The grand prize was a suit with *two
pairs* of *long* pants! (It would be at least three years before I would
be allowed to sport even one pair.) For weeks I rushed home from
school, no dallying on the way, to ask whether there was a big
package waiting for me. After a few weeks of feverish anticipation,
I received a letter from King's Kredit Kustomer Kompetition offering to name me a semi-finalist if I sent them ten dollars. I teetered
on the edge unbearably for a week, and then finally decided that
my entry was good enough to stand on its own (metrical) feet
without subsidy. To tell the truth, the young cynic smelled a rat,
I'm proud to say. And to this day I have been deprived of the joy of
owning a suit with two pairs of pants.

But radio was far more than children's programs, far more than
the comedy hours of Jack Benny and Fred Allen and Eddie Cantor
(or the daytime soap operas I listened to in bed when I was home
from school with a cold, like "One Man's Family," along with that
captivatingly folksy old rascal, Dad Rango, endlessly hawking his
snake oil from Tijuana, just out of reach of the feds). No, radio
meant music, music, music!

"How potent cheap music can be!" one of Noel Coward's characters murmurs dreamily in a love scene (*Private Lives,* I think). I remember being a passenger in Brosie's Ford V-8 coupe when he was a freshman on vacation from Yale, and I asked him why classical music was considered to be superior to popular music; I can even remember the very block on Milpas Street where I put this profound question. His answer came after a moment of sober reflection while shifting gears: "Well, I suppose because it appeals to a higher part of us." That may well be, and I accepted it as a reasonable answer. But if it's true, then Brosie and I don't have a higher part to our natures, or at least not one accessible by classical music. Nor did my father, Ambrose Cramer, though he was not man enough to admit it. I remember in my thirties attending a piano concert with him at his summer place in Camden, Maine: two grand pianos played with great flash and style by a Jewish refugee couple, the Luboshutzes, Genia a lovely-looking creature with a swan-like neck, and her maestro/husband Pierre, who pinched women's bottoms as adroitly as he tickled the ivories. Father fell asleep during every single piece, though he later denied it, and tried to make up for it when the music stopped with a furious clapping of hands and cries of "Bravo! Brava! Encore!" He was smitten with the woman's charms; otherwise he would have invented some excuse for staying home. Of course he loved classical music! It was part of a cultivated life! He huffed and puffed when I accused him of hypocrisy.

So it is cheap music, pop music, dreamy love songs that I remember so well from those days, and indeed all the days from then till now: songs that recall to me as sharply as Proust's madeleine the aura of a summer, or a term or a year at prep school, or the bittersweetness of young love. What was there in the lovers' song "Blue Moon" to catch at the heart of a little boy far too young even to think about love, let alone yearn for it? Or in "Winter Wonderland" that would make it nostalgic to a child who had never seen snow or even wanted to? Or in "The Little Town of Doona," with its sentimental picturing of a dreamlike town that couldn't possibly be as appealing as my own beloved Montecito?

In the '30s the airwaves were vibrating night and day with "big band" music. Recently I sloshed my way through a bottle of wine, instructing my usually random unconscious to dredge up some of the more obscure bands from that era. Here are a few that fought their way up into consciousness through the vinous fumes: Isham Jones, Jan "Idol of the Airwaves" Garber, Anson Weeks, Ben "Yowza" Bernie, Ted Weems, Carl Ravazza, Lud Gluskin (!), and Ted Fio Rito. Others sprang onto my mental screen much more easily, but these are the jewels of my collection, and I offer them to readers of my generation with no strings attached. When I was ten or so, I wrote down the names of all the band leaders I could think of and then ranked them according to my view of their excellence. How do you suppose I discriminated among such *maestri*? I think I must have done it on the basis of their names since I lacked the ability to make nice musical distinctions. I remember showing my long list of carefully ranked bands to a friend, George Crane, who took piano lessons. He thought it a foolish idea and snickered. But then George loved to snicker. I pointed out to him that it was at least harmless, unlike his ringing doorbells and making a nuisance of himself with his parents' friends and neighbors trying to talk them into buying Cloverine salve. (He got it from a distributor in the Midwest, who kept sending it to him in quantities far greater than he could dispose of, so it piled up in his closet till his father stumbled over it and in a fury sent it all back to Cedar Rapids.)

On a higher level, there were marvelous hour-long sponsored radio programs featuring the prominent opera singers of the day, or at least those with attractive personalities in addition to their golden voices. In the darkened room, I would lie by the hour on my back on the carpet next to the big Philco, lost in a dream of aural glory. I think of Lawrence Tibbett and Gladys Swarthout, Lily Pons, Vivian della Chiesa (I'm proud of myself for retrieving that name, though there is no face to go with it as there is for the others), and John Charles Thomas. The last-named caused consternation among the trustees of Montecito's Music Academy of the West in the early '50s when he used his position as musical director to take romantic advantage of young female singers in his charge. For is there anything lovelier than the human singing voice at its finest, stretched to capacity? What warm-blooded young woman wouldn't succumb to a passionate baritone, tenor, or bass, depending on her tastes? Let us be thankful there are so few of them to humiliate us voiceless ones with their splendor.

I don't want to give the impression that I became a devotee of opera. I just liked an occasional aria in the context of a commercial program. A contemporary of Isaac Newton's said of him after he had attended his first opera: "The first act he heard with pleasure, the second stretched his patience, at the third he ran away." Now, I have no feeling for or against his theory of gravity, but today I regard him as a very sound critic of music. (At the age of ten I was taken to hear a road company perform *Rigoletto* in the Granada Theater. That was supposed to be a treat?)

ENTHRALLING THOUGH THEY WERE, reading and radio were mere background activities because soon after we had moved to La Vereda Road, school began to dominate my life. In September of 1929, just days after my seventh birthday, I pedaled off to the Crane School, a rural mile away, on my new big-boy's Columbia bike with balloon tires and a basket for books in front. Crane was in its second year of operation and still lacked grades one and two, so I was skipped into the third grade. It must have been an easy transition into this all-boys' school because I remember no trepidation whatever. It felt totally natural and totally right, so much so that I have no memories of the first day. My teacher was a pleasant but commonplace young woman, who changed her name by marriage during the first year. I thought that a strange thing to do, though, come to think of it, my own mother had given me a precedent not long before. And another strange thing: she pronounced *fatigue* to rhyme with *pig*. I felt embarrassed for her but realized it was not my place to correct her. Still, it shook my faith a little. At the age of seven I realized that teachers were not infallible; was anyone? Probably not, I decided. One very important thing she did teach me, however: with regard to handwriting, anyone who failed to "close" his *a*'s could not keep a promise. Whew! That was a powerful discovery! And even though since then I suppose I have broken promises from time to time, I have *always* made sure that I go back to close a sloppily done *a*. On balance, at the time I felt that this bit of wisdom was as much a plus as the *fatig* thing was a minus. And, besides, she was a pleasant and fair-minded woman. (I did not know then that one might expect even more from a teacher: this I learned from another Crane teacher, one of my very few lifetime heroes, Arnold Lejeune, about whom I will have more to say presently.) When this worthy woman married in the course of the year, it was to a man who ran a gas station. She let it be known that he would be glad to provide tires for our parents' cars, so I made casual mention of the fact at our dinner table. Pop announced that he could use a set, and a deal was soon consummated. Soon after, my teacher gave me a crisp dollar bill as a commission, possibly the equivalent of $10 today. My reaction was not that of the budding young capitalist who would go on to found a retail empire; far from it. I was bewildered and embarrassed. I had thought I was doing a good deed; I certainly had no wish to make a profit. Now I was "unclean," yet my instinct told me it would hurt her feelings if I refused to accept it, so I kept it.

Irrational I know it to be, but it has always been my gut feeling that money and work are two separate things. For one thing, when I was growing up, men in Montecito didn't work for a living. Most were not rich, but they knew how to get by on what they had, and they all sent their children to private schools if they had any pretensions to gentility. So when I became a private school teacher at the age of thirty, I was embarrassed to receive my first pay check even though the money would come in very handy what with my newly acquired mortgage, and I continued to feel embarrassed bi-monthly for the next twenty-six years. But not embarrassed enough to return the checks uncashed. And it wasn't till I retired that I found myself in a position to volunteer my labor and so feel right within myself for the first time. And yes, I realize that it was my grandfather's fruitful efforts in the money line that prevented me from having to spend my life getting the better of others, often the fate in the business world of those who are so conditioned to "succeed" that they don't even realize that that is what they are doing.

Grade four meant a new teacher, one highly regarded by all. She was the descendant of a very old Santa Barbara family, though its origins were Danish rather than the usual Spanish or Mexican, and her pride in it did not prevent her from changing her name not just once, but twice during my years at Crane. I wonder if she was inspired by parental behavior, for, not to mention myself, hardly any of my classmates bore the same names as their parents. (Mother said Montecito had been called "a sunny place for shady people," but she never made it clear as to whether she agreed with that judgment.) As I have implied, this woman was both likable and competent, yet what struck me chiefly about her was that whenever she wore a bright, canary-yellow skirt and sweater ensemble, it brought into display quite a prominent little pot belly. I was fascinated by what I referred to among my classmates as her "pot of gold." I swear that it disappeared from view whenever she wore any other color. Now is that a peculiar and perhaps well-known property of yellow clothes, or was there something free-spirited and un-inhibited about this sunny outfit that made her just want to "let it all hang out"? At about this time, we were studying a rudimentary form of geometry and acquired a smattering of geometrical jargon. I soon came up with an imaginary sentence that was well received by my classmates as it blended one of these bizarre new words into a more familiar, homey context. "Hi, Mrs. Ludcke, is your pot in use?" Of course this was spoken offstage, not in the presence of the good woman herself, and stands as a fair sample of my fourth-grade humor—jaunty, irreverent, and just a touch pedantic. I like it even today.

In the fifth grade, we encountered Mrs. Learned. She was different in that unlike her predecessors, she was not instinctively drawn to children. It soon became clear that one had to earn her respect and affection, which was a novel idea indeed, and repellent to many of her charges. (What odd creatures our teachers were turning out to be! Mrs. Ludcke, who had seemed such a good friend when we were in her class, either ignored us or spoke sharply as we careered about the covered passageways now that we were no longer her little darlings.) Mrs. Learned was an arresting-looking woman, tall with auburn hair framing a white face accented by prominent cheekbones and deepset eyes, and all this over a long, shapeless body. Arresting, and formidable.

But not formidable to me. In fact, I very soon became "teacher's pet." This was usually the kiss of death for a boy, but it didn't work that way for me. I knew that I was being singled out for the quality of my work and not because I was that unforgivable thing, a "goody-goody," and my classmates were aware of and re-spected this distinction. On the contrary, I was mischievous like many bright children who finish their work quickly and have lots of time and energy left over to pester others. And besides being the best all-around student in my admittedly small grade (remember that this was an expensive one-sex school in the early and virulent stages of a massive depression), I was good company because of my quick wit and lively sense of fun. Respect came my way, too, on the sports field and tennis court, where I excelled at anything that had to do with running and rackets. I took it for granted, when we "chose up" sides, that I would be one team's first choice, or even one of the captains who would do the actual choosing, and it wasn't till years later that I developed enough empathy to realize the agonies that ill-coordinated boys must have endured when they were left dangling all the way to the end of the choosing process. This must have been especially destructive in the small world of Crane.

But though I soon became aware that I was blessed with above-normal abilities in certain areas, I found that in others I was mad-deningly deficient. My singing was erratic, to speak kindly of it; I never knew what note would come out when I tried to follow along in a song. It was a conscious effort for me to keep in tune, and by no means always a successful one. It was horrifying to hear my voice (softly, of course, for I had to be cautious) take off on a line of its own. My greatest fear all through Crane was that I would be obliged to sing a solo in front of a large group. Silly; who on earth would have asked me to? And my art work was contemptible. I never progressed beyond the level of a third-grader. Thursday, when we had our weekly art class, was the worst day of the week for me; I dreaded it for days before. Dear little Annie Cruickshank, noticing my Thursday dejection, would urge me to perk up, insist-ing that "School days are the best days of your life. Enjoy them while you can!" What bunk grownups do talk! What her remark boiled down to, I decided with the acuity of an eight-year-old, was that she preferred being a schoolgirl to being a chambermaid. But for me, it was hard to reconcile my easy triumphs in the classroom and on the sports field with my appalling performance beside the piano and on the drawing tables.

❧

AND I HAVEN'T EVEN MENTIONED "shop"—woodshop, that is. It was far more awful than music or art because unlike them it was not confined to one blessedly short class period, but rather lasted interminably, indeed completely wiping out my beloved sports on its appointed day, and I think even the final class period that preceded sports. It lasted *for hours!* Even as one may have a compulsion to probe a sore in the mouth with one's tongue or relentlessly pick at a stubborn scab, so do I now find a fearful pleasure in reconstructing, in revivifying, the horrors of shop. There were predecessors, but the shop teacher I best remember was a middle-aged man named Bill Dobson, who wore a sawdusty smock and was relentlessly upbeat and wholesome. If he temporarily forgot the name of an object, he referred to it as a "hootenanny." Any novel approach to a problem was introduced by "Now here's a new wrinkle." (At first, George Crane and I thought he was referring to his face, and wondered why he would be boasting about something most adults wanted to play down.) All things considered, he filled the position admirably.

So what was wrong? Well, the worst thing was that the tools wouldn't work for me the way they did for other boys. I always had to get help in making the first cut with a saw, whether a cross-cut or a rip saw. For me, the damned saw just bounced to left and right, refusing to bite into the wood. Not sometimes; always. If I was working with a plane, I became so involved with the rich, thick curls that were making a sort of bow-wave in front of my speeding hand that I would plane way below the pencilled line that I was shooting for; and then, of course, the piece of wood had to be discarded. With a spokeshave I cut great jagged splinters; nobody else could do that, even if he wanted to, which he didn't. My nails went in at an angle and came out the other side. My thumb was black and blue from the vicious hammering it took.

What sort of things did I make? Well, I remember spending an entire term on a plywood wastebasket, mitred at the corners and laced together with leather thongs. When I stained it, the stains made ugly runs that dried before I noticed them. Think of it: one whole term! Two hours should have sufficed. When the term was over and teachers' comments were mailed home, Mr. Dobson summed me up thus: "A slow but careful worker." Well, as I have already said, he was an upbeat kind of person. One reason I was so slow was that to pass the leaden hours I spent a great deal of time bothering my classmates, interfering with their projects but making them laugh at the same time. It was my hope to be sent out of class, but Mr. Dobson was just too kindly and long-suffering. One day I deliberately plunged a knife into the soft flesh under my left thumb. It spurted blood very satisfactorily, and I was bandaged and sent home in the early afternoon to my great joy. It got me out of shop for a week, and I still bear the proud scar.

Far and away my most ambitious project was building a twelve-foot skiff with centerboard, mast, and mainsail. This I built after a fashion in the eighth grade along with my classmate, John Demory, but with a great deal of help from Mr. Dobson. It took the entire year, and even then we didn't quite finish caulking the seams. When it was launched in Santa Barbara harbor, it filled with water during the first night and sank at its mooring. I didn't know a wooden boat *could* sink. It had to be rebuilt, pretty much from scratch, by a professional boatbuilder on Stearns Wharf. I will return to this ill-fated craft in the next chapter. Its sailing history is of a piece with that of its construction.

Not long ago I read a biography of Robert Louis Stevenson's American wife. She was quoted as making the point that RLS could do nothing right with his hands, so she coined a word to indicate the reverse of *handy;* she called him *handless.* Handless is what I was; handless is what I am. I come by it honestly, genetically. My enormous, powerful, and athletic grandfather was handless; so was his wife, Grace, who was astonished that her daughter Katharine Gray was able to remove the cap from a milk bottle. My mother to the end of her life could not figure out how to make a peanut butter and jelly sandwich, which she dearly loved. And I almost forgot to say that I was drummed out of the Cub Scouts for not being able to tie my shoelaces.

Perhaps my favorite "handless" story concerning me is one I was reminded of not long since by my former stepson, Piero Fenci. One day, many years ago, when he was seven or eight, I gave him a model airplane kit that turned out to be beyond his powers. Evidently I forgot my disability and pitched in with gusto. After about an hour of sweaty labor and juicy cursing, I was able to complete all but the last step. But the sub-assemblies just would not quite fit together. Clearly, to my mind there was only one solution left, one that Piero says he will never forget because it was such a shockingly unexpected climax. I took the wretched model, just a hair away from its completion, and with a foul oath smashed it to bits over my knee!

BEFORE GOING ON to specific memories of life in grades six, seven, and eight along with their teachers, I want to focus on a few tidbits that may add color to these reminiscences. We were served a hot lunch daily in the dining room after one of the heads said grace. The food was edible rather than delicious and relied heavily on macaroni and cheese and the like. I remember with particular distaste a loathsome vegetable called baked squash, which I refused to eat, exposing myself to a verbal whiplashing from Mr. Crane. (I threatened to vomit, which took the pressure off me.) Today my wife serves it to me now and again. She says I'll learn to like it. At seventy? Another thing besides squash that cut down on my schoolboy appetite was the pervasive odor of tobacco leaves that hung heavily in the dining room. It transpired that Alfred, the Filipino chef who lived on the premises, rolled his own Manila cigars in his quarters, whether for his own delectation or to supplement his salary one never learned. The smell lingered there as long as Alfred did. When he was not attending to his luncheon duties or working on his Manilas, Alfred used to wander out to the tennis court at recess to watch us at play. I can see him standing by the net, calling out the magic words that kept the game going, but giving them a Filipino twist: "Pom Pom Pool Avay! Pom Pom Pool Avay!" It was a fine game, Pom Pom Pull Away, but I don't remember a thing about it except Alfred. Have any of my readers ever heard of it?

After lunch we were issued rectangles of light-brown canvas known as ground sheets. We spread them out on the grass under broad oak trees and took our ease, reading or dozing, while our macaroni was digesting. Silence was the rule, but it took a very observant monitor to prevent acorns from flying through the air. At the end of the rest period we queued up with our sheets in front of a special closet, where a teacher waited to receive them and hang them up by their brass eyelets on protruding rods. A very neat procedure, undoubtedly the work of Mr. Lejeune, the headmaster. I look back upon this daily interlude very happily; I suppose the reason I didn't resent the loss of time from touch football or baseball was that I greatly enjoyed reading. Two books from the school library come to mind that I read with total absorption on those ground sheets: *For the Honor of the School* by one Ralph D. Barbour and *The Peterkin Papers* by a Boston lady, Lucretia Hale. Both were turn-of-the-century charmers. The first had a hero who was impossibly noble and pure, constantly challenged by a villainous lad who broke all the rules and cared only for self-aggrandizement. Of course there was a thrillingly climactic football game with a last-minute touchdown by our hero. The other book concerned a hopelessly inept family devoid of the most basic modicum of common sense. They were rescued from their predicaments over and over by the wisdom of the Lady from Philadelphia. I hope *The Peterkin Papers* is still in print; though they were very much of their period, I see no reason why the tales wouldn't be delightful reading today. When still very young, I came across James Russell Lowell's *Bigelow Papers* and assumed it would be something very similar. How wrong I was! I never trusted the word "papers" in a title again.

Murray. Murray Mathers (not his real name)—a classmate all the way through Crane until he went on to Thacher and I to Cate. What a curious fellow he was! He did a lot of twitching and jerking, so much so that it was said knowingly that he had St. Vitus' Dance, whatever that may be. He was certainly different from the rest of us. No one teased him; eccentric though he was, he had his own dignity. Boys said that he would disappear into the oak woods adjacent to the school and there strip off all his clothes. We thought this was bizarre in the extreme. But had anyone actually observed him in the forest, naked as a jaybird? I doubt it. I don't remember him at all on the playing fields, where my most joyful hours were spent. Can his parents have got him a special dispensation? His father, who drove him to school every day from the family's eyrie atop the Riviera, was just as twitchy and jerky as Murray; in fact I invented for him the name of "Wink 'em, Blink 'em, and Nod," taking liberties with the childhood rhyme. Mr. Mathers was thought to have been shellshocked in the Great War, and that could certainly have accounted for *his* twitching, but what about Murray's?

One weekend we went on a school-organized weekend trip to the Mt. Wilson observatory in the mountains back of Pasadena. We stared through the sixty-inch telescope and discovered that Saturn looked exactly the way it did in the funnies, as one called the comics then. We spent the night in rustic cabins on the mountain. I became very apprehensive when I learned that my roommate was to be Murray; I think we were even assigned to the same bed. I didn't know what might happen. Might he be a...vampire? He had already become proficient at taxidermy, his passion; what if he tried to stuff me while I slept? I was deeply worried because he was a very strange boy. We talked for a while in the dark, and then, thank God, he began to snore softly.

Fast forward for a moment. Just after graduation from our respective prep schools, I ran into Mr. Mathers somewhere. He took me aside conspiratorially and asked me *please* to keep an eye on Murray at Williams College while I attended Harvard (never mind that the two could hardly be farther apart and still be in Massachusetts). He told me he had great confidence in me and very little in his son, who needed a steadying hand. Me—a steadying hand? My one thought as I looked forward to college after five years of cramping confinement at Cate was to raise as much hell as I could. But I could hardly tell Mr. Mathers that. I never saw father or son again. What can have happened to Murray? I hope he broke new ground in taxidermy—back in Indianapolis, that is, where the family came from. For years I fretted over having Murray, my grandmother's maiden name, for a middle name.

In the sixth grade I encountered a male teacher for the first time, Paul Crawford. He was a fine fellow. I have no special recollections of his classroom presence, but he was a joy to have on the sports field. About six-foot-six, and a former varsity basketball player from Occidental College, he had grown up in China, where his father was a Presbyterian missionary. He was manly and genial and fair, and his presence on our field (think of it, a varsity basketballer, playing with us little squirts day after day!) gave dignity and importance to our track meets and football and baseball games.

In spite of his background, he never emphasized basketball; thank God, because I was terrible at it, yet excelled at all the other games. Perhaps he felt the game would be ruined for him if played with shrimpy ten-year-olds. He went on to become a highly respected teacher and administrator at Santa Barbara High School.

IN GRADES SEVEN AND EIGHT, when they were our teachers, we came to know well the two heads of the school, Mr. Crane, referred to as the principal, and Mr. Lejeune, the headmaster. I wonder how they divided their responsibilities. Probably they played to their different strengths. The division was so careful that they rotated the duty of saying grace before lunch. I must say I never saw fur fly between them, though they were both strong-willed. I think I'm right in saying that the Englishman Arnold Lejeune had already started a very small school in Carpinteria, spurred on by Mrs. Curtis Cate (of whom more in my Cate chapters), but that soon afterwards New Yorker Bill Crane, prepared by St. Mark's and polished by Harvard, who had left his post as an English instructor at Caltech, arrived in Montecito with his wife and two boys, itching to start a school for young boys. The two men were brought together and in 1928 founded with Crane money a proprietary school to be known as the Crane Country Day School. The impressive list of original trustees, headed by the president of Caltech, soon dwindled to the two men themselves plus Mrs. Cate, an intimidating woman indeed, and my mother. Why Mother, I've no idea. I never asked her, and she never told the story of her being invited. I feel pretty sure that Bill Crane was responsible, feeling that Mrs. Cate was in Mr. Lejeune's pocket and that he needed a vote he could count on. (The Lloyds had a social relationship with the Cranes.) I do know, presumably from Mother, that the board was often stalemated, two to two, along just those lines. A predictable situation, surely; why not remedy it with a fifth member? I don't know the answer to that, and it's too late to find out, since the four involved are long since dead. Can it be that they failed to find one impartial person in all of Montecito? I think that the meetings must often have been acrimonious because I never heard Mother say a kind word about either Mrs. Cate or Mr. Lejeune.

But from my point of view, Mr. Lejeune could do no wrong. For one thing, he made math and science interesting. In fact, I didn't know until I had left his tutelage that I detested both subjects. His own competence, thoroughness, and enthusiasm caused me to overlook (almost) the vile stench in the science room, in which there were unspeakable horrors suspended in jars, pickled in formaldehyde. We performed rudimentary experiments to prove that the ocean had a stabilizing effect upon the climate. We raised silkworms and fed them mulberry leaves from our own tree, and the worms actually produced what we were told was silk. We watched caterpillars turn into butterflies, or was it the other way around? Every day, first thing, I was assigned to read a special thermometer that registered the day's extremes in temperature, and somehow Mr. Lejeune made me feel that this was a privilege instead of a tiresome chore. After several months, he commended me for my faithfulness and exactitude in carrying out my task; he was testing my sense of responsibility, he said. Of course I swelled with pride. (My good wife would say, "It's just because you're a Virgo.")

He taught us geography, too. I remember researching (I suppose plagiarizing would be a more accurate word) piles of old *National Geographics* to find material for a long paper I did on the Gobi Desert. I can see him in my mind's eye handing this batch of papers back, and prefacing the return with these musical words: "Far and away the best one was Nevie's on the Gobi Desert." I don't think he read it aloud as it told a good deal more about that bleak land than anyone in the class would have wanted to know. All I remember of it was the name of the distinguished anthropologist, Roy Chapman Andrews, who provided me with most of my material. I hope I gave him credit. And I remember also that I did not, unlike my classmates, flesh out a skimpy paper with lots of pictures cut out from magazines. Even in those days, I knew that nothing is so satisfying as well-chosen words. To hell with the art work.

Another time I gave a detailed talk, complete with maps, on a subject assigned to me: "The Physical Features of South Africa." George Crane gave me a bad time for a long while over that title. It did have a pompous ring to it, but after all that *was* what it was about. He would mutter the words into my ear at odd moments and then snicker. Fortunately for me, one day in class he was asked to read aloud from a map the names of some obscure island groups in the South Pacific. When he came to the Society Islands, he pronounced their name as the "Soashety" Islands, and I let him have it with both barrels. I heard no more about the "physical features."

Mr. Lejeune was from Manchester and incurably English, to the point of chauvinism. George resented this, but I enjoyed it. Perhaps my Anglophilia began at this time. We heard endless stories about the great inventors of the Industrial Revolution. I learned far more about the home life of James Watt and Michael Faraday than I ever did about Thomas Alva Edison's, and of course everyone knew the Flying Scot was far superior to the 20th Century Limited. His kindly, florid face would glow with pleasure as he transferred some of his seemingly vast store of knowledge into our empty little heads. We heard a good deal about strange things called cooperatives, which were meant to usher in a utopian era for farmers and consumers alike. In 1932 the school held a "straw" ballot for the presidency. The students were unanimous for Hoover, the faculty mostly for the new man, Roosevelt; and there was one ballot for Norman Thomas, the Socialist. Of course that quixotic vote was Mr. Lejeune's. I thought it quite dashing—no, that is not the *mot juste* for Mr. Lejeune—independent and fearless, perhaps. And I had grown more tolerant of the strange ways of grownups since the election of 1928, when I had been a six-year-old at Green Lane and was outraged that the maids vocally and without shame supported Al Smith against Hoover. (Lest this be misconstrued, let me say that I have never cast a *real* ballot for a Republican, except maybe once for Earl Warren, and I considered him an honorary Democrat.)

Mr. Lejeune was so unreconstructed an Englishman that when Paul Crawford was sick and not available for sports, he would take over and have us play something called rounders, which he declared to be a great favorite with British boys. It was no favorite with us, being a sort of half-assed baseball—exactly the sort of thing, said George, the British *would* like. And he introduced a pastime called Morris dancing during our music period in the assembly hall, a species of English folk dancing handed down through the centuries. (And while we were dancing, there was no chance that I might have to sing a solo!) Very physical with lots of movement, the dances were quite good fun. We formed in opposite rows and, spurred on by a walloping piano, would whirl down the length of the room as we sang out traditional words: "A-hunting we will go, a-hunting we will go; we'll catch a fox and put him in a box, and then we'll let him go!" Mr. Lejeune took a very active part. I can see his long flanneled legs like great scissors as they covered the ground, swinging up and down the room on the hardwood floor, feet noiseless in his beloved rubber-soled Footjoy shoes ("They're so comfortable I never wear anything else"), his face glossy from exertion, but his coat and tie impeccably neat.

Only once did I ever see this controlled, even-tempered man knocked off balance, and that literally. During a nighttime Halloween party at the school, when we all wore silly costumes and masks that pretty well hid our identities, George Crane muttered to the boys around him, "C'mon, let's get Lejeune!" And, seeing his man only a few feet away, he launched a flying tackle that brought his lanky prey crashing to the ground. I turned away, horrified. But Mr. Lejeune took it in good part, got up, dusted himself off with his hands and went about his business. I must admit it took a lot of nerve on George's part to do that. Perhaps he felt secure in being his father's son; perhaps, too, the animosity that underlay the tackle sprang from the fact that he saw Mr. Lejeune as a dangerous rival to his father. Or maybe he was just sick of hearing about the Industrial Revolution in Old Blighty when what he really wanted to focus on in class was the American Revolution, in which the Lejeunes of the world had got their comeuppance. As for me, I noted the fact that Mr. Lejeune's mouth movements, when chewing his food at the lunch table, were exactly those of a rabbit. This was a discovery of great pith and moment, and I had to share it with George. Together we watched him as he nibbled his lunch, and tittered behind our napkins. Then one day we managed to sneak into his office and leave on his desk a plate with nothing on it but a lettuce leaf. I wonder what he thought of that. I like to think he nibbled it and went about his business refreshed. I liked and respected the man enormously.

William Dwight Crane, known to his friends as Bill and to his two sons as "Da," was a different kettle of fish. Unlike the coolly rational Arnold Lejeune, he was all emotion. English and history were his fields. In addition, he was in charge of dramatics and con-

75

ducted the daily assembly that brought the school together. To these responsibilities he brought great but wavering enthusiasm; I would say he lacked emotional staying power, and refractory children tested him beyond endurance. He could switch from extreme affability to rage more quickly than any other adult of my aquaintance. (Pop of course wasn't even in the running because he didn't have the affability to start with.)

Mr. Crane would get so wound up with enthusiasm in front of the class that he would generate foam in the corners of his mouth. Naturally George and I hopped on to that little trick, but we couldn't mimic it. One either is or is not a foamer; it is not a trick one can learn. But we would exchange smiles as Da stood before us, carried away with his excitement over the Boston Tea Party, and of course he would see us laughing inappropriately and lash out—at poor George, invariably.

He was always ready to take it out on his own children. One day he found out—I can't imagine how—that George's toenails were too long. Perhaps his wife, Kitty, had phoned him the news and told him to do something about it. He stormed down to the ball field, made George expose his offending toes and delivered a fierce tongue lashing quite out of proportion to the offense. Hysterical, really. But the nails *were* awfully long.

I've gone too far in painting a picture of a very emotional man. He had a lot of charm and warmth and a radiant nature. It's just that he wasn't all of a piece, like Mr. Lejeune. One felt that he was trying too hard to be a loving and beloved schoolmaster, that he saw himself playing that role and kept grimly at it even when it didn't feel right. He wrote his own quirky textbooks and printed them on his home press. He wrote anti-war plays that the boys acted in (I think he'd been gassed in the Great War). Then he went through a period when the big thing in his life was scouting and scoutmastering; and that role didn't really fit him either. George and I thought he was obsessed with the idea of being wholesome. We were not.

One day he was reading something aloud to a group of boys outdoors under the spreading oaks. He read out the words, "and they came upon a pair of asses, munching the grass." We could hardly believe our ears. Obviously the same vivid, forbidden picture flashed into our minds, and we both burst out simultaneously with uncontrollable guffaws. Mr. Crane tried to carry on, and addressed us with withering scorn, but we didn't wither. He shouted. More laughter from us. Then Mr. Lejeune came swiftly up behind us and without a word whisked us away to a classroom and shut the door behind us. No one ever referred to the incident again. No one, that is, except for George and me, and we laughed about it at Cate, we laughed about it at Harvard, and when we were old men in his mother's house forty-five years after the incident, we laughed about it again.... Think what you wish, but remember that when all is said and done, people aren't *forced* to teach twelve-year-old boys.

A singularly pleasant memory I have concerning Mr. Crane is of the annual evening in December at the Crane house when he would gather his seventh- and eighth-grade students about him and read Dickens's *A Christmas Carol* to us before a hospitable fire. He was a genial host and he read aloud very well.

But there was a great deal more to life than just going to school, and that is what the next chapter is about.

Above: Mother, her sons, and assorted pets at La Villetta.
Below: On the beach at Miramar. Nevie, Joanie, Grandmother Meeker,
Horace Gray, Jr., and Aunt Katharine Gray.

Above: Brosie and Nevie at La Villetta.
Below: The puppy on page 78 has grown a little.

Above: At Edgecliffe Beach we were known as Carrot Top and Cotton Top.
Innocent as we may look, this was the summer of our shoplifting escapades.
Below: The only picture I have of Pop, in Palm Canyon, Palm Springs.

I like this one, so it gets a page to itself.

Above: With my sister, Nancy Lloyd, at Constantia.
Middle: Gymkhana practice at Cate.
Below: With Unky at his Swiss chalet near Luzern.

Above: After rehearsal for the Latin play. Richard de Mille (extreme right),
when I asked him recently to account for my expression,
said instantly, "You're thinking, 'What am I doing
with all these ghastly people?' "

Below: Cate's Class of 1940, an unusually small one.
Front row: Kendal Forman, Mr. and Mrs. Cate, Michael Macauley.
Middle row: Philip Hamilton, Richard de Mille, Ned Donohoe,
Nion Tucker, Stewart Sargent, Bill Savage, and N.C.
(the oddly folded hands were to ward off the Evil Eye).
Back row: George Crane, Robin Skewes-Cox, Willard Porter.

CHAPTER FOUR

🌀 Time Off

WHEN I WAS A NEW ADMINISTRATOR at Laguna Blanca School in the early 1950s, we decided to institute a dress code that severely limited students' choice of clothes. The latter complained that they would be deprived of a chance to wear their own favorite clothes (yes, of course, that was the whole point of it). After a little figuring on my fingers, however, I was able to establish the fact that at a day school, students spend more days at home than at school in the course of a calendar year, and that therefore we were not seriously infringing upon their rights to adorn themselves. This shut them up for many years.

And so it was for me that though my life at Crane looms large indeed as I think back upon it, its significance shrinks before the sheer bulk of my time off, as it were, and the rich variety and complexity of experiences to be lived through as a member of a family, a family dominated by its tyrannical and ill-tempered head, who set the tone, established the rules, and prescribed the way of life for the household on La Vereda Road.

Brosie and I still today delight, because of our fondness for mimicry and fun-poking, in addressing each other in the manner of Pop: "Brosay! Nevay! You young jackass! You young whippersnapper! God damn it, why can't you...!" It was unending. Nothing we ever did was right. And of course the converse was that everything *his* children, Pick and little Nancy, did was perfect. In order to be able to walk freely about in our carpeted quarters upstairs without his bellowing up the staircase to shut up and not make so much damned noise, we hit upon the protective device of stamping about as noisily as we possibly could so that he would think it was the guiltless staggering of his little girl. Of course this gave us double satisfaction: the joy of hoodwinking him as well as the keen pleasure derived from knowing that the noise was driving him nuts and he couldn't do a thing about it.

Mealtimes were grim. I daresay my table manners left something to be desired (my wife says they still do), but his behavior left even more. The slightest infraction on my part led to a sharp whack with a heavy silver spoon across the knuckles; a few moments later, his tall torso would slump in his chair as he lunged forward with his feet to kick my ankles savagely. At these times, we thought we could see steam hissing out from his ears. Amusing today, less so then. Mother often left the table in tears, but as far as I know, she never scolded the old wretch. And I never complained to her or to anyone else. He didn't hate one; he just had a poor disposition and a vile temper. ("Just"?) Never as long as she lived did we so much as hint to Mother that we felt any resentment over her choice of a second husband. There was nothing Hamlet-like about our resentment; we liked the idea of her marrying again. But why not to a nice man? We had friends who were pleased with their stepfathers, who were, in fact, on such easygoing terms that they called them by their first names. Genial, smiling men, and besides much younger than our old grouch. We picked out a bachelor that we christened (without his knowledge, of course) "the ideal stepfather": Charlie Hague, a banker with a pepper-and-salt moustache, an ever-ready smile, and a kindly chuckle. We couldn't imagine that he would ever lose his temper; in fact, that was the only qualification for the title we awarded him. Besides, he was the golf champion of the Valley Club, whereas our old duffer broke out the bootleg champagne on those very rare occasions when he broke 90 there.

In the early '30s there was a popular song whose words went, more or less:

All I do the whole day through
Is dream of you;
(Da da dum, da da dum)
Morning, noon and nighttime, too;
All I do the whole day through
Is dream—of—you!

Not well remembered, but the best I can do. The important thing is that whenever we sang it to each other, and we sang it frequently, we substituted "crab at" for "dream of." We called it "the Pop song." "Pop is a weas-el" was another and more obvious alteration of an original. These were some of the petty ways in which we expressed our displeasure with the tyrant. To the outside world, we breathed nothing. Like Resistance fighters on the continent in World War II, we went underground. We had each other; that was sufficient. Some day we would emerge to wreak our vengeance. And meanwhile we would make him ridiculous, at least in our minds.

I must add that my elder brother, fortunate fellow, and I did not share equally in absorbing Pop's verbal blows for the simple reason that even as I was enrolling in 1929 as a new student in the third grade at Crane, he escaped by going off to board at the Cate School on a hilltop in Carpinteria. That means that I had a more or less unrelieved diet of Pop until he died in 1935, whereas Brosie had only to endure him during vacations.

Besides a conventional two-car garage connected to the back door of our house by a covered passage (along which I once chased a tormenting Brosie, armed with a Daisy air rifle that I intended to kill him with except that he slammed a glass door on my forearm, requiring an emergency trip to the surgeon and lots of tears at the injustice of it all), there was a free-standing building that contained both a single garage and a playroom that opened on to a sizable lawn area available to us for fooling around with baseballs and footballs. Now this was a good setup, obviously, and we made excellent use of it, both indoors and out. The playroom contained all the usual things, especially games and costumes and model boats and ships, but it must also have served, partially at least, as a storeroom for Pop. Because there, in a chest of drawers, we came across some of his Great War memorabilia. I remember a weighty official history of the 315th Infantry, in which he had served in the front lines in France. I read through it, unnourishing though it was. And one fine day we came across a dozen printed copies of a poem, a long, long piece of the rankest doggerel, written by an enlisted man in Pop's battalion which, as a major, he had commanded.

This poem consisted, to our astonishment and disgust, of endless stanzas in praise of Major Lloyd. Each stanza ended with the refrain, "Behind bold Major Lloyd." The gist of it was that he was a model of bravery, and never asked his men to do anything he wouldn't have done himself. Could this be the same Francis Vernon Lloyd that by then we knew so well? One stanza near the beginning opened with "He left his family house / A mansion, I am told", and went on to paint a picture of the noble gentleman leaving his teary wife, child, and law practice behind to become a heroic *citoyen-soldat*. Alas, that's the only line besides the refrain that either Brosie or I have been able to remember over the years. Of course it was insupportable to have Pop immortalized as a hero; but the deed was done, and how could it best be countered?

What we did was, with a pen, to blank out the second "b" in the refrain "Behind bold Major Lloyd." And because there were a great many stanzas and we wanted to make a neat job of it, it took us a long time. Oh, but it was worth it.... But why, we wondered, had he ever left his beloved army if it suited him so well? And what could we do to get him back in? Alas, a rhetorical question.

Another day we made an enormously gratifying discovery. Pop was forever boasting about the exploits of the undefeated Princeton football team in his year of graduation (the "Class of Oughty-ought," he called it, i.e., 1900). He had played left tackle on the varsity, and carried a gold charm to commemorate the distinction. So far, so good—for him. But, while rummaging in the drawers of a chest in the playroom, Brosie came up with a yellowed newspaper clipping and proceeded to scan it for a minute or two. "Listen to this!" he ordered, his voice crackling with excitement. As he summarized it, it seemed to be a eulogistic critique of the victorious team's season. But then, eyes sparkling, he put his finger on a sentence and handed it to me. "Read this out! Just that one sentence. It's the only one where he's even mentioned." I did as I was told. And there came into focus before my eyes these magical words that we still love to repeat to each other some sixty years later: *Lloyd plays too high in the line.*

MEANWHILE, he had two very substantial toys to play with, Depression or no Depression. Picture first his yacht, or *yatch*, as he

spelt it, the John Alden-designed schooner *Wanderlure II,* moored in
a harbor with no marinas and a mere dozen or so sailing yachts.
She was thirty-eight feet long, a sensible size, big enough to be sea-
worthy on cruises to the treacherous waters around the Channel Islands and yet easy to manage with a small crew. Speaking of crews,
Brosie and his good friend Jack Manning fell into that category;
Mother and I did not. Jack served ably for years and by way of
thanking the skipper crafted for him a beautiful scale model of the
schooner, about a foot long, housed in a glass case. Brosie owns it
today and displays it proudly. Mother was early judged to be value-
less on board and was given the permanent chore of coiling loose
ends of lines and sheets—ropes, to the layman. This kept her out of
Pop's way. Occasionally he would invite a friend aboard to serve as
deckhand for an afternoon sail in the channel. As one might imagine, he was a veritable Captain Bligh, roaring like a tormented lion
at the slightest misstep on the part of one of these "friends." Only
very rarely did they pass muster and receive a second invitation;
even more rarely did they accept that second chance to serve.

And what was my role aboard? I really didn't have one. It seems
to me I spent most of my time avoiding the critical eye of the skipper, sitting disconsolately on a hatch cover or moving swiftly up to
the bowsprit ("One hand for the boat, one hand for yourself, you
young jackass!") to get out of shouting range. I loved sailboats,
power boats too, as long as I wasn't on them. I was sensitive to
their beauty even as I was to cars', whether they were at anchor or
in motion (and provided I was not). I loved the sense of movement
and speed in a car and felt utterly secure at any speed and with any
driver at the wheel. On a boat, however, I was either numb with
ennui or scared out of my wits when the boat heeled over farther
and farther as the skipper hauled in the main sheet. I remarked that
if God had wanted us to sail that way, he would have made us with
one leg shorter than the other. This was thought by the quarterdeck
to be a good witticism, but the skipper was not about to mend his
ways for little Nevie-pie (or just plain "the Pie," as I was often foolishly called).

All the time we were headed away from port, I was glum and
withdrawn, sulky even, thinking every nautical mile we covered
meant we were just that much farther from port, but there came a

point in the afternoon when the skipper finally, reluctantly, grudgingly, altered our heading so that the boat was steering for the breakwater, the dear old breakwater, and suddenly I was joyful and sure that sailing was the sport of sports and I the most fortunate of children.

MY OWN PERSONAL SAILING HISTORY came a few years later, after Pop had been permanently bedded with heart disease, but this seems to me to be the place to insert it in my narrative; in other words, put all the sailing stuff together and get rid of it. So here I am eleven years old, having just finished the seventh grade at Crane. The little sailing skiff, belonging to the "moon boat" class, has just sunk at its mooring. Mother concludes shrewdly that we (Mr. Dobson, John Demory, and I) have not built it properly and has it hauled out of its watery grave to be rebuilt by a professional.

It took the man forever, and you may be sure I was not there spurring him on, but one day he announced he was satisfied that it was time for the skipper to take over his new responsibilities. I think my shop-class partner must have bowed out at this point because I don't see him in the boat at all, just in shop class, endlessly caulking. Now Brosie, near the end of his Cate years and almost ready for Yale, had built a moon boat with a classmate and called it *Moon Mullins* as a tribute to the chief character in the comic strip of that name. It was summer time, and the sizable fleet of moon boats had already raced many times in the harbor before mine was re-launched. *Moon Mullins* was a distinct success; Brosie and his partner took turns winning many a race. Deciding to capitalize on his new fame as a skipper, I named my craft *Kayo,* after Moon's little brother in the strip, the one who slept in a bureau drawer. Now it was time for me to take a deep breath and plunge into the world of racing. But suddenly I realized the hideous truth: in spite of all those years aboard our schooner, I hadn't the slightest notion of how to sail a boat!

Not the slightest. I had never held the wheel or noticed under what circumstances it was a good idea to "come about" or known when to let the mainsail out or haul it in. I had been content to serve merely as ballast. And now what had I let myself in for? One tends to forget things one doesn't want to remember, so I find I have no real memory of taking a lesson or two from Brosie, but I must have—surely one, at least. The rudiments of sailing are not complex, and the little boat was only twelve feet long, with a mast in proportion. How much can there have been to learn? Once one identified the direction the wind was coming from, surely all action flowed naturally from that. But there, of course, was the problem. I never did figure out where the wind was coming from, and therefore I never did sail properly.

That summer was one in which I became master of the art of evasion. Mother would say as we lunched peacefully at Edgecliffe Beach Club, "Look, dear, there's going to be a perfect sailing breeze this afternoon." Out to sea there were angry whitecaps; not my idea of a perfect sailing breeze at all—not for anything under eighty feet. "Gee, too bad! I've got a court reserved for 2:00, and you know how mad Mr. White gets if anybody cancels out." "What a shame! Well, tomorrow, then."

And tomorrow: "Oh, there's not enough breeze. I'd just get becalmed if I went out."

And so it went. Then, towards the end of the summer, I learned that Brosie, the wretch, had signed me up to take part in the big race of the season, from the harbor all the way down to Miramar, and then, after a lunch break, all the way back. I was paralyzed. My pleas were ignored, and the ghastly day rolled around. He agreed to sail with me downwind to Miramar. (I didn't realize that was the easy leg that any landlubber could have done alone.) So he relaxed comfortably, encouraging me to take the tiller occasionally and filling me with false confidence while his partner sailed their boat and placed very well. The *Kayo* finished dead last because it was the heaviest, carrying two bodies. Though I have just mentioned the name again, I must tell you that I never liked the boat well enough to have that name painted on its counter. I probably felt that if I didn't make its name official, then perhaps the boat didn't even exist.

On the last leg, headed for home, I was alone in my boat for the first (and last) time in my life. I had just learned that this would be a leg involving endless coming about and tacking, since the wind was coming from dead ahead. I'd never tacked in my life. I had to now. I overdid it. I must have, because I made virtually no progress forward. All my motion seemed to be at right angles to the course I needed to follow—back and forth, zig and zag. It was like being trapped in a maze. Suddenly I saw another moon boat, closer to shore than I was; I made out that it was skippered by a girl who seemed to be in trouble, having apparently lost control. She suddenly stood up, the little boat slammed right into a groin jutting out from the beach, and she went overboard. Well, thought I gallantly, now I won't be the last to finish.

No, but the next to last. Half an hour later the wind died completely. I was picked up by the Coast Guard cutter, the only pretty sight I'd seen all day, and watched moodily from the afterdeck as my horrible little boat thrashed around in the cutter's wake. That was my first and last race. I never set foot in it again. Soon it began to take on water at its mooring, and someone had to be hired to bail it out periodically.

But it had one more role to play. Not long after I had given up on it, a British naval cruiser anchored in our roadstead, a magnificent vessel. The Santa Barbara Yacht Club hospitably offered the ship's officers a chance for a busman's holiday: they were invited to unwind by racing the fleet of twenty or so moon boats among themselves, with the yacht club to provide a trophy. And the race took place as planned, though I went nowhere near the waterfront on race day. A couple of days later a story was printed in the *News-Press* complete with race results. At or near the top (I don't remember which) stood the *Moon Mullins,* belonging to Ambrose Cramer and his partner, and at the very bottom, number twenty in a field of twenty, was the good ship *No Name,* belonging to Nevill Cramer. I expect the fellow who sailed her had to bail every nautical foot of the way.

The young people who had lent their craft were offered a guided tour and tea aboard the cruiser, a handsome gesture. Guess which one of the twenty boat owners regretted the invitation. I couldn't bear to look that poor officer in the eye because he never had a chance.

POP'S OTHER TOY dwarfed the schooner; in fact it was 5800

acres big. He had lived for many years with the persona and trappings of the gentleman yachtsman and foxhunter and felt it was time to try out another macho role: himself as a Westerner, a bigtime cattle rancher with Stetson and spurs. He and a golf crony named Ed Gilbert, a Santa Barbara real estate man with similar Western yearnings, scouted around the Santa Ynez Valley until they found their dream, the Brinkerhoff ranch, known only to Valley oldtimers because of its isolated but (some would say) idyllic situation. They leased it for two years to see how they liked ranching.

The ranch has been in the news as I write because, now known as the Sedgwick ranch, it has been the cause of litigation. The details are not a part of my story, but the essence is that "Duke" Sedgwick willed it to go to UC Santa Barbara after his wife's death, but the latter changed the will somehow to enable a relatively small but valuable part of it to go to their surviving children to beef up their parental inheritance. The legal and moral question now is whether UCSB is to be allowed to sell off another portion of it to raise cash for other university projects or must keep its large share intact as a nature preserve. In our day, the early '30s, the ranch was hard to find. It may still be. One drove there via the San Marcos Pass and stayed on that route, known today as Highway 154, until shortly before Los Olivos, at which point one turned right and drove for several miles until one sensed that it was time to turn left on a private road. That road, rough and bumpy, presently turned into a mini-pass over whose summit one drove gingerly in a low gear until, spread before one, lay the first view of a very private domain: level, fertile fields with crops and nearby numerous small canyons rising to meet the big mountains behind them. The experience gave one, if romantically inclined (I wasn't), the sort of feeling experienced a few years later by readers and viewers of Shangri-la in *Lost Horizon*. In fact, as one wound down the pass, a yet finer view unrolled before one to the left. Beyond the simple ranch buildings, canyons led the eye onwards with singular grace to hills that rose to meet the burly slope of Figueroa Mountain. Almost everywhere one looked one could see nothing but our ranch property. It was not at all the usual wide, sweeping view of the Santa Ynez Valley, which my grandmother, who was awfully good at complaining, criticized because, as she put it, it didn't "compose."

The scale was just right, impressive but not awesome or overbearing, and all the details of the views were pleasing to the eye and harmonious with each other. In my memory I see the ranch as painted in the tawny shades of summer and autumn, but of course there were winter and spring's vibrant greens as well.

Views don't mean much to a nine-year-old. I wanted to see the house and the barn. The former was a very simple but pleasing old brown ranch house, single-wall board-and-batten, not duded up for rich owners. No electricity. Smelly kerosene lanterns. Cooking with bottled gas. Fireplace and a woodstove for heat. One bathroom with toilet. In back a bunkhouse. The house was really a perfect stage set for a game of cowboys, and I suppose that's exactly what it was for us.

Between the house and the barn was the foreman's cottage, similar to ours, though smaller. There lived tall, drawling Henry Cox, his part-Indian wife, Juanita, and their little boy, Henry, Jr., who became my frequent playmate.

The barn was huge and weathered. Pop had bought a half-dozen or so horses, mindful of each family member's horsemanship. I was given what was always referred to as an Indian pony, though I never asked what exactly that meant; one was supposed to know. He was small, black, and ugly. He had a mind of his own, and it was a very different mind from mine. His worst habit was rolling whenever he had crossed a live stream. "Nevay, you fool, pull his head up!" But the moment I felt his knees buckling, I learned to jump off instantly because there was no way of influencing him to stay upright. Fortunately, most of the time there were no live streams, but all year round he had rotten little gaits. It was Mother who named him Zaca. She loved to give romantic Spanish names to the horses. Her sleepy strawberry roan mare she named Madulce, meaning wild strawberry, she *said*. It was also the name of a local mountain peak, but she was the only person in the county aware of this fact. Pickie's big bay horse she named San Marcos. Pop would have none of these phony Hispanicisms and called his fire-breathing buckskin gelding Dynamite. She had the last word(s), though, because she named the place "Rancho Dos Robles" after the two towering Valley oaks in front of the ranch house. But that's nothing compared with the name Duke Sedgwick chose for it when his turn came: "Rancho La Laguna de San Francisco"!

We took a lot of rides in those two years, up hill and down dale. I felt pretty much about them as I did about afternoon sails aboard the schooner—glum on the way out, happy when headed for home; and Zaca was the same. Pop's temper was no sweeter in the back country than it had been on the coast. "Grace, sit up straight! You look like a sack of potatoes on that horse!"

I remember one special moment in the barn. The wind was sighing softly through the ramshackle old building. It was late on a Sunday afternoon. In an hour we'd be packing up to go back to Montecito and another week of dreary old school. Zaca was munching hay in his stall. Something possessed me to throw my arms around his neck and bury my nose in his soft, smelly neck fur, murmuring rather stagily to myself with my eyes closed, "I'll never forget this moment as long as I live! Never!" And for years I thought of it, not because the moment was a really precious one, the way it would have been in a sentimental horse story for children, but to be true to my vow. Then it slipped from my mind as other memories crowded in with the years, to surface again now for the first time in many, many years. I'm glad it came back, stagy or not.

There was no bedroom for me, so I was given a bed in the surprisingly large dining room. I remember that on bitter-cold mornings typical of the Valley's inland climate in winter, Pop would rise and dress early and then come into "my" room and feed the stove that was close to my drowsy head. It was blissful lying back and feeling the warmth radiate out from the roaring little stove, but I knew I had to get up and throw on my clothes before the dining room was filled with Lloyds and Gilberts hungry for breakfast. The kitchen was about what one would expect in a basic ranch house and certainly not its nerve center. From my recollection of the food, Mrs. Gilbert must not have been a cook any more than Mother was. I remember that breakfasts were either corn flakes or fried eggs, the latter prepared by the men. (I wonder why choosing fried eggs is thought to be a sign of virility. Could it be that they are favored because they are bad for one, and to be concerned with health is for sissies? One didn't know about cholesterol in 1930, but in general we men do seem to gravitate towards all the wrong foods. But, come to think of it, women go to ruin in their own way with their rich desserts.) I have no recollection whatever of lunches, but I do remember the dinners, which came out of cans. The only actual dish I can recall, because it was repeated over and over, was called "chicken a la king," a misnomer if ever there was one. It was declared to be "perfectly delicious, and so easy to prepare." If, dear reader, you should ever be called upon for an example of a half-truth, I urge you to remember that one. Uncalled-for pieces of spicy pimientos floated about in the thick, greasy sauce that overwhelmed the tiny bits of meat.

The worst meal of all was provided not by the pretend-ranchers, but rather by the real thing, the foreman's wife. Mrs. Cox was paid to prepare the Sunday midday meal and serve it in her house as a treat for the city slickers who had been roughing it in their own kitchen since Friday night. The idea was to pull up a chair, let out your belt a couple of notches, plant your fork vertically in your left hand and your knife similarly in the right, and let 'er rip. *Hombre,* it was terrible! Yellow gravy with great blobs of congealed flour obscuring chunks of stringy chicken, partially mashed potatoes, and a side dish of canned fruit salad in lime jello. And the helpings were gigantic. But I can hear Pop, as we left the Coxes', clumping down the wooden steps in his boots, smacking his lips and pronouncing his ultimate accolade for tasty food, "That hit the spot!"

Roundups were an exciting event in the Valley. Each big ranch in turn would hold one, and the neighboring ranchers were supposed to go over and lend a hand. Their reward was a fine steak barbecue at long tables set festively by the womenfolk. I especially remember one at Rancho San Julian, the celebrated ranch long in the family of the Dibblees, Poetts, and their Spanish forebears the de la Guerras. The barbecue was pleasurable; the roundup much less so, since its purpose was to castrate and brand the young cattle, a procedure causing great discomfort to the animals, whose bawlings conveyed their misery. The stench of a red-hot branding iron searing the hide of a trapped animal is not one to gladden the heart or nose.

There was one thing about our ranch, or at least going to it, that I loved unequivocally. Mother and Pop would frequently drive there from Montecito in mid-week. I of course wasn't free to leave school till Friday afternoon, so arrangements had to be made for someone to drive me over in one of our cars and then return the car without me to Montecito. We family members would all return together on Sunday. The young man engaged to drive me over was a very agreeable fellow and fell in with my heartfelt plea to let me "step on the gas," as I called it, almost all the way over. For safety's sake, we would avoid the San Marcos Pass in favor of the longer but much straighter 101. This was a delicious experience, and Friday afternoons couldn't roll around fast enough to suit me. I could barely see over the hood of the car, but that was no deterrent, and the driver was at hand to take over in any sort of emergency. The feeling of response from the accelerator was one of the most satisfying feelings I have ever known and remains so to this day.

The first year of the ranch lease was a wet one; the grass grew mightily and the books showed a profit from the cattle operation. The second year was dry, dry, dry. Because there was no feed for the cattle, they had to be shipped north to Bridgeport and fattened there at great expense; the books this time showed a substantial loss. What's more, corporate dividends out in the real world kept dropping. So the lease was not renewed and the Lloyd-Gilbert partnership was dissolved. We were out of the ranching business. I shed no tears.

SUMMER VACATIONS would have been poor things without Edgecliffe Beach Club. It was owned by the philanthropist George Owen Knapp. Besides the main structure, which wasn't an essential part of the club operation, there was a fine beach with facilities for serving a daily buffet lunch. Of course there were dressing rooms for both sexes. (To satisfy the morals of the day, all males had to wear tops to their bathing trunks, and all females had to be skirted. Fortunately, girls were allowed to have skirts that were very short and tight. Even more fortunately, older women wore voluminous skirts that hid everything—except varicose veins.) There was ample non-sandy space behind the beach to provide for games that didn't lend themselves to sand. I am thinking of organized games, in and out of the water, because there was a thriving summer day camp presided over by one Paul Gerrish with two amiable college-boy assistants. This camp was great fun as it emphasized the acquisition of athletic skills and competition in exercising those skills; this was meat and drink to me, except that I had to slink away from water competition since I was a very indifferent swimmer. For one thing, I hated to put my head under water. That meant no diving and a slow, tiring head-up crawl. I feel even today that it's highly unnatural to go under, and I cannot understand why practically no one seems to feel as I do.

Then, too, I never felt safe or comfortable with the procedure taught for "floating," which was supposed to keep one afloat for hours while waiting for help to arrive. Legs were extended and arms, too, the latter at right angles to the body, head all the way back. The trouble was, to keep even partially afloat I had to tilt my head back so far that my ears filled disagreeably with water. The idea of lying in that preposterous position, with nothing sticking up out of the water but my nose and a few toes, was repellent in the extreme. I told Mr. Gerrish that I would far rather drown. Mother said, and demonstrated, that she could float standing up with only the merest treading of water. "It's so easy. You just stand there.... Stop flailing!" But I had to flail to keep myself from sinking to the bottom of the Pacific. She floated; I sank. We were apparently made of different ingredients. Years later, when I had grown fat, I concluded that our ingredients were after all the same, but that some people had more of these same ingredients than did others, and that those with a superabundance floated without effort. But now, old and tubby, what wouldn't I give to be young and scrawny again even if it meant plummeting right down to the bottom.

Edgecliffe had three rafts, connected to one another by ropes that floated, more or less, thanks to regularly spaced wooden buoys. The first raft was conventional and my favorite because it was nearest to shore. The second one was a teaching raft, in effect a salt-water swimming pool that rolled and pitched with the swells. It had deep wooden sides, slatted to let in the sea water. A clever idea; I've never seen a raft like it. I had many a lesson in it but never improved because as soon as the lessons were over, I went back to my versions of the crawl, the breast stroke, and the side stroke—with head well up in the air. Sensibly; like a dog, come to think of it, only I had the advantage there because all dogs can do is paddle. But the sound basic instinct is the same: Keep your head up. And then there was a third raft, quite far out by my standards. Its feature was a towering slide, anathema to me because whether one slid down feet first or head first, one went under and the water rushed deafeningly about one's ears. I had to feign chronic sinus trouble to keep away from that one, which all my contemporaries loved. But I did well enough in land-based games to earn a decent respect from them.

I think today's sport of surfing must have had its California beginnings around the time that I am reminiscing about, the early '30s. It was imported from Hawaii, as I remember. The boards were immensely long, made of wood, and of course extremely heavy. The legendary master of the sport was Duke Kahanamoku of Honolulu. I remember Edgecliffe's surfing brothers from Pasadena, the Caulks, and our own lifeguard, Gates Foss, as being very adept. There were others. But most of us small fry contented ourselves with riding the waves on rubber mattresses that required no skill but gave immoderate pleasure and a wholly unmerited sense of reckless abandon.

One of the best things about the summer camp, and indeed membership in Edgecliffe, was the chance to widen my circle of friends. There I met boys (and a few girls) from the other private schools in the area, and many from out of town and out of state whose parents were looking for a cool place to spend the summer. There was an especially large number from Pasadena, whose upper crust have always been rich enough and wise enough to flee their summer inferno, even before the days of smog. So I met dozens of children that I would not have known otherwise, boys and girls in some cases that became my good friends and remained friends for many years.

When the sand disappeared from Edgecliffe Point, the children of privilege lost a charming and wholesome pleasure ground that was irreplaceable. The Biltmore had a beach club of sorts with a few cabanas up the coast a quarter-mile, but it held little appeal for the young; and the hotel's glamorous Coral Casino that opened in the late '30s was intended to satisfy more sophisticated adult needs. It became the favorite summer hangout for me and my friends in my late teens, from about 1938 to 1942.

ANOTHER CENTER of activity was the Montecito Country
Club. It was a tradition for Montecito families to gather there Sunday evenings for a buffet dinner and movies viewed from chairs set
up in the ballroom. Before the lights were dimmed, the mild little
manager, Mr. Genung, used to stand before us and announce the
choice for the next week. On one night that I recall, Mr. Genung
was unable to command the respectful attention he needed and de-
served in order to make his announcement. He cleared his little
throat, but the babble of conversation would not be stilled. At last,
frustrated beyond endurance, he summoned up from some deep reserve within him a thunderous and commanding baritone cry of
"Si-gno-o-ri!" Nothing could have been more arresting. The
whole room was shocked speechless. The resounding voice, and in
Italian, too! Our Mr. *Genung?* After that, we would have listened in
perfect silence to a recitation from Mother Goose, but instead he
told us, in his usual unassuming way, that next week's treat (I
daresay) would be yet another of Martin and Osa Johnson's African
adventure films. Or perhaps Frank Buck's *Bring 'em Back Alive.* (You
couldn't go wrong with intrepid Bwana and Mrs. Bwana fighting
their way across raging, muddy rivers, and pythons devouring wild
boars inch by inch.) But sometimes we got spicier fare. One of my
very favorites was the musical *Gold Diggers of 1933.* I fell in love
with Ruby Keeler. It was so marvelous, the way that she could be a
plain little secretary with horn-rimmed glasses at the beginning and
a ravishing beauty at the end. The few secretaries and receptionists
that I was aware of never changed their looks. They started plain
and, as far as I could tell, they ended plain. And they couldn't tap-
dance either. But at least they had the good sense not to marry Al
Jolson. That was a blunder I could not comprehend. I wasn't jealous, exactly; disenchanted, rather. For I had just come up prema-
turely against the conundrum posed so starkly and so memorably by
Sigmund Freud: What do women want?

The same large, high-ceilinged room that provided cinematic
delights became associated during the winter with a far more dubious pleasure—dancing classes. These were taught by a tall and dignified lady, Kathleen Page Wheeler, who during the summers ran
Edgecliffe and at intervals throughout the year taught our parents to

play bridge. A woman of many talents, clearly; one too many, in my opinion, because I did not look forward to dancing school. White flannels, dark blue blazer, and a dry mouth: picture me thus on my first day. I knew before I even tried that dancing was going to be added to music, art, and woodworking as debits on the balance sheet of my childhood. The girls, still pre-pubertal, looked silly, though they smelled better than the boys. I picked out two as my favorites because of their adornments: one carried a very pretty purse embroidered all over with tiny pearls, and the other wore around her neck an engrossing little crystal ball that was in fact a watch. (If she had had a bosom, that watch would have provided me with a very plausible excuse to look down into it. I say, "If.")

We lined up in ranks across the ballroom behind Mrs. Wheeler and Mrs. Basham, her accompanist on the piano who pounded out the rhythms with gusto. The former stood with her back to us, one hand holding up a corner of the skirt of her long dress of plum-colored lace while she demonstrated and called out the commands for the "box" step as the foundation of the foxtrot, which, along with the waltz, was to form our entire repertoire. Way too soon the day came when we were cast adrift to dance with each other, boys and girls. I've no idea how partners were assigned; it must have been by lot because nothing else could explain the gross disparity in the couple of whom I formed the male half—or more properly, the male quarter. The girl, from one of Santa Barbara's tallest families, was in her second year of dancing whereas I, with the top of my tow head level with her lofty and ample midsection, was the rawest of rookies. Almost desperate, frequently out of step, I stumbled with my partner around the edges of the ballroom, hoping to escape notice in the general confusion. Only once did I sneak a look upwards to see if there was a face attached to this towering body I was trying to maneuver around the room, and just as I did so, she shot a savage look to a girl dancing nearby that said it all without a word: "You think *you're* in trouble? Look what *I'm* stuck with!" After that first evening, things improved, but never by very much. I still hate dancing.

And the Country Club meant tennis. The Valley Club meant old people, entertaining each other sedately and playing golf. Golf? No red-blooded boy that I knew would have anything to do with it. Sport meant running and sweating and competing with other boys. Tennis, of all the games I'm familiar with, is the one that makes a beginner look most like a fool, so I submitted with unaccustomed grace to a course of lessons. (Throughout my long life I have for the most part enjoyed teaching and disliked being taught. It has seemed to me that if a thing is worth doing, one ought to be able to figure out how to do it and do it well without someone else's spoiling it for one with his notions. This is probably a foolish idea for most people, but it's mine and I like it, even though it seems to invalidate my years of teaching. I have been largely content to learn from experience, books, and intuition. Tennis was an exception.)

The person who as teaching "pro" stood for tennis at the Country Club in those days was an interesting man, Harwood White, known to his friends as "Beece" or "Beecie." He belonged to a talented group of brothers who had migrated to Santa Barbara from Michigan early in the century. The best known of the brothers was Stewart Edward White, a very popular, nationally known writer of fiction and non-fiction of the day, very much an outdoorsman. The other brother, Roderick, was a musician (violinist?), who lived in a charming Spanish cottage with a tower to be found just off the 900-block of Garden Street in that delightful complex called *El Caserio,* the Settlement. How Beecie got on to tennis, I can't imagine, because he was intellectual in his interests. He became a close friend of my uncle, Dr. Horace Gray, who was a very serious-minded student and later practitioner of Jungian depth psychology. But how would they have come to know each other? The only time I ever heard of Uncle Horace's playing tennis was in what must have been a memorable match, never repeated, with Pop. Pop came home steaming mad after the game. "That damn brother-in-law of yours!" he grumbled to Mother. "All he did was chop and lob!" One didn't need to ask who had won.

But it wasn't tennis that originally brought the two men together. It must have been backs. Uncle Horace had a plaguy sacroiliac problem, and Beecie fixed backs. Between lessons, the latter was often to be seen bending over a man lying prone on a bench by the teaching court, poking and pulling and twisting the poor wretch until suddenly one heard a distinct crack, if one was nearby, and lo! the man rose healed from his bed of pain. Those cracking sounds began the Gray-White friendship, and Dr. Jung's theories sealed it.

Mr. White, as I called him, was a fine teacher. His much younger wife, Alex, he turned into one of the town's top women players. He had married her when she was a girl of fifteen, unskilled in domestic economy. He was not a patient husband, and whenever a dish of hers turned out to be beneath his reasonable expectations, he flung it out the window. She didn't "file for dissolution," as young wives would today, citing "irreconcilable differences"; instead she became a very good cook. And, later, for the same reason, I suppose, a very good tennis player.

I don't think I started out very well; I was certainly no prodigy. But in time, after several summers of lessons and games with other children, especially my cousin Joan Gray, I developed into a tolerably good player. There were tournaments for children at the Club and on the Biltmore courts, where I played often, too; I won my share. Young and old, all wore white ducks; no shorts in those days. And one spring George Crane and I got to the semi-finals in doubles in our age group in the prestigious Ojai tournament.

And, as was the case with Edgecliffe, the Club introduced me to children from all over that I wouldn't have met otherwise. Montecito was such a small and seemingly self-enclosed world in those days that I emphasize the importance to me and my peers of the community-wide contacts provided by Edgecliffe, the tennis courts, and yes, even the abominated dancing class. Those who are relatively new to this area may find it hard to appreciate what a small community Santa Barbara was in the 1930s. It was indeed possible, through the social mingling mentioned above, for all the children of the *gente de razón* in the same age group to know one another, no matter how many miles within the county separated them. I am no demographer, but I remember the population of the city as being between 30,000 and 40,000; and that's where virtually the whole population lived. I doubt if there were more than 3,000 in Montecito. Carpinteria was just the little town and surrounding orchards—no tracts. Goleta town had one real street and a school; no tracts, no shopping centers, just ranches and farms. Summerland had oil derricks and temperance and spiritualist kooks. Santa Ynez village looked like a Western ghost town. There was one gas pump there, pumping out Gilmore Red Lion gas by hand. The little corner store where we often stopped on the way to our ranch was the world's smallest, surely. We used to buy chocolate bars called Horsefeathers from the proprietress, Mrs. Edelblute (four syllables), and Nehi sodas. So just in case you thought they were, note that brand names are not eternal. Solvang had today's overhanging arches down the main street but hadn't thought of going Danish, even though its main store was called Nielsen and Petersen. (Its slogan was the memorable "We've got it, we'll get it, or it's not to be had!" For years I longed to put that to the test but was never allowed to.)

I NEVER AGAIN had a Christmas as special as the one featuring Fanny Brown-Browne and the wieners on the tree at La Villetta, but the memory of one from the early '30s at La Vereda Road has delighted me for some sixty years. Actually, this incident took place just before Christmas. Mother and Pop were at a party. Dinner, including mine, was being held for their arrival. At last the front door opened, and I went to greet them. Mother came in first, plainly flustered. "Don't pay any attention to Pop. He had too much to drink at the Ogilvys'." Naturally I couldn't take my eyes off him when he did come in, but we quickly made our way into the dining room lest the dinner be spoiled. And there the big man sat, at his place at the end of the table. His movements were clumsy. He spilled the salt and a glass of water. His voice was thick, and he said the same things over and over. I'd never seen anyone out of control before. It was most interesting, but frightening, too; in fact, more frightening than interesting. I was afraid he would lunge at me. It was a long and awkward meal, with Mother looking pained throughout. We left the dining room, crossed the large entrance hall, and started down the narrow hall that led to the panelled study where we spent our evenings. He caromed off the walls in turn before he lurched into the study, where he slumped to the carpeted floor and sat there, looking around bemusedly.

Then it dawned on him that it was almost Christmas, and that he hadn't yet wrapped his presents for his wife. "Get me the flower potsh," he ordered me. "I'm going to wrap them." He had bought a half-dozen flower pots bright with glazes, blue and green and yellow, as a surprise for Mother. And now he proposed to wrap them right in front of her. I did as I was ordered and brought him the red tissue paper that was the only paper he felt comfortable with. Apprehensive as I was, I couldn't help smiling as I watched the ridiculous scene. There was Mother, pretending to be deeply involved with her murder mystery but sneaking glances at the action on the carpet. And there he was, the cynosure, trying to wrap the pots with clumsy motions, then giving up and just jamming the paper in frustration into the maw of the pots. I thought of poor Eeyore on his birthday, gamely making the best of a bad job, stuffing the popped balloon from Pooh and Piglet into the empty jar and pulling it out again, over and over, pretending everything was all right. I must admit the scene humanized Pop in my mind, and I never did see him drunk again. On Christmas Day the pots appeared nude under the big tree without a wisp of wrapping, but bright and gay and glossy, and Mother reacted as though they were a complete surprise.

The next summer Pop had a heart attack. He and Mother were at Edgecliffe (I wasn't that day) and had just stepped into the ocean to take a swim. Apparently he keeled over with no warning. I imagine he was pulled ashore and that people swarmed around him as they always do in a calamity. A doctor from Montecito who was a club member and happened to be present stepped forward with his black bag and did something that saved Pop's life. (In a few days the doctor, who lived a quarter-mile away from us and whose daughter was a friend of mine, sent a bill for $2,000, which would be about $20,000 in today's money. Understandably, this caused a great deal of grumbling at home, where the ethics of the medical profession were called into question. The Hippocratic oath was reviewed scornfully.)

It transpired that Pop had had a serious illness (rheumatic fever?) when young that had weakened his heart. He had never mentioned this to Mother. From now on, said the cardiologist, he was to lead a sedentary life and be pretty much housebound. This must have been very hard for such a physical person to accept, but as far as I can remember he endured his plight stoically. Of course he became even shorter of temper, if that is possible, and I did my best to avoid him. He hadn't much in the way of inner resources: his reading tastes ran to the *Saturday Evening Post,* sacred because it was published in Philly, Zane Gray, the cowboy Will James, and P.G. Wodehouse. "Just Plain Bill" and "Amos and Andy" he loved. He started to whittle blocks of wood into animals for his little daughter, Nancy. I would sum them up by saying that he was not inept, but that he was not very ept, either; his ducks, for example, were recognizably, but not attractively, ducky. He whittled a great many animals and then ran dry of ideas about how to spend his time. At this point Mother, who according to her sister Katharine did not have a way with sick people, engaged a trained nurse, as R.N.s were called at that time. This was a smart move as it got him off her back—he was growing increasingly restive and irritable—and mine. Lucky Brosie was at Cate.

The nurse was named (Mrs.) Abigail Conroy, and she was a trimly attractive, small, grey-haired woman. To Pop's great joy she had served overseas in the War as a lieutenant. She called him "Major," which was the sweetest sound he had heard since he had been mustered out. He was usually irritable with Mother but ponderously jocose with "Connie," as she soon came to be called by her patient. The two endlessly swapped yarns about the good old days overseas. Brosie and I did an imitation for anyone who would listen that purported to be Pop's differing responses to morning greetings from each of his two women: first a grouchily resentful "Good morning, Grace," followed by a beaming *"Good morning, Connay!"*—a line delivered with all the skittishness of an elephant greeting its favorite *mahout.*

WHY DO MANY PARENTS think that children need planned activities during the summer vacation? Every year we tried to fight off efforts to fill our days with wholesome busy-ness. One summer I spent endless hours in a pottery-making class, where I tortured coils of damp clay into ugly bowls and mugs and fashioned a tiger that came back from the glazing works all white so that my father thanked me for a magnificent polar bear. Couldn't he see the tiger's lean, muscular body under the glaze? (Mother used to send him most of the things I made, probably as a punishment for having spoiled their marriage.) Another year Cousin Joan and I were sent every morning all the way to Mission Canyon to study nature lore along with other listless children. No sports, no competition, no fun. But at least we were ferried back and forth in Grandfather Meeker's enormous skyblue-and-black Excelsior limousine, a supremely visible vehicle of Belgian origin with the prized feature of an extra pedal called a cutout, which, if the chauffeur was in a good mood and let me step on it, had the function of bypassing the muffler and producing a sound so terrifying that pedestrians clapped their hands to their ears and ran out of sight.

Brosie by now was a licensed driver and had been given Pickie's outgrown Model A Ford, a charming little tan roadster with lots of dash and style. He "allowed" me to help him wash it and polish the beautiful chromed headlights, separate in those days from the body. But of course I was given many a ride in it to compensate. I especially enjoyed watching the speedometer, which was of an extraordinary gelatinous consistency and moved horizontally. The little car had forty horse power and sounded like a tractor.

Brosie had inherited Pickie's name for the car and the lame little joke that went with it:

"Its name is David Hunt."

"Why?"

"Because it's as good as any other name." It didn't seem to me that it was. But if that was Pickie's Stanford humor, who was I at ten to scorn it?

I call to mind one magical trip from this period. Because Pop was not present and yet I see myself as being ten or so, it must have taken place during the time Pop was an invalid. In fact, he probably gave orders to Mother to get the Cramers out of the damned house for a while before he went berserk. Mother, Brosie, and I travelled on the glorious white steamer to Catalina. That would have been exciting enough, but on board with us were the two English members of that year's Wightman Cup team, Dorothy Round and Mary Healy, who were like goddesses to me because of their fame in the world of tennis. We had a chance to see them play an exhibition game, and we did the glass-bottom boat ride and saw zillions of flying fish and wandered through the touristy little town of Avalon and spent happy hours poking around the grounds of the old St. Catherine resort hotel, a cove or two away from Avalon.

But what I chiefly wish to shine the glaring beam of memory on is something that took place in that very hotel, in our twin-bedded room next to Mother's. As we were getting ready to call it a day, one of us chanced to look under his bed. What an extraordinary discovery—a potty!... "And here's another, under *my* bed!" How old-world could one get? What a fusty old dump we were in! We were absolutely enchanted, and our hands went instantly to our flies. In mere seconds we had peed our libations into the bowls and, howling with laughter, opened the door to Mother's room to show her what good use we had made of our treasures. Like Queen Victoria, she was not amused. In fact, she became angrier than I ever saw her, before or after. She was apoplectic, almost shouting. "I'll never take you horrible children on a trip again. Never!" We could not understand the depth of her anger. Apparently we had transgressed in some extraordinarily provocative way. "Now go to bed, and I don't want to hear another word from you! I'm ashamed of you both!" We weren't ashamed in the least, just astonished and even embarrassed by her performance. Grownups were impossible to figure out.... And besides, she had ruined our sleep the night before with her snoring.

Mother had a short fuse and we were fond of lighting it, but it sputtered out quickly. Here are some examples of her fury that she hurled at us over and over in childhood: "You boys must think I'm made of money!" "*Will* you stop tormenting your brother!" "*Will* you stop that constant bickering!" "I'll wash your mouth out with soap!" "I don't know what I've done to deserve two such children!" After all, as we occasionally reminded her, we didn't ask to be born.

I HAVE MADE IT PLAIN that though I certainly had friends in my life, they did not mean a great deal to me. Perhaps it would be more accurate to say that I enjoyed their company during daytime activities on neutral ground but had no wish to have them over for a meal or—especially not—to spend the night. George was forever badgering me to spend the night with him on those occasions when his older brother was away and had vacated his bed next to

George's. Once or twice I agreed to spend the night with him, but I didn't enjoy it. The atmosphere was tense because his high-strung parents frequently blew up at each other without regard for their audience. Mrs. Crane in a fury shied a tennis shoe at Mr. Crane in my presence. I was greatly embarrassed at witnessing it, but when I was home again I decided the incident was comical. And I didn't twit George about it even though it was the kind of thing that grownups did only in the funny papers, certainly not at home. With roles reversed he would have given me a bad time over it, as he did over Mother's wig. I never knew how to handle that one. Brosie and I laughed endlessly about the wig, but never to outsiders. (I christened her "Mrs. Wiggs of the Cabbage Patch," the title of a well-known children's book.)

I often shared with my friends one great pleasure from this period of my life, a pleasure that lasted through the entire period covered by this memoir. El Camino Pharmacy—what happy recollections that magical name revives! "L. Miratti, prop." (Because of that sign, Brosie and I thought and spoke of him as Elmer Atti even though we knew his name was Louis.) The store must have opened around 1930. After a long day at Crane, we boys would bike directly to El Camino, which was across from the Montecito Inn in the building nearest Olive Mill Road, there to restore our depleted energies with sugary food and drink from the long counter. All the customers were friends or parents of friends; it was Montecito's prime meeting place. The milkshakes were ambrosial—*thin* so that one could taste the chocolate and actually drink it, not like today's monstrosities that offer blobby mouthfuls of tasteless, chewy slush. And the perfectly toasted peanut butter and jelly sandwiches! And rack after rack of comic books to riffle the pages of. And my favorite Street and Smith pulps, especially ones with rousing baseball stories, not to mention, as I grew a bit older, the furtively bought copies of *Spicy Detective,* long on titillation but nothing below the belt. Mr. Miratti wouldn't have tolerated that. A shrewd businessman, he left El Camino to tap the rich Upper Montecito market by founding San Ysidro Pharmacy on East Valley Road, which soon became a much more sophisticated gathering place for Montecitans. But El Camino, with its matchless counter, lingered on for years in other capable hands.

I have dozens of memories of El Camino, but one comical one that I'd like to share with male readers, wondering if they were ever in my position. It concerns my first jockstrap, comparable, I suppose, to a girl's first bra, though even more intimate. Of course it would be a woman that waited on me. "An athletic supporter," I muttered to her, my head down. Fortunately I remembered that generic name, less gross than its common one. "What size?" she asked, loud as a pistol shot. My God, what do I do now? I thought. And thought. "Large" would be preposterous in a twelve-year-old, but "small" was out of the question for obvious reasons. After a long pause, I leaned across the counter and whispered, "Medium." It wasn't till years later that I learned that the article in question is graded according to waist size.

My only intimate friend was my cousin, Joanie Gray, but because at this period of my life the Grays lived in San Francisco, we saw each other only in the summers, which they spent in their house in Montecito. Our families were very close, and we were thrown together a good deal. I will write about our relationship at some length in the chapter in Book II called "The Grays."

THE PERSON whose company I most intensely enjoyed was my brother. Opposites in most ways, he the classic extrovert conformist and I the introvert non-conformist, we shared and still share our sense of humor. There were times when he directed the full strength of his pleasure-loving nature in my direction, and that made me very happy indeed. At such times we got on beautifully and I could not imagine a greater happiness. However, there was a five-year gap between us with all that that implies, and it must be said that no matter what fun we might be having, if anybody better (i.e., older) turned up, male or (especially) female, little brother got dumped. This was inevitable and part of me understood it, but it was a betrayal, repeated many times, and it always hurt. I must admit that I became skillful at playing the role of obnoxious little brother with girlfriends I didn't like, and bright, perky little mascot with ones that I did.

I was of course able to benefit from his sophistication. He it was who got us started on coin collecting. Our favorite sources were intoxicating catalogs from Otto Odehon and B. Max Mehling, numismatists based in far-off Midwestern cities. We had an envelope for each foreign country's coins, and I went so far as to make, astonishingly, quite an acceptable box in woodworking class to hold them. My favorites, probably because of my fondness for classical myths, were the Roman coins, which may well have been stamped out and antiqued in Kansas City, but to me they were glorious artifacts of almost unimaginably far-off times. Yet we had our share of more humdrum modern European coins of the sort that might have been useful in riding the trams in Budapest.

One summer we fired off requests for autographs to dozens of major-league ballplayers, and a surprising number responded. That summer's mail was far and away the most thrilling I have ever received. With what feverish anticipation did I flip open the lid of the mailbox, peering to see if there were self-addressed envelopes with my childish printing to identify them! And then to return to the house, gloating, to empty out their contents and compare my treasures with Brosie's. (A few years ago Brosie suggested we sell the collection, which he had kept intact all those years. He found a buyer in Los Angeles who paid us $2500 for the lot. With my share I bought a motor scooter, something I had always wanted, at the age of sixty-five.)

We were both hopelessly in love with baseball. We knew everybody's batting averages, RBIs, homers, and other bewitching data. Besides, I carried this interest over to track and field, for which sport I knew all the current records in every event. ("Virgo, pure virgo," my wife would say.) If anyone "misspoke," I corrected him instantly. These were important matters; error must not be tolerated. To this day, my brother remains a rabid sports fan, watching all of the major sports on TV. As for me, I may watch bits and pieces of a tennis tournament, but that's about it. Oh, and for old times' sake, the last game in each World Series. And, come to think of it, though I detest active sailing, I love watching the America's Cup races from my armchair.

We invented a way of playing baseball with playing cards. Simply by dealing cards, we recorded balls and strikes, base hits of all kinds, and anything else needed to make the game work. We made up our own scoring system since we didn't know the regulation way of keeping score, and it worked very well indeed. We formed our own highly specialized competitive teams, of which I remember but two. One consisted solely of old ladies, the more wildly improbable the better. One player was an extravagantly ugly old woman we often saw at Edgecliffe in her grim black bathing suit. We thought of her, a Pasadena beldame, as "the Belle of the Beach," and she went on the lineup as Belle. Another was our own grandmother, as unathletic an old lady as ever lived. We visualized her in bloomers. Two of them were our cleaning women. Yet another was a friend of our grandmother's whom we called (because we'd seen her at the beach in her swimsuit) "Potato on toothpicks"; she became a nifty shortstop. Every woman was superbly miscast in her role, but the cards had them rapping out doubles and homers, as well as striking out or hitting pop flies. A team they often competed against was made up of local male characters who were important threads in the fabric of our daily lives. One man was on our batting order as E.C. Walker. He had his own name in real life, but as he seemed to spend his entire day endlessly walking, walking, back and forth from his home on Channel Drive to El Camino Pharmacy, we called him the El Camino Walker. We marveled at how little he seemed to expect from life, but in our games he was a tireless outfielder. A surprisingly heavy hitter was the fellow known to us, and to others I think, as the Milpas Street dwarf, about four feet tall, who was often to be seen on his favorite street, right smack in the middle of the Haley Street intersection, with a policeman's whistle in his mouth, trying to direct traffic before he was gently forced back to the curb by an indulgent cop. Then there was a man we called Amos Safeway, the manager of the Safeway store on Milpas. This was the only big market in town, referred to in those days not as a supermarket, but as a "cash and carry" store. Amos, with a protuberant Adam's apple like Andy Gump's in the funnies, was the manager, who caught our fascinated attention because we decided that the blue sweater he habitually wore was fashioned of pieces of string tied together. Evidently Safeway's Depression clothes allowance for managers was a meager one. But he was one of our outstanding pitchers, master of a very tricky, though illegal, spitball.... A stimulating game.

Brosie occasionally took me to see professional wrestling in a dilapidated old tin-roofed building that stank of cigar smoke some-where on the lower Eastside. I loved every moment of it. Of course the matches were staged, even as they are on TV today, but they were exciting and funny at the same time. I enjoyed learning each man's specialty that distinguished his performance from all others. One favored the "elbow smash"; another took flying jumps onto his opponent's supine body; yet another harassed the referee outrageously. We usually sat near the ring, and I lived in fear that one of these huge monsters would land in my lap; I was ready to bolt at any moment to save my skin. I loved the way a "wrestler" would use the ropes like a slingshot, propelling himself across the ring at his opponent, who would neatly dodge him and then whack him down with a neat chop on his neck. Very much a part of the performance was our mailman, "Hippo" Espinosa, who did the Montecito rounds daily in his own "woodie" station wagon. He was the announcer, a man for whom the epithet "leather-lunged" must have been invented. His face did look a good deal like that of an elderly and kindly hippopotamus but with some-thing of Popeye's Wimpy thrown in because his cheeks seemed to seal his eyes shut.

And once Brosie took me to a carnival on the old circus grounds, small in scale but big in sleaze. The only activity that I re-member clearly took place in a small tent, for which Brosie paid a special admission fee for both of us. The tent was filled with slouching, seedy-looking middle-aged men, foreheads sweating and lighted cigarettes or cigars drooping from their mouths. Recorded music was tinnily playing "In a sailboat, in the moonlight" while a faded and fattish woman of about forty dressed in nothing but a g-string shook and shimmied before us. This was the first mature naked woman I had ever seen. She was not a good example of the species. At least I hoped she wasn't.

AS TIME WENT ON, Pop grew no better. He hardly ever left his bed. Dinner time was depressing because there were only Mother, Nurse Conroy, and I at the big table. (Where were Davie and her charge, little Nancy? I don't know. Not at our table, at any rate. They must have supped earlier, fortunate ones.) The talk was of the latest doctor's report, of medicines and laxatives, of changing diagnoses and treatments.

The months passed drearily by, and it was spring vacation of 1935. Brosie was home. He was on the verge of graduating and moving on to Yale, our father's college and our maternal grandfather's, too.

One morning very early Brosie pushed open my bedroom door. "Wake up," he commanded. He paused for dramatic effect.... "Pop died last night." I could think of nothing to say.

"You're supposed to cry!" I couldn't have cried to save my life. There were no tears in Brosie's eyes either.

A new era had begun; we knew that. There was no one to be afraid of any more. Mother would be a pushover.... Let the good times roll!

But it didn't turn out that way. Does it ever?

CHAPTER FIVE

🐚 Cate I

MOTHER WAS WEEPY for quite a while following Pop's death. To Brosie and me, "The oldest man he seemed that ever wore grey hairs," in Wordsworth's telling verse, yet Pop was a mere fifty-six when he died. About twenty years ago, on Brosie's fifty-seventh birthday, I found pleasure in reminding him, who had always gloried during our childhood in being the elder by five years, that he had now outlived his stepfather and was officially a very old man. "Don't think I don't know it," he said glumly.

Mother wore "widow's weeds," as black mourning clothes were called in those and earlier days, and Brosie longed to be allowed to sport a black armband on his coatsleeve because a Cate classmate, a handsome, elegant Eastern boy, had set that particular style a year earlier when his stepfather had died. It was seen by his classmates as something very chic, a clothing option not available, after all, to the average boy, something, in fact, that money couldn't buy. Unfortunately for Brosie, our Episcopalian minister said it was quite unnecessary. I could have hugged him because at the level of twelve-year-olds, I knew it would be a social disaster. George Crane alone would have made life hell for me.

From this time forward and for many, many years (she outlived him in contented widowhood by forty-eight years), Mother referred to her late husband in our hearing as "Poor dear Pop." (Between ourselves, we changed that to "PDP.") Many years later she took to referring to him as simply "Pops." Since his death by then was far in the past, "poor dear" had come to seem inappropriate. Adding an *s* seemed to give it that little emotional fillip that she was looking for. Needless to say, he remained just plain old Pop to us.

The other day in writing to a friend, I mentioned that I was enjoying myself greatly by writing a book. I knew that he was try-ing to start one himself and might need a little encouragement, so I added, "It doesn't take much to make writing a book worthwhile. In my case I am savoring the chance to pillory my stepfather, who died when I was only twelve, but not before wrecking my nervous system." That was meant to be funny, but it was also true. He really did damage my nervous system to the extent that I go to pieces when I am under what I feel to be intense pressure. Up to a certain point, I function as I should: the adrenalin flows, and I fully accept the challenge to succeed. But if the pressure gets to be extreme, then I go to pieces and fall into what today is called a clinical de-pression. I don't intend to go into the symptoms, but they have been strong enough to require therapy and medication. I suffered such a depression when I was twenty-one in the Army Air Force during World War II and again when I was a teacher in my late for-ties. After the first episode, I underwent a Jungian analysis to find out what lay behind my collapse. Dream after dream pointed to the same source: Pop, and the harshness of his commands and demands. When the going gets really tough, I become flustered and can't function, just as I became all thumbs literally and figuratively when he would bark and bellow at me. A child with a different makeup would very likely not have reacted as I did, but I was a sensitive, even hyper-sensitive child. Let me stress once more that I never said anything to Mother concerning my true feelings about Pop. What good would it have done? He couldn't change his disposition, and if I had complained about him after his death, Mother would have felt guilty. Better to let her live with the strange illusion that he was a dear fellow. Brosie and I knew better; that was enough. And writ-ing him out of my system in these pages helps, too. If my concern with him has seemed a little obsessive, my readers will now, I hope, better understand my reasons for that concern. Perhaps I have suc-ceeded in laying his large and angry ghost. R.I.P. (Rest, Ill-tempered Pop.)

Mother's income was diminished by Pop's death, though her fa-ther continued his generous subsidies. One-third of the Lloyd estate went to her, a third to little Nancy, aged about five, and a third to Pickie, who was now out of Stanford, independent and about to beome a teacher. It was necessary to reduce the household expenses. At this point a most extraordinary woman came into our lives.

Emma Krick, known as Emmy, must have been about forty when she came to La Vereda Road, and she made her home with Mother for the rest of her beautiful life, more than twenty-five years. Emmy was apple-cheeked, with black hair drawn back into a bun. She was earthy and physical, a peasant type, and German to the core. A superb natural cook, she busied herself during all her waking hours doing useful work in and around the house. There was no stopping her. If there was nothing that obviously needed doing, she'd get down on the floor and wax the tiles of the large entrance hall or polish the brass doorknobs of the double front doors. Everything was clean, shining, sparkling. She not only cooked the delicious meals, she served them, did the dishes, and made all the beds. She did the laundry and ironing, this at a time when there were no washing machines, just scrubbing boards and laundry sinks. In later years, as labor-saving inventions became popular, she would have none of them until they had proven themselves for ten years at least and some respected German friend nearby gave unqualified approval; otherwise, they were just inventions of the devil. She took sole care of Mother's Sealyhams. She grew vegetables and flowers, arranging the latter to perfection and displaying them in the main rooms and bedrooms of the house. The only help she would allow Mother to provide was a cleaning woman, and I am not sure what the latter accomplished other than going over what Emmy had already done, but I do believe the bathrooms were the special province of the cleaning woman.

Selfless, she was—the only person I have known of whom I can say that. Virtually everything she did was to give pleasure and satisfaction and show kindness and love to others. And instinctively, not consciously. Quite different from me; I have done a lot of what most people would consider "good," especially during the years of my retirement, but I am always regrettably *aware* that I am doing good, and that removes a lot of the goodness. Emmy was all instinct with a minimum of self-awareness. Mother often referred to her as "the peerless Emmy," a loving and accurate phrase. "Peerless" indeed; I have never known anyone who was even in her league.

It was Emmy who, right around my thirteenth birthday in early

September of 1935, gave me a cram course in bed making, starting from scratch. Why then? Because in a matter of days I would be off to board at Cate. My dream of being greatly indulged, of getting away with everything, that had seemed so almost shockingly attainable a few months before when Pop died, was now in tatters. In fact, I realized that I would have to submit to a discipline far more severe and all-embracing than Pop's, though better-tempered and more evenly administered, I hoped.

I THINK THERE WERE TWO CHIEF REASONS why families that could afford the tuition in those days chose to send their sons away to school. The dominant one, I believe, was the understandable desire to get them out from under foot. Teenage males, by and large, are not fun to have in the house. Ancillary to this was the thought that growing up in an all-male environment, away from debilitating feminine influences, would tend to make a boy "manly," whatever that means or should mean; and it was hoped that the boy might acquire some spiritual values, whatever that means, through regular exposure to the King James Bible and the Book of Common Prayer. This paragraph accurately explains why Brosie and I were sent to Cate.

The other chief, though undeclared, reason for sending a son away was the social cachet that was thought to be a concomitant of 1) writing whopping checks for tuition and 2) having the son associate with other boys of high social standing.

There is a third reason that may well be the dominant one among today's parents, but it was not in the forefront of parents' minds in the 1930s: getting a first-rate education that would ease entry into a superior college or university and so put one on the road to a lucrative career.

Apprehensive by nature, I nonetheless felt no qualms when the time came for leaving home. This was not a step I dreaded. Far from it. During all that summer, in my dreams I was already at Cate. Here was a rite of passage that I could hardly wait to undergo. After all, for years I had been exposed to its glamorous side by attending inter-scholastic sports events, first at Deane (where Westmont College is now) in Pickie's day, and a little later at Cate in Brosie's. And Brosie, who adored the school, had stuffed my mind with absorbing details of life there. I had a clear idea of what to expect, and I very much liked the sound of it.

Once again, as was the case at Crane, Brosie's and my attendance was not to overlap. This caused no regret on my part in spite of my affection for him because I welcomed the idea of being independent, the idea that success or failure would be in my hands alone. I wanted neither help from an older brother, nor the occasional stab in the back that that same brother was capable of delivering. I had learned in growing up with him that he had a jealous nature and that his loyalty was not a thing I could completely depend on. Looking back, I would say that his feelings towards me, and mine towards him, were ambivalent, but certainly more affectionate than otherwise. Nothing sinister there. Isn't that usually the case with brothers, with sisters?

I can't remember the original impact that the school made upon me when I was dropped off there in September 1935 because of the many baseball games and track meets and the like that I had been attending during Brosie's five years there. But it was plain that it was a singularly beautiful place, richly endowed by nature as well as by the skill of man. The buildings stood near the edge of a mesa or small plateau overlooking the Carpinteria Valley, planted in those days chiefly to walnuts. No housing tracts, no hideous floral greenhouses. As one looked towards the coast, to the left one saw broad-shouldered Rincon Mountain; ahead of one—across the blue channel—Anacapa and Santa Cruz islands; and to the right, one gazed all the way up the coast to Santa Barbara. Then if one turned around and faced north, one saw the magnificent mountains of the coastal range, separated from the school by high hills.

The buildings, superbly appropriate to their setting and function, had been designed by Reginald Johnson of Pasadena, architect of the Santa Barbara Biltmore and the downtown post office. They were a mixture of one- and two-storey construction, of beige-colored reinforced concrete topped with shake roofs. Each bedrooom in the dormitories had its own balcony. I suppose the whole might be said to be of that Monterey style that many consider to be California's most pleasing contribution to the history of architecture.

The school was divided academically and residentially into five "forms" in the English manner, in which the second form equaled the eighth grade and the sixth form the twelfth grade. George Crane and I entered the second form. Though this fact might suggest a frustrating repeat of our eighth grade experience, in fact it was not. We were to study Latin, French, and algebra all for the first time, as well as a history course and natural science (and music appreciation plus my old friend woodworking). In English we were to read Dickens and Sir Walter Scott. All of this was far more intense than anything we had been exposed to at Crane. I found myself once again the youngest boy in my class, a fact that suggests that all the others had been similarly held back, presumably because "feeder" schools in those days didn't feed very hard.

There was a common misconception in my day on the part of boys who attended public schools that boys in boarding schools, if they even knew that such existed, were pampered sissies. Let me give you an idea of what a typical day at Cate was like in the 1930s, and you can decide for yourself as to the merits of that notion.

At 6:30 A.M. a centrally controlled electric bell went off that sounded like an air raid alert in all the dormitories. I got up ten minutes early to beat the rush of half-asleep students pushing and shoving their way down the stairs to their dorm's "barn room," where one sloughed off pyjamas and eased into outgrown and usually repulsive clothes (washed only at the end of the year) that were thought by their owners to be suitable for barn duties. Then down the long hill on the mountain side to the school barns, dark and bitter cold as the days grew shorter. Every boy was required to own a horse—character-building, of course. And for the next thirty to forty minutes that horse had to be curried and brushed and his box stall and corral made neat and sanitary with rake and pitchfork. One's handiwork was subject to inspection, and penalties were assessed for sloppy work. The whole procedure was supervised by Mr. Conover, in charge of the horse program, and his underling, Bert Rogers, who did all the dirty work in between spasms of frightful coughing brought on by his addiction to roll-your-owns. (I cannot resist relating a tidbit concerning Mr. Conover. It was said that he had greeted a student named Hanchett one day as the latter returned from a ride with the innocuous question, "How's your horse, Hanchett?" But it came out, à la Dr. Spooner, as "How's your hand, Horchett?" Too good to be true, I fear.)

And then the long trudge up the hill to the dorm again. The next step was to shed our reeking barn clothes and head, soap and towel in hand, for the shower room, where, supervised by the sixth former in charge of our dorm, we were forced to take cold showers. This was an obsession of Mr. Cate's, something to do with closing the pores, as I remember. Of all the nonsense! As far as I know, the only sensible thing to do with pores is to leave them alone. If they truly need to open and close, which I doubt, I am sure they can do that automatically as needed. The only result of cold showering that I am aware of was that we went through the day less clean than if we had had a hot shower, which was deferred till late afternoon, after sports. I suspect the real reason for the cold showers was that they cost the school much less than hot ones.

Then we dressed for the day. Levis, because it was a horse school. Many affected cowboy boots. I often did. For breakfast, we converged by diverse routes upon the dining room, where we were waited upon by the resident Chinese staff. I never got interested in breakfasts till many years later, but I remember that the food at lunch and dinner was almost invariably delicious by institutional standards. After breakfast, we returned to our rooms to prepare them for inspection.

And then the day's real work began. First, to the beautiful paneled library, which comfortably held the eighty or so assembled students and faculty (all men, of course) for morning prayers and announcements, conducted by Mr. Cate, a man of the cloth *manqué* who tore into holy scripture with gusto. I shall naturally have lots to say about him in due time.

After prayers began the long day's classes. There were three classes followed by a recess featuring milk and crackers to still the stomach rumbles. Older boys said knowingly, "Go easy on the milk. It's full of saltpetre." Then three more class periods before lunch, after which we retired to our rooms for a rest period (or "detention," i.e., supervised makeup work, for delinquent scholars). Then we rode our horses for an hour or so to exercise them, after which we reported in sports clothes to whatever athletic group we had been assigned to. Then, after a long workout at soccer or baseball, hot showers in the dorm. After that, no more blue jeans. Instead, a suit and a shirt with a separate stiff collar. We must have been the only people in the country at that time, except Herbert Hoover, to wear stiff collars nightly. Mr. Cate did not know that they had gone out of fashion years before, or if he did know, he was still detemined to make us pay for the laxity of being in jeans all day long. Year after year, it was amusing to watch the young new boys, known as "Jimmies," streaming frantically across the lawn to get to class or study hall before the late bell rang, their collars flapping at their necks because they hadn't succeeded in mooring the wretched things with metal collar studs, or whatever they were called, that fastened the collar front and rear and made it possible to insert a necktie. And many of the Jimmies were new to tying four-in-hand knots as well.

So two more class periods after showers, and then the evening meal, which in turn was followed by Mr. Cate's reading aloud a relaxing book in the elegant McIntosh Room just off the dining room, beautifully paneled like the library. After a half-hour's reading, we lined up to shake Mrs. Cate's hand and exchange good nights before trickling out to an hour or two of study hall before bedtime and lights out at staggered times, beginning at nine o'clock for the second formers, but early for all.

I never heard of anyone who had trouble sleeping during my years at the school. My days were fuller than they ever were in later life, and yet besides all the scheduled activities, there was time for adolescent daydreaming and horseplay with one's friends. It was a very good life for one like me who enjoyed both lessons and sports.

On weekends we had cause to bless our horses because they allowed us to roam the valley and the hills and mountains near the school. In the morning we picked up our brown-bag lunches and signed out with our destination for the day, and off I would go with my favorite friend of the moment, not planning to return till mid-afternoon at least. Carpinteria itself had very few attractions. We congregated at the drugstore for milkshakes, magazines, and pinball machines, not to mention huge quantities of Milky Ways and Snickers to munch on at leisure back at school. The old fleabag of a movie theater was out of bounds; one couldn't even sneak in because the tied-up horse nearby would be telling evidence, and

Ober's restaurant was also out of bounds since several boys had contracted ptomaine poisoning there, but the school had its own rustic cottage right on the sands of "The World's Safest Beach," as a banner that spanned Carpinteria Avenue foolishly claimed. There we changed into swimming trunks and swam in season or rode our horses bareback in the ocean or the mouth of the slough.

Other days we rode on the trails, of which there was a pleasing variety. My favorite was a broad one that wound up the big hill behind the school barn till one reached a minor summit, after which the trail descended narrowly to a wooded canyon called "Three-cornered Corral" that made an ideal spot for a picnic. But enough was enough; by now you know me well enough to realize that the best part of any ride for me was the ride back to civilization, in this case the school buildings.

My horse Ben was of the same mind, only much more so. A lively and pretty strawberry-roan-and-white pinto, he was an inheritance from Brosie. No, "inheritance" is not the right word because every hand-me-down I received from Brosie during the Cate years, mostly but not exclusively such horse-related objects as saddle and bridle, had to be bought back from him by poor Mother, the original donor, and then presented again, this time to me. No sentimentalist, he drove a hard bargain, but it was obviously still cheaper for Mother than buying me new things. So Ben was not inherited from Brosie; he was bought from Brosie. And he was a fine, spirited horse with one intolerable flaw. The moment I turned his head towards home, he started prancing and dancing and throwing his head. Older boys with more experience than I tried to calm him down. They failed. Mr. Conover added a martingale to his bridle. That failed. I had to accept him as he was even though he ruined exactly half of every ride. But he came into his own excitingly during gymkhana season. More of that later. And I turned him into a pretty fair jumper under the guidance of a rigid old Belgian cavalry officer.

The only bad thing about weekends was that, dressed in dark-blue suits and our stiffest stiff collars, we had to endure an interminable religious service after dinner on Sundays. I'll have more to say on religion at school on another page.

THE SCHOOL WAS RUN to some extent on the prefect system, modelled after the English "public" (i.e., private) schools whose discipline and concentration on team sports prepared their students to administer the far-flung Empire in the British Victorian heyday. The head boy was the senior prefect, and lesser prefects, who were all sixth formers, ran the dorms, even though there was usually a resident bachelor master (as teachers were called in the English manner), who was supposed to oversee dorm life but in practice preferred to close his door and prepare for his classes or just take his ease.

The prefect in charge of our "Jimmy" dorm was a generally amiable fellow, built like a bull, with an irascible Irish temperament. He made it plain the very first week that we would have to eat out of his hand. He stood a few of us at a time flat against the walls of the hallway and ordered us to slide our backs downwards until we looked in profile as though we were sitting on chairs. The tough part was that there was nothing to support our butts. Soon our muscles began to tremble from the strain. At this point he brought out a huge bullwhip and cracked it several times a few inches from our bodies. When he felt he had made his point about dominance and submission, he smiled pleasantly and let us go. We always behaved very, very well when he was around. One boy he took a dislike to he punished by making him sit down on a bench in the shower room while he proceeded to shave off his pubic hair with an electric shaver. His power, I suppose, was virtually limitless. He rarely abused it. He didn't have to.

We soon learned that the one act sure to bring swift retribution was to be disrespectful to sixth formers, individually or collectively. It could mean a belting that left angry welts on a boy's behind or a shaving of the head down to the skin. These punishments were especially mortifying because their visible and shaming effects lasted for a long time. But the most serious punishment was called "horse-troughing."

In our first term we had a chance to witness this curious folk custom. As we were currying our horses at the barn on a cold, bleak December dawn, the rumor spread: "There's gonna be a horse troughing!" We looked about us and noted that no seniors were anywhere to be seen. There were their horses untouched in their stalls. We went about our business, fascinated but frightened, too. After a while, down the narrow dirt path that led from the school buildings to the barn, the sixth formers filed, a grimly self-important procession. We stood aside from our horses to stare at the proceedings. My heart beat hard and fast as they strode past me, turned a corner and disappeared. Presently they returned with their prey, a second-former like me. They marched him to the central horse trough, a large cement structure. Several grabbed the boy and dumped him in, face up. Then the big boys leaned over and pummeled him so that he sank under the water. When he surfaced, they pummeled him down again. And again. As it was December, the water temperature in the trough must have been in the thirties or forties. Then the seniors dispersed, their ritual completed.

We put away our curry combs and brushes and walked up the hill in silence. The victim, dripping wet, walked alone, holding his head high, trying to make it seem as though nothing had happened. He's brave, I thought; I wouldn't have guessed it. But what else could he have done, the poor wretch? The boy was notorious for boasting and seemed to have a personality that rubbed people the wrong way; and he must have sassed a sixth former. Second formers through fifth formers, we all felt cowed. We were supposed to feel cowed.... The message was clear: "We don't want any uppity Jimmies around here. If you step out of line, you're going to pay for it. You're not at home; you're at Cate. We don't care if your parents love you; we don't. You're on your own here."

I wasn't an uppity Jimmy. I was polite and deferential to older students. What I thought and said behind their backs was another matter, but in general I tried to please. Why wouldn't I? This was where I wanted to be. Because Brosie had won the scholarship trophy in his second-form year and had performed very well thereafter, classmates and masters alike expected me to do well. I did well.

WE RECEIVED GRADES every month. As soon as the faculty had recorded them at night during a faculty meeting, they would be posted on a bulletin board for all to peruse. Whether the grade was 91 percent or 37 percent, it instantly became common knowledge. The concept of confidentiality was unknown and probably would have been considered unmanly. And as the '30s were not a time of grade inflation, there were very few high marks (90 percent or over) handed out. Along with many other boys, I would wake up very early on the morning that followed the midnight posting of the grades and tear over to the building where they were to be seen. No matter how early it was, there were others there too, huddled around the bulletin board. The etiquette was to say nothing but instead to absorb silently whatever was of interest to one before heading back to bed, elated, relieved, or depressed. But the next day, no matter how one really felt, one had to be nonchalant about the whole thing.

One matter of great practical interest to me was the sheet next to the grades that indicated whether one's grades had earned one first or second privileges or, for most students, none at all. First privileges exempted one from detestable after-dinner study hall, whereas second privileges allowed one to spend all free periods in the dorm, a right that I greatly enjoyed even in the dead of winter, when its unheated rooms and cement-floored hallways were less than inviting (one solved the problem by jumping into bed). I soon got into the routine of earning second privileges and consequently have very few memories connected with compulsory study halls. But I have a great many connected with the study hall itself because all the two-to-three-hour exams that concluded each term— fall, winter, and spring—were given in there, not to mention the four dreaded three-hour essay-type College Board exams that were administered the week following graduation and constituted, for the more able students, the full range of Board testing in those days.

There was one school exam that remains in my mind in horrid vividness as distinct from all the others that have melted away. It was at the end of my very first term, in December, one of the first round of long exams that any of us second-formers had ever been exposed to—in Algebra 1. I had been very competent in arithmetic at Crane, even quite enjoying word problems that seemed to baffle many students. I had scored 100 percent in Cate's arithmetic entrance test, and up to now algebra had posed no serious problems. I looked at the first question and solved it without much difficulty. Then I went on cheerfully to the second, another equation.

Hmmm. My first try was a failure; and my second. Hmmm. Hmmm.… I was upset by now. I'd never known failure. I went on to the next, badly rattled. I couldn't do it either. I felt close to despair. I looked out the study hall window. There was Martin Westcott, the overalled gardener, who had never been known to speak a word, gently raking a path, obviously without a care in the world. Why, why couldn't I be a gardener, with no worries worth mentioning, thinking my own green thoughts, endlessly mowing and raking? …Somehow I got through the exam. I don't remember my grade, but it certainly wasn't an A. This was my first intimation that I would not after all be an academic superboy. Later I was to conclude that my strengths and interests lay with language and human beings, preferably combined. With abstractions, whether numerical or verbal, I was never to be at home.

In spite of this now-exposed Achilles' heel, my first year was a very successful one. I got along well with boys and masters and developed a small reputation as a wit and mimic. Our dorm master and English teacher, a young man named Mr. Rice, must have been advised before setting out on his career to be hard-nosed right from the beginning. His half-hearted attempts to smile ended up as sneers. He lashed out with his sarcastic tongue. Except with me: his sneers became genial smiles, and he lavished compliments upon me. I don't know why my classmates didn't rebuke or chastise me for this special treatment, but as with my former classmates at Crane, they showed no resentment. Perhaps my sense of humor was thought to be a saving grace. And I was not conceited; or not so that it showed.

I DON'T REMEMBER BEING HOMESICK. We were allowed to spend a Sunday with parents—that meant lunch and a movie—at regular intervals. Was it once a month or once a term? And once each term we were allowed to spend a Saturday night away from school, the home leave beginning late in the afternoon after a scheduled series of soccer or baseball games with a rival school. So, as a boy who lived only ten miles from the school, I had no advantage over those who lived hundreds of miles away, except that Mother was very faithful in visiting me most Sundays, late in the day; we would sit in her car and chat while I munched Emmy's chocolate chip cookies and drank milk from a thermos. She would also bring me funnies from the Sunday papers, which I didn't ask for but found strangely comforting when I read them later in my room.

A tradition that was supposed to relieve the grimness of life for Jimmies was to gather occasionally, dressed in pyjamas, in the master's sitting room in our dorm (he must have gone into hiding somewhere) while Mrs. Cate read aloud to us. The only book I re-member, and indeed it may well have lasted the whole year, was J.M. Barrie's dreary novel *Sentimental Tommy*. Mrs. Cate's voice, which was deep and gruff, was no treat to hear at the best of times; add to it an ill-advised attempt at a Scottish accent and one had the makings of an aural disaster. I didn't listen to a word but enjoyed greatly the peanut brittle that she brought along in generous quan-tities. To protect and even increase my share, I was prepared to fight, even to maim.

At that stage in my life, taking part in sports continued to be a source of joy, but runty thirteen-year-olds are not likely to distin-guish themselves against burly older boys. I played on low-level teams in soccer and baseball. I'm amused to remember the fourth-team field we played baseball on at Thacher in Ojai, our major ri-val. It was dirt with patches of grass here and there, and nearly ver-tical. If one knocked the ball out of the infield (upfield?) and the outfielders failed to field it properly, it rolled back down briskly to the infielders. (But it wasn't anything like so bad as a field in the Santa Ynez Valley I had once had to play on when captain of the Crane baseball team. It was thrilling to be playing a game away from our home field, but when we got there, the site turned out to be a cow pasture. The field was Swiss-cheesed with gopher holes and flecked with thousands of stones typical of Valley soil, and the whole strewn with dozens of cow patties, both wet and dry. As shortstop, I didn't get a decent bounce all afternoon.)

I distinguished myself only once athletically that first year. I ad-vanced to the semi-finals of the school tennis tournament, where I was opposed by one Charles d'Autremont, a towering sixth-former. As time wore on into the third and final set, word got out that an upset might be in the making, with a little five-foot Jimmy putting up a good fight against a popular sixth-former, and boys began to stream towards the courts, which were rather far removed from the playing fields. Soon we had a considerable audience, a situation that often made me choke up and play wretchedly; but not this time. The audience was with me and I rose to the occasion, winning the set 6-4.

However, in the finals the next day I had to face all six-foot-six of Andy McLaglen (son of the then-famous actor, Victor, and himself today a well-known director of Hollywood Westerns) who was a brilliant player cut out of different cloth from the rest of us. I never had a chance, and my head shrank to its normal size.

For me, the Cate experience had proved to be exhilarating. I felt I had been tested in important ways. Timorous by nature and sheltered by upbringing, I had had to stand on my own feet in a way that no boy at a public school or a private day school could really grasp. When things went wrong, and there were so many ways they could go wrong, there was absolutely no one to turn to because the unspoken code wouldn't allow it. Things had to go right. For me, that first year things did go right. And I was the one who made them go right. That was a matchless feeling.

COMMENCEMENT DAY was everyone's favorite day of the year. There were no classes, just a bustle of activity as the setting was made ready for the day's events. I learned over the years that, with regard to choosing a site for the formal exercises, Mr. Cate was like an indecisive but finicky hostess who keeps rearranging her living-room furniture without ever finding the right combination. In 1936 he chose to hold the exercises in the McIntosh Room, filled to over-capacity with folding chairs. Other years, other sites.

I remember only one part of the program. There must have been the usual pompous speeches by three seniors on subjects of arcane interest. Mr. Cate no doubt delivered his well-phrased but forgettable remarks. And then came time for the awarding of trophies and prizes for everything but athletic endeavor, these last being handed out by alumni informally during the alfresco luncheon that followed the exercises.

In the fullness of time came the moment for the presentation of the huge scholarship trophy, engraved with the names of all the previous winners, along with their winning averages. In spite of my troubles with algebra, I knew I had a chance to win, though probably not a very big one. Some of my classmates were sure I would be named, but that was just class loyalty at work. I doubt that even the faculty knew the answer until the final grades were recorded and laborious computations completed.... Mr. Cate reached for the trophy, adjusted his glasses, and proceeded to read aloud the names of the earlier winners. And finally he read out the name of "this year's winner—Charles d'Autremont!"

Well, good for him, I pretended. He'd won it the year before and was an outstanding student. Sixth formers had a lot of demands on their time, I knew, and didn't often win the scholarship competition. And besides, he needed to restore his *amour propre* after losing to me in the tennis semi-finals. But of course I was disappointed. The lanky senior walked up to the lectern and received the trophy and due applause.

Then a master walked up to Mr. Cate as he stood at the lectern and handed him a note before slipping back into the audience. Mr. Cate glanced at it, then looked intently at it. A very visible flush suffused his cheeks. He faced his audience.

"I'm embarrassed to say that I have made a mistake. I have just awarded the trophy to the boy who won it last year. His name is of course the last one on the trophy because we haven't yet had time to engrave the name of this year's winner, with an average of 93 percent, a score equaled only once before—Nevill Murray Cramer."

Poor d'Autremont. First the tennis and now this. He had to walk up and give the trophy back. I was in heaven.... For one year, that is. I never won it again. From then on, there was always another boy who, unlike me, had no chinks in his academic armor. I was a modest winner, and I was learning to lose gracefully, too, because style had become important to me.

MY THIRD-FORM YEAR I remember as one of athletic triumphs for me. In the fall, I was promoted to the second soccer team, which scrimmaged daily with the first team under the guidance of that elegant and arrogant Englishman, Captain Davy, the chief math and science master. Under him I learned the rudiments of the game and became familiar with the duties of a forward.

The first part of the winter term was always devoted to gymkhana practice in preparation for the climactic competition with Thacher. There was endless practice every day, and then three all-school gymkhanas from which the five highest scorers were chosen to play on the team against Thacher. My spirited horse Ben loved competition and performed very well in three of the eight-or-so events. He and I were the school's top combination in the sack race, which to my mind was the most thrilling race of all. In it the half-dozen horses in their own lanes would converge at full speed upon six carefully spaced sacks loosely stuffed with straw, swing a bit wide while reining-in, then perform a 180-degree turn around the sack while horse and rider leaned like racing motorcy-clists, and the rider snatched up the sack and whipped the horse back up to full speed as they raced back to the start/finish line a hundred yards away. It depended on precise timing and a close inti-macy between boy and horse. Ben and I were supreme in this event and by winning points in other events, too, qualified for the team that would ride against Thacher in winter of 1937.

I remember little about the Thacher meet, which was really the high point of each year's sporting calendar. (The next year, when I had a new horse because Ben was so unpleasant to ride on an ev-eryday basis, I didn't make the team; that was the year that *Life* magazine, then at its zenith as a weekly featuring photo-journalism, covered the Cate-Thacher gymkhana with a big spread.) I was ex-tremely nervous, and I remember being taken out for a soothing early-morning ride by an older boy, also on the team, who was so superbly in tune with his horse that the two of them looked like one centaur. During the afternoon gymkhana I picked up points in the figure-8 and the bending (a slalom, really), and then it was time for the sack race, which I was determined to win for the school.

The six contestants lined up, the starting flag went down, and five of the horses bolted ahead full-speed, with the sixth one pok-ing along behind. I galloped faster than I ever had before, and so apparently did the other fast four because we were all neck and neck as we prepared to make our turn. Then, incredibly, every single one of the leading five swung wide of his sack. We leaned way over, all of us, and grabbed at—air! And the five horses, feeling no disgrace, raced for the finish line. What a humiliation! Of course the one tortoise won in record slow time. It was Mr. Cate's nephew, Peter Cate. And the rest of us were sizzling mad at ourselves. The race had to be re-run to determine the remaining prize-winners. This time everything went as it should have in the first place, and Ben and I ran a perfect race, finishing first in very fast time. I refused to draw the obvious and repulsive moral that this race seemed to offer. To hell with Peter Cate. I was glad to be a hare, win or lose.

In the late winter there was an intra-school track meet for younger boys, with the second and third formers divided up into two more or less equal teams competing with each other. In track at Crane, I had never run more than a 50-yard dash. Now I ran my first hundred. It was very exciting and felt just right; I finished first. Then I won the broad jump as the long jump was then called. Next, time for the 220; halfway around, in staggered lanes, the big 440-yard oval. I started fast, but because of the staggering, it was impossible to tell where I stood. As we rounded the final bend and came on to the homestretch, I discovered I was in the lead but was definitely beginning to falter. And no wonder, since I had never practiced this distance and had no idea of how to pace myself. A big third former came up fast in the final yards and would have passed me if the race had been a yard longer, but I broke the tape. And then I anchored my team in the 4 x 110 relay, coming from way behind my opponent and passing him handily in the final twenty yards so that my team won the meet. Heady stuff! This was a day of days for me, as anyone could imagine. Cliff Greene, a sixth former, said to someone in my hearing, "If you think he's fast now, wait till he's a fourth former next year!"

In fact, that day was the end of my running triumphs. Next year, everybody else got faster and I got slower. I never figured out why, but I swallowed the disappointment. So I wasn't going to be a sprinter. What of it? Anyway, in spring of third-form year I beat out Cliff Greene, the sixth former who thought I was such a track star, for second base on the first baseball team. That meant two first teams in major sports and qualified me to earn my letter on Commencement Day, the youngest and smallest boy to do so in my years at school, as well as the coveted Junior Horsemanship trophy. I remember an older boy saying to me one day that year, "God, but you're lucky, Cramer, to be so good at your work and sports, too. I really envy you."

I was indeed lucky, and certainly very proud and happy. Of course, if I had been mature enough to take stock of myself at fourteen, I would have had to admit that I was neither handsome nor well built, had no musical sense, was very weak in drawing and painting, and couldn't make or even repair things. Great for prep school, much less so for life. Proud? I should have been crying my heart out.

Next year, for better or for worse, I was to become a very different person, with interests that went far beyond conventional studies and sports. But that transformation belongs in the next chapter.

INTERESTING THINGS were going on in my academic life, meanwhile. I had enjoyed my first year of Latin, and when Mr. Cate suggested at the start of the second year that another boy and I might enjoy studying Greek, I saw no reason to object, though I certainly did not clap my hands with joy. So Richard de Mille and I began our four-year apprenticeship to that strange tongue under the tutelage of O.C. Crawford, known to his colleagues as Curt and to us, sometimes, as Old Rumbleguts. He remained as our Latin master as well throughout our years at school. Mr. Crawford was a strict and demanding teacher whose obvious interest in his subjects provoked a corresponding interest in me. He was someone I wanted to please, and most of the time I was able to do so because language study came very easily to me. De Mille, son of Cecil B., a very bright but rather prickly boy, was equally capable, and we competed in amicable fashion during our years together as Mr. Crawford's top students. We often said to each other that we had taught Mr. Crawford all the Greek he ever knew. At the very least, we stimulated him. I have very happy memories of the three of us, O.C. with his pipe, seated in his study in late afternoon during the last pre-prandial period of the day, working away at our translations of Xenophon or Homer or Euripides.

Though his manner in Latin classes, which, being compulsory, were of course much larger, was severe and unbending, he had a bawdy sense of humor and a zest for gossip, predilections that were right up my alley. Also, he had a very appealing crescent-moon smile that irradiated his face when he chose to flash it. He loved his bourbon much more than was wise, but I was not fully aware of that failing until after I had graduated. (At the end of senior year, de Mille and I found the place where he kept his whiskey bottle, dumped out most of it and added strong tea to what remained. We took great pleasure in imagining his discomfiture when the time came to chug-a-lug. When we were both freshmen, de Mille at Columbia and I at Harvard, we met one weekend in New York and, after a long night on the town, found a little place on Times Square that specialized in cutting and mailing very brief phonograph records. We ran one off for Mr. Crawford in which we cheerfully confessed to the crime of whiskey dilution and expressed the hope that the new mixture was to his liking. He was vexed.)

There's a curious thing about Greek; it doesn't stay with one. Fifty-three years later, I can still write the alphabet, both capitals and lower-case letters, and can read aloud prose, at least, without hesitation, but I can't translate it even though I can trace the derivation of many English words from the meanings that I recall of their Greek roots. My Cicero or Virgil, on the other hand, I'm sure I could revive with a few days' serious application. Not that I intend to try. I don't see any important benefit from the study of the classics, but I thoroughly enjoyed it, much as a musically inclined student enjoys learning to play the piano or violin without any thought of a career in music. There are those who insist that a knowledge of Latin provides a fine foundation for the study and practice of the English language, and to a certain extent I agree, but more time devoted to a thorough study of our own tongue, grievously neglected in today's high-school curricula, would be far more beneficial. Latin and English really aren't very closely allied. And of the two, English is by far the subtler and richer and more flexible.

Studying Greek got me out of studying history. Something had to be skimped to provide time for the former, and someone, probably Mr. Cate, made that decision for de Mille and me. I don't regret it because history was lamely taught at Cate in my day. I have read fairly widely since that time in the areas of history that interest me, and it has always been a delight not to have a well-meaning but ill-equipped master coming between me and a lively and literate text.

On an earlier page I mentioned that I would become noted for my imitations while at Cate. My first notable one was of the school matron, Mrs. Van Horne, who was responsible for the smooth functioning of the housekeeping side of school life, an important post indeed. She was born a Stow of Goleta's La Patera Ranch, and odd coincidence that it is, my wife Pat and I have owned and lived in her sister Anne Stow Fithian's house on Picacho Lane in Montecito for thirty-odd years, while below us on the same street lives her grandson David Van Horne with his wife and children. Mrs. Van Horne was a warm-hearted, wise, and delightful woman, but she was very deaf and as a consequence had the loud, scratchy voice often characteristic of people with that affliction. I imitated it to perfection and invented a patter that included all her earthy folk sayings, of which I can remember only one, that she used of a boy about to play in his first soccer game: "He's as nervous as a pregnant mare!" I strung them all together to my hearers' delight and one day was forced by Mr. Crawford, with what motivation I do not know, to perform my act in front of her, which I did very reluctantly. I like to think that she was too deaf to hear a word I said, but she laughed like the good sport she was. Not long after, during a tea for Jimmies at her house at the foot of the school hill, I bent down to stroke her shaggy little dog, upon which he leaped up and bit me fiercely on my nose. I had the feeling that it might have been a case of thought transference from mistress to pet, and I could hardly blame either one, but it was painful, and I felt I had to pretend that nothing had happened. I said I had a sudden nosebleed.

I also mimicked the way various masters walked or gestured or talked. Mr. Cate himself was especially fond of my version of the gorilla-like gait of a stiffly self-important young master, and made me do it over and over while his face grew red with laughter. And of course all the guest speakers that appeared from time to time to vary our routine were fair game for my verbal caricatures. My pulse would quicken whenever one of these unfortunates revealed a weakness in content or delivery (and it seems to me our speakers were unusually rich in such deficiencies), and I would spend leisure moments in polishing my burlesques before trying them out on my public: immensely satisfying.

Every school day began with an assembly in the library that featured readings by Mr. Cate from the Holy Bible followed by other readings, both quasi-holy and secular, but uniformly soporific in their effect upon me. Besides, I did not regard myself as a miserable sinner (even less so, I am sure, did Mr. Cate regard himself), and I took a very dim view of Jehovah's vengeful shenanigans. I do not have a spiritual nature, and I do have a very low threshold of boredom; the Bible is not my book. For years I daydreamed and dozed through those wretched assemblies and their much longer and holier Sunday night versions. At least during the assemblies there were announcements of general interest to palliate the tedium. Also, there were times when Mr. Cate used to solicit "observations," as he called them, from boys sharp-eyed enough to have spotted the first barn swallow of the season or to have noticed that the gate on a certain trail needed repairs or that Sagittarius was visible from one's dorm room at a certain hour of the night. I tried for years to think of something to contribute, but such sharp-eyed perceptions were simply foreign to my nature. Besides, I noticed that those who did make observations tended to be "establishment" types, though of course that particular word had not yet come into its present-day usage. And I was most emphatically not an establishment kind of boy.

I tried to figure out why I was never the one to spy the flowering bush or the infestation of nematodes in a lawn. The answer was simple: *people* didn't count in those matters. If I had been encouraged to make observations about the human beings I lived among, I would have pointed out that a certain fourth-former was picking his nose during prayers for the third straight day, or that Mr. Eric (of whom more later) had fallen asleep during the reading from Thomas à Kempis's *Imitation of Christ*. And would I have been praised for my observational powers? I think not. And so it was when I came to study mathematics or, later, physics, or, later still, philosophy: remove the human element and I am struck dumb.

❦

FROM TIME TO TIME the rector of All Saints by the Sea, Montecito's Episcopal church, would conduct a worship service in the library, and Holy Communion would be offered by the Rev. Edgar Owens (not his real name, for reasons that will presently be revealed) to boys and masters who had been "confirmed." I decided there was something rather chic about being one of this elite group and signed up for the winter's confirmation classes. I wish I could say that Bible study spiritualized my materialistic nature, but I discovered that my eyes would glaze over at the merest whisper of a "he saith" or "she doth" or "thou hast." Mr. Owens, who had a marvelously rich, deep, and mellifluous voice, truly a golden voice, did his best to turn our minds to matters above and beyond the Cate Mesa, and I like to think that he succeeded with some. One day the Bishop of Los Angeles appeared at All Saints and proceeded to lay his hands upon the candidates for confirmation; at that moment I became a most unworthy member of the Protestant Episcopal Church and soon took my place among the elect at school who were qualified to kneel in full view before their fellows and receive the bread and wine of Holy Communion.

I suppose I was a "whited sepulchre" in biblical terminology, but not nearly so much so as was the Rev. Mr. Owens himself, as came to light some years later. When the scandal broke in the mid-'40s, I was not greatly surprised because George Crane had often confided, during our Cate years, that Mr. Owens had made unwelcome passes at George's girl friend of those days, who sang in the All Saints choir. I'm not sure whether I believed him or not. After all, the rector was not only married, but the father of three children with chronically running noses and jammy mouths, who used to play on the rectory lawn right beside the sidewalk on Eucalyptus Lane. Perhaps, I thought, he merely took an avuncular interest in George's Rachel.

Perhaps; perhaps not. In 1948, eight years after my graduation, a parishioner spotted a furtive-looking Mr. Owens emerging with an attractive young woman from one of the cottages at Mattei's Tavern in Los Olivos, some forty miles away, a popular trysting place in those days. He was summoned before the vestry and, when called to account, replied that his private life was none of their business. The vestrymen took a different view and sent him packing.

A year or two later, Mother, a devout parishioner, received a Christmas card from him saying that he was now running a gas station in Jonesboro, Arkansas. The New Testament quotes Jesus as saying, "In my Father's house are many mansions," so let us hope that in that ample and hospitable dwelling there is room for a gas station or two. But it seemed a pity that Mr. Owens's golden theological voice should be reduced to mouthing, "Fill 'er up, Bubba?"

While on the subject of religion, I remember a paper that I wrote, my only experiment in creative theology, for third-form English class. I called it "Courage at Calvary," and in it I expounded the radical notion that the two thieves were the brave ones, because they knew the penalty for their crime was death by crucifixion, whereas Jesus had every reason to think he would soon be ascending into heaven as the Son of God. Nobody complained when it was read aloud, as my papers invariably were; probably only George Crane bothered to listen. And after class he taxed me with regurgitating something I'd heard from Mr. Owens in confirmation class.

"But that's preposterous," I said hotly. "What I wrote is blasphemous. No minister in his right mind would come up with an idea like that."

"You stole it. You know you did." What can one do with such a person?

I bided my time. One day we were given the jejune assignment of writing about some place that meant a great deal to us. A few days later George's, among others, was read aloud. Lucky fellow, he and his family had spent a whole summer in England not long before, and he had chosen to write about his desire to revisit a peaceful little town named Appledore. It was a reasonably effective description; and then, to my great joy, out oozed the concluding sentence: "As for me, give me my wish or give me death!"

The whole class roared.

I teased him about it for years, and I still think of it whenever I come across the word *bathos*. (He survived the shame of it, though, since he earned a Ph.D. in English at Berkeley and enjoyed a long professorial career at Cal State Long Beach. We kept in touch till his death in 1982.)

A PLEASANT CODA to my second year at Cate was a visit, just a few days into summer vacation, to the Oregon lodge of my classmate, Nion Tucker. Tucker's mother was the youngest of the De Young sisters, the daughters of M.H. De Young, founder and publisher of the San Francisco *Chronicle* and the man after whom the De Young Museum in Golden Gate Park is named. I rode the train to the Tuckers' in Burlingame, a huge sprawling one-storey house built on several levels, enjoyed a meal at the baronial Burlingame Club, and then caught a night train for Oregon with Tucker, his cousin, and a Burlingame friend. We woke in the morning at Medford, where we were greeted by the family chauffeur in an enormous station wagon and driven some miles up the Rogue River to the family lodge, "Rogue's Roost." It was a marvelous place. I remember a large central wooden lodge with a huge, rustic living room and great windows giving on the river, which flowed so swiftly that it made a ceaseless roaring sound as it went rushing and whirling by. Elegant meals were served by a white-coated butler. Mrs. Tucker, ensconced in a luxurious cabin of her own, never appeared till lunch, but she was worth waiting for as she turned out to be a woman of exceptional charm and vivacity, and I fell for her right away. I think she spent most of her time in bed telephoning friends all over the country. Mr. Tucker was a large, hearty man clearly fond of the outdoors; undoubtedly the lodge was primarily for him and Nion, Jr. And there was a third cabin with lots of guestrooms, one of which, with a huge tree trunk smack in its middle and projecting up through the ceiling and roof, was home during my stay. The everlasting sound of the river stayed with me a long time after; surely rushing water is one of the greatest blessings that nature can afford. I longed to take the river back to Santa Barbara with me, but not if it meant importing the rainfall that created it.

I had a memorable adventure on the Rogue. One day three of us boys went fishing on the river in a skiff. To stabilize us in the rushing current, Tucker threw an anchor overboard—not a wise thing to do, apparently, as the bow headed upstream and, suddenly dipping, the skiff began to take on water. In about ten seconds the boat had filled with water and we were cast adrift. Somehow the others made it to shore without incident, but I was swept downstream by the current. My frantic stroking was useless. For a moment I caught onto an overhanging branch, but the charging current swept me away again. I knew I was drowning, that there was no hope. Contrary to folklore, my whole life (all fourteen years of it) did not flash before me. Instead, there welled up within me a cry of raw egotism, "This can't be happening to me! Not to *me!*"

Ready to give up the hopeless battle, I was almost too tired to care when the current suddenly dumped me into a backwater near the shore. I crawled on my knees to shore and rested there, heaving and panting. That was the closest I have ever come to death. The second closest took place a year later, also at "Rogue's Roost," but this time on dry land, as I shall relate in the next chapter.

CHAPTER SIX

🐚 Cate II

A CHANGE took place in me the next year, when, aged fifteen, I had become a fourth former, a change that gave a focus and direction to my life from that day to this. But before I elaborate upon that cryptic, even (I hope) tantalizing remark, I feel it is time for me to come to grips with those looming presences, Mr. and Mrs. Cate, known informally at the school as the King and Queen, behind-the-back titles that they made no attempt to deplore or disavow.

Curtis Wolsey Cate and his wife, Katharine Thayer Cate, were both Proper Bostonians, though I am fairly sure they met in Santa Barbara. Mrs. Cate was the widow of yet another Proper Bostonian, by whom she had a son, Harry Russell, who ran a lemon ranch where his parents had once lived, near the foot of the school's hill. They were a most formidable pair, Mr. and Mrs. Cate, autocratic and imperious.

An incident related years later by a master who had observed it captures definitively a certain aspect of their personalities. The gravel driveway to their handsome Spanish house, set a comfortable distance from the nearest school buildings and invisible from the latter, ended in a circular forecourt. On the day that concerns us, their cars were parked facing each other and some little distance apart. Each got behind the wheel, started the engine, and prepared to put it in gear. They tried to stare each other down, but neither one flinched. They glared for a few pregnant seconds, and then each proceeded straight ahead in first gear with all the low-end torque that the big V-8's of those days could command. There was of course massive front-end damage to both cars. Unfortunately the anecdote as it came down to me does not relate what happened next. Probably the witness thought it injudicious to become embroiled and took to his heels.... It is a good thing that the Cates had separate bedrooms.

Mrs. Cate had a deep, gruff voice and a curt manner. It was said of her that she had a heart of gold, but my experience tells me that that is what people say of those who blend an habitual unpleasantness with an occasional spark of geniality. In appearance she was short, with dark-brown hair, usually hatted with a mannish felt. I remember her in a tailored suit, except, I suppose, when she occasionally came to school to dine. The darkish skin of her face appeared to be made of leather, but it was very high-quality leather, as though fashioned from those same carefully selected Connolly hides that distinguish the seats and interior trim of Rolls-Royces. It was fissured by decades of heavy cigarette smoking. Her speech, which came usually in the form of pronouncements, consisted of growls and barks punctuated with fits of coughing.

I found I could make her laugh in spite of herself if I put my mind to it, but she liked her boys to be (unlike me) strong, silent, and none too quick on the intellectual draw, and ideally with the right Boston background. By now, I liked older women to be in the mold of my Oregon hostess, Phyllis Tucker, who was warm-hearted, genial, lively, and worldly. So early on, Mrs. Cate and I sized each other up and found each other seriously wanting.

By now I was in the forward line of the school's soccer team, coached by the chief math and science master, the Englishman, Captain Davy. He was demanding but knowledgeable, the only amateur coach in my day of whom one could use either of those adjectives. He was also a bad sport and the terror of the other amateur coaches in our league. I wasn't much at scoring goals, but I became very sharp at passing, the very essence of the game. ("Well, hardly," as Mr. Crawford, my Latin and Greek master, used to say. The essence of the game is scoring, but you know what I mean: no passee, no scoree.) I mention soccer because Mrs. Cate used to attend our home games. I can see her sitting in our grandstand, watching the action through a haze of cigarette smoke. My position, unlike most, involved following the ball, running tirelessly from one end of the field to the other and back and forth. Sometimes I was just plain exhausted and didn't fully live up to that responsibility; those were the times that Mrs. Cate would choose to bark out, "Get Cramer mad! Get him mad!" And in an exceedingly loud undertone, "That's the only way he'll play hard!" Did she succeed? Did she get me mad? And if so, how? For the sake of my narrative, I wish I could remember. Probably she accused me of being lazy, and possibly I did get mad and tried even harder, but it's also possible that I, being I, tried less hard just to spite her.... Poor woman, she died of cancer a decade or so after my 1940 graduation. Mr. Cate lived on into his nineties.

Mr. Cate, the King, would have stood out in any group, anywhere. He was about six feet tall and held himself rigidly erect. Elegantly and tastefully dressed at all hours of the day, he was incapable of committing an undignified act. He enunciated with unusual clarity, though his speech (unlike his wife's) bore few signs of its Boston origins. A couple of amusing quirks were his pronunciation of *soon* with a vowel sound to rhyme with that of *foot* and *shone* to rhyme with *on*. I like to think that those oddities may have been vintage Ralph Waldo Emerson or even Bronson Alcott. A stickler for neatness and order, he was a compulsive picture-straightener and picker-up of litter. He was clearly a person born to command, and when I saw him in company with the headmasters of the nearby boarding schools with which we engaged in interscholastic competition, his patrician looks made me proud that he was "mine." He dominated any group he was in. (Soon after Pearl Harbor, which occurred a little over a year after my graduation, the vulnerable Catalina Island School was forced to leave its oceanside campus outside of Avalon and, with a welcome infusion of new students, was folded into Cate's Mesa campus in a joint-headmastership arrangement. It didn't take more than a year or two for its likable headmaster, Keith Vosburg, along with any special Catalina customs and traditions, to sink without a trace.)

I feel certain that Mr. Cate's was the guiding hand and intellect, along with his architect's, that created the extraordinary beauty of the school, a beauty that permeated our lives whether we admitted it or not. There was an esthetic rightness about all the structures and their furnishings that complemented the perfection of the natural scene. Visiting parents would "ooh" and "ah" as they walked about the grounds, savoring the sights their good tuition money had paid for, and of course we would groan at the notion that pretty views could make up for the rigors of boarding-school life. But they did, though we were not aware of it at the time. Rare is the king who has the chance to create his own kingdom. Mr. Cate had that chance, and he took royal advantage of it.

He could be jovial (Jovial?). In fact, his face lit up marvelously when he heard something said that caught his fancy, and he would communicate his pleasure with a look of extraordinary radiance and delighted laughter. This was likely to be accompanied, if one was seated next to him, by a quick, confirming grip of one's upper thigh. And not only was he appreciative of others' wit, but he could be witty himself. I remember one example in particular that I have chuckled over for years. The school barber, an estimable man, devoted to poetry, who came to us once a week from his shop in Santa Barbara, had a wife who taught painting and a son who had attained a degree of fame beyond Santa Barbara as an artist. These facts having been laid before him, Mr. Cate wondered aloud if the son belonged to any particular school of painting. Then he answered his own question: "He must belong to the Barber's-son school." For that I could forgive him much.

And there was much to forgive. He himself recorded that his maiden aunt, Miss Marion Cate, who was extremely helpful to him in the early, struggling days of the school both in Mission Canyon and later at the foot of the Mesa, made the following astringent criticism: "You run roughshod over people." True, true, true. He would fly into a rage without warning or without making any effort to get at the root of whatever had upset him. And there was no talking back. Time and again in front of others he humiliated hapless students or was curtly rude to young masters and even certain parents. We all have tempers, and we all lose them now and then, but when one has total, unquestioned power, as he did, surely one must take extra pains not to abuse that power. Apparently this thought never occurred to him. I observed that favored students and longtime masters and rich parents never felt the whiplash of his tongue, and, I must admit, for this and other reasons I came to question his real commitment to the Christian ethics he so ardently professed.

As far as I could tell, what he lacked in humility he made up for with overweening pride, a lamentable inversion of the tradi-

tional Christian view of behavior. And I have to assign reponsibility
to him for allowing, perhaps even encouraging, the physical brutal-
ity that I have described in the previous chapter. I suppose he felt
that such behavior was sanctioned by generations of physical abuse
in the fashionable English "public" schools; but their headmasters
used to have the excuse that they were hardening boys for their future role as administrators and warriors in the farflung Empire. Cate
boys by and large went in for business and the professions. But one
seriously questions the validity of encouraging or even tolerating,
for any reason, physical abuse in twentieth-century American
society.

Though Mr. Cate was respected and even admired by almost all
the boys, over the years a wide gap had opened up between him
and the students. In my day, hardly any boy was at ease with him.
There was almost always a forced quality, a stiffness, to any inter-
course with him—on our parts by all means, but also to a degree
on his. He often spoke with enthusiasm of the days of the little
school in its simple wooden buildings at the foot of the Mesa.
There of course he had been a younger man, fraternizing with the
boys, all of whom he knew intimately; there they had set off together on carefree camping trips in the mountains. He was never
able in my day to re-establish that intimacy, that members-of-a-
family feeling from the old days. I think there were times when this
disturbed him. Was this country club (as boys from other schools
were wont to call it) what he had wanted after all?... On balance I
think it was.

He retired some dozen years after I had received my diploma,
though he continued to live in his handsome Spanish villa, Mesa
House, a formidable presence in the background for his successors.
He traveled a good deal, to Italy and Greece and the Holy Land.
He took courses in Italian so that he could read Dante. But he had
almost thirty years of retirement to get through, and the time began
to hang heavily. One year, in his annual birthday card to me, he
wrote, "Lucky you! You have something to do." Indeed I did, as a
beleaguered schoolmaster in the turbulent '60s who didn't see himself as being exactly lucky. Poor Mr. Cate, he really couldn't think
of being anything but a headmaster. The motto he had chosen for
his school was *Servons,* "Let us serve," but he had very limited ideas

as to what service should consist of, at least for himself. Isolated from Santa Barbara for so long, he had apparently no interest in inserting himself into the dense and rich charitable world of that community that might have given a sense of purpose to his last years. Or perhaps he understood himself well enough to know that he might not be a welcome addition to groups in the outside world, since he was in the habit of ruling, rather than cooperating.

A flawed man, but an impressive and memorable one. If he had a message, I must have tuned it out, because I have never had the faintest memory of anything he ever said or of the moralizing he indulged in during the hundreds of carefully planned and carefully articulated speeches and sermons that I listened to over five long years—that is, except for one thing: "Remember that *like* is a preposition, not a conjunction!" The fact that that is what my unconscious has chosen to remember tells far more, I must admit, about me than about Mr. Cate, but it's true that he stood foursquare against verbal infelicities and the adulteration of the language. There are worse epitaphs than that.

ONE DAY MY FOURTH-FORM ENGLISH TEACHER (a bustling and officious man known as "Wee-wee" because a fanciful boy—not I—had observed that the way he stood before the class with his hands in his pockets made it seem that he had just peed in his pants) said to me after looking over my list of books read outside of class, "Cramer, I thought you were a reader."

Well, I had thought so, too, but I suppose that my efforts to keep my grades high, combined with being on interscholastic teams most of the year and spending endless hours riding and training my new horse, Cyclone, had deflected my natural love for books to some degree. His words, spoken with sarcasm, shocked me.... But it really wasn't much of a list. Wee-wee was right.

So I began to read, with increasing ardor. Over my last three years as a schoolboy, I read almost everything in the school library (but not *The Life and Letters of Walter Hines Page*) and a great deal that wasn't. During those years I invariably won the annual prize for the length and breadth of "outside" reading. I discovered the magic of poetry when as a fifteen-year-old I read Keats's "The Eve of St. Agnes" under my blankets with a flashlight after lights out. During Christmas vacation I visited and soon began to haunt the Tecolote Bookshop in the de la Guerra adobe that formed at that time a part of the El Paseo shops. It was presided over by dear old Roger Boutell, Sr., a real bookman who provided endless help and encouragement in his high, whining voice. My first serious literary purchase was Amy Lowell's biography of Keats, which I still have.

Soon I discovered that there existed a category of books about books and their authors. The first one of this sort, found at the Tecolote, opened up for me the thrilling, almost overwhelming world of modern American literature. Entitled *I Hear America*, by one Vernon Loggins, it was an English professor's way of introducing with relatively brief biographical and critical entries the various writers who had made their mark in the first third of our century. Of course virtually every entry filled me with the urge to read that author's works, and almost at once I sat down to absorb all I could of the significant writers of those times, most of them members of the avant-garde. What the school library lacked could usually be provided by the Tecolote's stock of Modern Library titles. What a blessing they were! The smaller ones sold for 95 cents and the "giants" for $1.25. I would give the obliging Mrs. Van Horne, the school's matron, a shopping list when she went to town, and my joy was intense when she returned and I could spill out the contents of the parcel she had brought me. Louis Untermeyer's *Modern American Poetry* introduced me to a representative sampling from the works of modern masters of the art, and thus prepared, I was in a position to comb the Tecolote bookshelves for individual works by the poets (in particular at that time T.S. Eliot and Robinson Jeffers, the latter of whom became a good friend years later in Carmel when he was an old man and I a young one). I was indiscriminate; I loved them all: Ezra Pound and e.e. cummings along with Carl Sandburg, William Carlos Williams along with Vachel Lindsey, Wallace Stevens with Robert Frost, Marianne Moore with Conrad Aiken, Edward Arlington Robinson with Hart Crane, and Robinson Jeffers with Edgar Lee Masters. How lucky I was! Can there ever have been a more propitious time for a boy to fall in love with poetry?

I don't remember how I discovered James Joyce during my

fourth-form year, but he soon became my foremost literary idol. First *A Portrait of the Artist as a Young Man* took possession of me, and not long after, *Ulysses*, which had only recently, in a landmark legal decision, been allowed into the country, though like me it had been born fifteen years earlier in Paris in 1922. I was poring over my own copy in the library one day when who should approach stealthily from behind but Wee-wee himself, who promptly snatched it away. He must have thought I would turn into a dangerous sex fiend; hypocrite that he was, that dubious prospect apparently counted for more in his mind than the fact that I had now embarked upon a sophisticated and discriminating reading binge. Sour grapes, too, I daresay; he was not the kind who could have derived any pleasure from Molly Bloom's soliloquy. (He returned it to me on the last day of school, leaving me with the whole of summer vacation to savor its extraordinary wonders.) Then Mr. Cate cancelled my subscription to *Esquire*. Those were not enlightened times.

Somewhere I came across a catalog from Frances Steloff's Gotham Book Mart, unique at that time in specializing in avantgarde first editions. I decided, in the face of that embarrassment of riches, to focus on James Joyce. Over the next two years I spent all the money I could save from my allowance, plus birthday and Christmas presents, on building up a collection of Joyce first editions. By happenstance, no modern author could have been more of a delight to collect when judged by the physical appearance of the books. The very earliest, a rarity by any standards, was a mere pamphlet of a few pages consisting of an essay, "The Day of the Rabblement," written by Joyce in 1901, when he was was a college student. I remember the huge pride I felt when, the very incarnation of the Boy Collector, I commissioned a local craftsman to fashion a leather slipcover for it. Next in sequence of publication were his two books of poems (unexpected throwbacks to Elizabethan lyrics), *Chamber Music* and *Pomes Penyeach,* the latter of which, a real charmer, was no more than about three inches square. During Christmas vacation I spied in the latest catalog two copies of *Ulysses*. One was a first edition, printed of course by Sylvia Beach's famous Paris bookshop, Shakespeare & Co.; the other was the second edition, exactly similar in appearance with its thin, light-blue paper binding. It was a presentation copy, signed by the author. The first edition was priced at $125, the presentation copy at $17.50. It can be foolish to be thrifty, and I regret to say that in this case I was thrifty. Much as I loved collecting Joyce, I was damned if I would spend *all* my precious Christmas money on a book, so I settled for second-best. I wonder what a *Ulysses* first is worth today. (No matter, really, since in the 1960s I donated my Joyce collection to UC Santa Barbara, where it is housed in the Special Collections section of the library.) Let me add that it was my regular trade edition of the book that Wee-wee confiscated.

Nor were these all. Soon I was able to add individual published fragments of what then was called *Work in Progress* and later was published as *Finnegans Wake,* his most controversial because essentially unreadable work. These fragments were ravishingly attractive examples of the printer's art, large, slender volumes printed on the most expensive paper, marvels of tactile as well as visual perfection. In one of them, the capitals that began each section were gorgeously "illuminated," in the medieval sense, by Joyce's mad daughter, Lucia. These volumes were sold as expensive limited editions, the proceeds from which helped to sustain Joyce and his wife during the 1930s. To round out the group I added an attractive book of essays by critics of the period; its editor gave it the delightfully Joycean title of *Our Exagmination Round His Factification of Work in Progress.* And one day there arrived in the mail to my almost uncontrollable excitement a record of Joyce reading a selection from the fragment "Anna Livia Plurabelle," into which he had woven the names of I forget how many hundreds of rivers. I can see myself, having torn the record from its packing, hunched over the only record player allowed at school in the Boys' Room (not a lavatory, but a bleak lounge where we received our mail), hoping no one would intrude to break the spell of the great man's lilting Irish brogue.

And from this time forth reading has been the chief joy of my long life—with one exception: during my two and a half years at college. I am so perverse that, unlike most American males, whose only reading experiences worth mentioning come under benign professorial direction, I read practically nothing at college, assigned or unassigned. How did I survive? By elevating the craft of bull-slinging into a fine art. And what did I do with the time I should have spent reading and studying? Ah, that's another story altogether, one that doesn't come within the scope of this memoir.

AS SOON AS SCHOOL WAS OVER, I went a second time to "Rogue's Roost" in Oregon along with my classmate/host, Nion Tucker, and a sizable houseparty. Once more I found the atmosphere congenial, a highly luxurious version of "roughing it" that was very much to my taste. I took along one huge volume of my newly acquired *Remembrance of Things Past* to get me through dull patches. Everyone else was either reading or talking about the new runaway bestseller *Gone with the Wind* while I looked down my nose at the intellectual peasantry.

One afternoon we all went riding. As a skilled horseman, I was given one of the more spirited horses, one that hadn't been ridden in quite a while. I swung my leg across the saddle and prepared to settle in, but the horse had something else in mind and immediately reared, throwing himself and me into a heap on the ground. I wasn't hurt beyond a soreness in the groin area, but it seemed clear to me that there were malign spirits in the area that were trying to do me in or at the very least warn me that there was no place for me, product of a decadent suburbia, in God's country. So I went back to the lodge by the rushing river and spent the afternoon lost in the enthralling complexities of Proust's characters while the others went thrashing pointlessly about on their horses under the distant pines.

OVER THE YEARS Mother had fallen in love with Lake Tahoe, and she rented summer cottages in different communities along the Nevada shore for a number of years before finally settling on one that suited her very well within the confines of the Glenbrook Inn compound, but on privately owned land. She favored the Nevada side because the California mountains, being far grander and higher, could be seen and appreciated better from across the lake. And Glenbrook was an enchanting place. The inn itself was a flavorful old two-storey structure dating from the last century, when

Glenbrook had been a thriving lumber camp. Near it were other mellow old buildings, all painted the same shade of pale pea-soup green. Near the main building were a dozen or so cottages for guests and a tennis court. (Because of the altitude, tennis balls floated interminably, giving an eerily bothersome slow-motion quality to the game.) A few yards away was the beginning of a fine small beach (that extended to and beyond our cottage) with the typically coarse tan sand of the Tahoe shore. A low, weathered pier led into the lake directly in front of the inn; at its end, fifty yards out from shore, I often rented an outboard skiff from the inn's ancient mariner, Hank, who wore a stained cowboy hat and an enormous pair of handlebar moustaches. It was a great treat to putt and glide around the nearby coves, and to peer deep down past huge rocks to the bottom through the transparent water.

Mother's house, which she rented for many years from June to September, was a half-mile beyond the inn, near the Glenbrook golf course, but fronting on the lake. It was a simple two-storey pine cottage, unpretentious but thoroughly comfortable inside. Emmy took care of all the housekeeping while Davie led sister Nancy on nearby nature hikes and trail rides and Mother planned picnics and hikes for all of us into the lake-bejeweled mountains and excursions to such far-off points as Carson City, the state capital, where a jailbird made a face at Nancy through a barred window and scared her out of her wits; Virginia City (the famous silver-mining town that helped to finance the Civil War for the Union side and founded many a San Francisco fortune); and Reno, "the biggest little city in the world." Minors were allowed to gamble in those simple, uncrowded times, and I won a useful amount at roulette one evening; not long afterwards, I tried roulette again, hoping for a killing. Instead, I lost a month's allowance—most inconvenient. But that—bang!—was the end of my gambling.... So why didn't I quit after my first carton of cigarettes or my first drunk? Genes, that's why.

Mother was a great one for activities. A relentless "doer" and extrovert, she wanted to have something going on every day. An introvert, I did not. With my new passion for reading, especially of a highbrow sort that she didn't try to appreciate and didn't approve of, I wanted nothing but to be left alone "with my nose in a book," as she would put it scornfully, though of course I appreciated the Sierra scenery and the sparkling air and the ever-changing lake. Who wouldn't? But they were mere backdrops to the book I was reading, perhaps De Quincey or Laurence Sterne, to be savored for a moment between chapters. And I did enjoy swimming in the cold lake, even though it lacked the easy buoyancy of the salty Pacific, and paddling in our kayaks, especially when the wind kicked up waves.

All in all, I look back extremely happily upon the partial summers spent on the shores of Tahoe from the age of fourteen to the age of eighteen, though as I grew older I wanted to spend more and more of my time in dear old decadent Montecito. Which, thanks to my grandparents' hospitality, is exactly what I did. I'll describe my long visits with them in chapter 8, "The Meekers in Montecito."

A FEW DAYS AFTER MY SIXTEENTH BIRTHDAY, I returned to school for my fifth-form year, ready to enjoy the elevated status of an older boy. My own form, whose faces and numbers shifted slightly each year, was both smaller and duller than most, a fact that depressed me as I contemplated the two years remaining of the prep-school period of my life. Each new year upon arrival at school, I would rush to the bulletin board to learn the names of new boys, hoping, hoping that one or two of these would turn into flesh-and-blood persons who would make life on the Mesa more stimulating and enjoyable. More often than not, my hopes were unfulfilled.

At English "public" schools, inter-class friendships were either frowned upon or flatly forbidden because of the incidence of homosexuality among the upper classes, the thought being that nothing could bring together an older and a younger boy except the unnatural lust of the former and the susceptibility of the latter. At Cate there were no such prohibitions, though in practice any boy who looked for friendship in a form more remote than the one just below his own was usually a misfit (of the uninteresting sort; God bless the interesting ones) who couldn't relate satisfactorily to boys his age. I depended greatly for social variety and stimulation upon boys in the form ahead of me. Many of them were two years older than I and consequently much more "sophisticated," a condition that had great appeal for me in those days. Those from the form above who were my friends knew more about girls, parties, drinking, travel, and luxurious living than I did, and much less about literature and sports. I learned quite a lot from them, and they learned little from me, but they enjoyed my witticisms and irreverent attitude.

During my fifth-form year, Mr. Crawford staged the first of a long line of Latin plays, with performers from the top two classes spouting their lines in metrical Latin (Mr. Crawford spent most of his summer vacation working out the complex meters of Plautus's *Menaechmi,* a rowdy play that formed the basis for Shakespeare's *A Comedy of Errors*). The rehearsals were a lot of fun, with both fifth and sixth formers involved and many chances for me to display my special brand of mischief. Not long ago, my old friend and classmate Richard de Mille came across a snapshot of half a dozen of the costumed fifth-form members of the cast relaxing in Mr. Crawford's study. Everyone looks cheerful and either smiling or on the verge of it—except for me. My mind is far away from this foolishness; the look is one of ineffable boredom and superiority. When Richard gave me a print not long ago, I asked him what he thought was running through my mind. His answer was instantaneous: "What am I doing with these ghastly people?" Actually, I was fond of four of the five pictured and no worse than neutral towards the fifth. A disdainful world-weariness was my pose of the moment. There were many others.

IN THE SMALL WORLD of Cate, the masters, of necessity, played very important roles in our lives. One significant one whom I haven't had occasion to mention was Mr. Eric Parson, known as "Mr. Eric," to distinguish him from his brother, "Uncle John." The two Parsons had been "imported" by Mr. Cate many years before my time and had grown gray in service. Their provenance was impeccable: Boston, plus a large summer home in Brooklin, Maine, and of course B.A. degrees from Harvard. They were probably put into baggy gray flannels and tweed coats with leather patches at the elbows at the age of five. Uncle John was a bachelor and nearly blind; during most of my Cate years he was on an extended sabbatical, traveling often in Europe, from which he would send letters for Mr. Cate to read aloud, studded with such remarks as that he had just finished "munchin' luncheon in Munchen," for which I continue to berate him since I have never been able to forget it, much as I would like to. He was a history teacher, and because of my conflicting Greek classes I was never exposed to his teaching style. Brosie remembers that Uncle John spent the class periods reading aloud from the text, held about two inches from his poor old eyes. His students snoozed, or worse.

Mr. Eric, on the other hand, I encountered in both algebra and English, the latter in my last two years. He was a gentle and lovable man of the genus *Mr. Chips.* Nearly as confused by math as I was, he was at least tolerant of one's mistakes, if indeed he was even capable of identifying them. Under him, at least I did not have to dread the whiplash of Captain Davy's mathematical scorn. On the other hand, Mr. Eric's explanations cleared away no cobwebs of misunderstanding. (Captain Davy once set us a geometry problem that he said would "separate the sheep from the goats." That's a silly expression because both words are pejorative. I'm pretty sure I turned out to be a goat. But why would one want to be a sheep? At any rate, of course I missed the problem.)

English was thought to be Mr. Eric's subject, and he was in fact the senior English master. I don't think he had ever read a poem more recent than the Victorian verse in his beloved Palgrave's *Golden Treasury.* The only time, for instance, that I ever heard him mention T.S. Eliot, who may well have been his contemporary at Harvard, was to refer to him as "Peace of God" Eliot (that peace "which passeth all understanding"—a nice remark but far too witty to have been original). He was full of homely anecdotes, usually with a New England background; they would often begin with "When I was fogbound off the coast of Maine...." Poor man, he was fogbound no matter where he was and no matter what the weather. A class that came along a few years after I had graduated aptly christened him "The Fog." He went through his days in a state of genial and harmless confusion, loyal and helpful and infinitely kind, devoted to the school, always ready to pinchhit as needed, whether as math teacher or baseball or track or drama coach, and always the amateur in a world becoming more and more professional.

As my English master, he was about as inspiring as cabbage. He led, or perhaps followed, us through Hardy and H.G. Wells and Arnold Bennett, enthusiasms from his youth. I'm sure he thought of them as moderns. Our class read some Thackeray, too, and Trollope, but we were spared George Eliot, one of his pets. I can't remember how we got through class day after day. I pinched and poked and tweaked the ears of people within range to help pass the time, and was never suspected of being the guilty one because top students of course wouldn't behave so childishly. And I invented a little game that provided a bit of suspense. Mr. Eric always wore or carried an old brown fedora hat, which he would place meticulously on the shelf below the seat of his chair. He would position it so that his right hand could meet it easily without having to grope when class was over. Our class was the last one of the day for him, so the hat lay there all morning unprotected, giving me easy access. I would slide it over several inches from its normal resting place and wait restlessly till the end of class. Then, after alerting friends to what was going on, I would watch as he called out the next day's dreary assignment while his hand dropped confidently down to pluck the hat. But his fingers closed upon themselves, not upon brown felt! He tried again. Still it eluded him. Finally he rose perplexed from his chair and bent way over to see what on earth could be wrong.... And the next day he went to special pains to be certain that *this* time the hat was placed exactly as it should have been. Imagine his consternation when, for the second time and *incredibly, inexplicably,* the hat proved to be again out of reach.

At some point Mr. Eric concluded that I did not need to attend the weekly class devoted to the rules of the language and told me instead to repair to the library, just across the hallway, read the works of some reputable author, and eventually write a paper based on my readings. In this way, joyfully alone in that lovely paneled room and sprawled on a long green leather sofa, I read right through all of Shaw's plays and their prefaces. And of course Mr. Eric forgot completely about the paper.... He was a dear man.

Captain Algernon A. Spearmint Davy (can his mother have

been a Wrigley heiress?) was not a dear man. On the other hand, he was never, never fogbound. A colleague years later remembered that at faculty meetings he was audibly scornful of the mistakes masters made when figuring and recording their grades. "I never make mistakes," he harumphed. "And," added the colleague, "he never did." I revere his memory not for his teaching skills, soccer coaching, drawling elegance, or arrogant personality, but because of two "masters' comments" he is alleged to have sent home at term's end, when the faculty had to cudgel their brains and write appropriate remarks about their students' "progress." One of his gems went out as "Continues to attend class." A second read, "Capable of carrying out simple tasks under close supervision." How well those would have served me in my teaching years if only I had had the Davy ability to terrify parents and children alike, not to mention apparent *carte blanche* from the headmaster.

The second of those comments might have served as a good description of me as a sixth-form physics student, especially when trying to perform lab experiments. I was unfortunately paired with a boy who, though intelligent, was even more inept with his hands than I was. Time after time our data failed to prove what they were supposed to prove, and after the first experiments we grew increasingly alarmed. I realize now that we were at least fortunate in that we knew exactly what the results should have been. (I believe today's science students are supposed to experiment in the dark so that they will know the same thrill of discovery enjoyed by Mr. Lejeune's Michael Faraday and James Watt. Humph!) So it came to us that the only way we could possibly pass the course was to make each experiment's results do our bidding. Therefore we cooked the books and went on cooking them throughout the year but never lost a moment's sleep over it, our consciences clear because we had never been warned not to falsify results (very likely because the crime was so obviously heinous that it never occurred to Captain Davy to forbid it). And at year's end we managed to get through our three-hour College Board exam in physics.

An interesting man was our French master, Marcel Hawkins. Half-French, Mr. Hawkins was a tall, shambling man of thirty or so who always looked depressed. I don't think he ever laughed, but he was not unamiable. His arrival in class was invariably announced by a loud bellow, "Will you siddown and shudup!"—a not unreasonable request, though ungracious. In his class I paid attention because I was very fond of the language and well disposed toward its teacher. In those days French was taught in English, so although I soon learned to pronounce, read, and write it with a high degree of competence, I rarely had a chance, alas, to try to practice or understand the spoken language. (As a freshman at Harvard, on the strength of my College Board exam, I was allowed to take a sophomore course in French civilization that consisted of lectures given by Frenchmen in their native tongue. I soon developed the ability to follow what was being said, and, though my attendance at the lectures was no more than sporadic, I can still see the professorial comment scrawled on the outside of the first blue book containing my answers for the final exam for the course—"A+; travail extraordinaire!") By the way, by the time I arrived at Cate, I had forgotten every bit of the language which had been my only tongue during the first few years of my life.

Mr. Hawkins had a strange, brooding presence. Clearly an intellectual, he was not on the same wavelength as his students. He probably should not have been teaching at the secondary-school level, but the degree he held from Yale was "Bachelor of Philosophy." I never knew anyone else with a similar degree, nor do I know what it signified, but it did not qualify him for college-level employment. When it was his turn to read aloud secular material during morning prayers, he was apt to read something like Livingston Lowes's *The Road to Xanadu,* that masterly but esoteric treatise on the sources for Coleridge's *The Ancient Mariner.* (His audience was not attentive.) He singled me out awkwardly, almost with embarrassment, as one who would benefit from reading important books. In this way, I came to read on my own, having been excused from routine French classes, those glorious novels *Madame Bovary* and Stendahl's *La Chartreuse de Parme.* And conscious, as other masters were not, of my interest in literature and literary criticism, he lent me his own copy of a wonderfully stimulating book, *From These Roots,* by the Irish critic Mary Colum. Perhaps, too, he was aware of my developing passion for things Irish. At any rate, I have long owed him a debt for reaching out to me in his inarticulate but helpful way.... I was crushed to hear, some years later, that the poor man had committed suicide. I never learned why, but the propensity was written on his face. There is probably nothing anyone could have done that would have made him a happy man. I think he was one of those, some of our finest, who are born to suffer.

IN THE COURSE of my random reading from the school's library, I came across Thomas Cravens's *Men of Art,* which served me as an introduction to the lives and works of some of the great masters and thus started me off on the road to art appreciation. In spring vacation of fifth-form year, 1939, I visited the San Francisco World's Fair at Mare Island, and there saw, or at least appreciated, for the first time a large show of masterpieces, in this case paintings sent over for the Fair by the French government, and visiting art museums has been a delight to me ever since. But in 1939, the art had to share pride of place in my mind, and now in my memory, with Sally Rand, the fan dancer who had made a huge hit at the Chicago Fair a few years earlier. In San Francisco her offering was the "D-nude Ranch," a set behind glass in which half-a-dozen cuties wearing almost nothing but cowboy hats and boots played endless games of volleyball in a ranch atmosphere while the customers filed by. Miss Rand, by now a bit long in the tooth and elsewhere, wisely kept herself out of the exhibit. I visited the D-nude Ranch several times, for wasn't this, after all, a form of visual art? (I figured that this show amply made up for the sleazy bumps-and-grinds *artiste* that Brosie had guided me to years before at the carnival in Santa Barbara.)

I have already referred to the passion that overwhelmed me in my last two years of school for Ireland and the Irish Literary Revival. I cannot remember exactly what set it in motion. One book led to another, I expect, and I came to identify myself with the political movement for independence that developed along with the literary movement, and for a few years at least my Anglophilia turned to Anglophobia because of the barbarous treatment England had inflicted on the Irish over hundreds of years. My attention was riveted by the romance and pathos that seemed to surround this tiny island and the people, real and imagined, whose lives seemed to have cast an aureole upon it. Whatever may have been the cause of this near-obsession of mine, during my last two years I devoured the works of Irish writers in addition to my already discovered Joyce, such people as Yeats, Lady Gregory, Edward Martyn, George Moore, J.M. Synge, AE, James Stevens, and Sean O'Casey. And I reveled in reading about the political turmoil and the revolutionary heroes of the years leading up to the establishment of the Republic of Eire with Eamon de Valera at its head. It is more truth than hyperbole to say that for two years I was drunk with Ireland. And, to prolong the alcoholic metaphor, I went on an extended Irish binge when, at the age of sixteen during the summer of 1939, I joined Brosie, just graduated like his father before him as a Phi Beta Kappa from Yale, and cousin Joan Gray for a six-week bicycle trip through Ireland before spending the rest of the summer on the continent. That September we were halfway across the Atlantic headed for New York when war broke out in Europe.

Grandfather Meeker had grumped with some justice since he was paying for the trip, "Why would they want to spend time in a third-rate little country like Ireland?" (Readers will have a chance to become acquainted with that outspoken man in Book II, and when they have done so, they will realize that there was no answer that would have satisfied him, so no one even tried to come up with one.)

The Irish/European trip is one of my happiest memories, compounded of equal parts of joy and laughter, but since it does not come even remotely near the purview suggested by the title of this book, I propose to pass it by at this time. My memories of it are so green, however, that I want to revisit it in my mind in detail, and so I have decided to work it up as my next writing project, to be followed by yet another: recollections, both serious and comical, of my experiences with some of the cars I have owned (numbering ninety-one as I write, though thirty-two of these I bought to give to others).

My fifth-form year closed out, of course, just before the trip with commencement exercises held this time on the lawn between the library and the study hall. Two things stand out in my memory, one proud, one shameful. The proud one was that I won an extraordinary number of prizes. The mother of one of my Cate friends, whom I came to know in my Monterey years when I was in my late twenties, said she was astonished at hearing the same name called out so many times and swore that I had worn a brown path in the lawn going up to receive my awards and returning to my seat before the ceremony was over. But the pleasure, mixed with a little embarrassment, was greatly diminished when, at a prearranged point in the schedule, I had to appear yet again before the audience and mumble (the only time I have ever mumbled in public) a written statement that Mr. Cate had handed me just before the exercises began. I made a point of forgetting all about it by that very evening and have never thought about it since. I seem to remember that a boy in the graduating class handed me some object in a very stilted speechlet similar to the one I had been issued and that I had to respond on the spot on behalf of the incoming sixth-formers that I swore to keep it safely (whatever "it" may have been—probably a sort of poor man's Holy Grail— but heavily symbolic of the HONOR OF THE CLASS) during the next year so that I could hand it on "untarnished" (that is the only word I remember, but it gives the flavor of the thing) to the class that followed ours. Even Mr. Cate must in time have realized that this little charade was not only corny, but in view of our class's soon-to-be-notorious lack of school spirit, would be out of the question as a repeat performance for June of 1940. The incident was never referred to and never repeated.

SIXTH-FORM YEAR was an anti-climax, as I knew it would be. I was ready for something new. The school was simply too small in those days to stimulate one for five long years. Today Cate School numbers its students in the two hundreds, is coeducational, and keeps students for only four years; boredom and restlessness must be far less prevalent. And my class had shown itself to be apathetic under the best of circumstances. Soon after the year began, we were all driven to the Montecito house of an alumnus, Gimmie Hollister, that turned out to be La Villetta, the house Mother had built when I was a little boy, the house that saw us through the famous earthquake of 1925 and in whose garden we had "joined forces" with the Lloyds. After a pleasant enough dinner, we were earnestly yet amiably scolded by half a dozen or so alumni from all over southern Calfornia for our lack of school spirit.

Why did they bother to tell us that? We knew it better than they did. What did they think we could do about it? One either has it or one doesn't. We didn't. I tuned out while they harangued us. Two or three boys were impressed and swore to do better.

Academically, things were much as before. I did most of my work while nobody was looking, anxious to give the impression that everything came very easily to me, which for the most part it did. Mr. Cate's American history teacher dropped out just before the year began, too late for a replacement, so Mr. Crawford stepped into the breach with two consecutive courses, one in Greek history and the other in Roman. He used college-level texts and expected us to absorb a great deal of what should have been tiresome detail but which I found fascinating. To me this was the most interesting course in all my five years, but I doubt that any of my classmates would have agreed with me. Mr. Cate said that we must promise to study American history at college to make up for this glaring, and probably illegal, lack in our preparation. I promised, but with my fingers crossed. I have yet to read the Federalist papers and can tell you very little about either John Calhoun or the Dred Scott case.

But, along with de Mille, I did translate the *Alcestis* of Euripides in our continuing Greek studies. Not only that, but under Mr. Crawford's direction de Mille and I put on an outdoor performance of the play, he impersonating Heracles in an animal skin and I the royal Admetus in a robe made from an old sheet. Of course the whole school attended as well as a passel of withered old retired classical scholars from the Santa Barbara area. It was a coup for Mr. Crawford and damned boring for everyone else; it went on incomprehensibly and interminably. I wonder the students didn't pelt us with rotten vegetables. (He had us make a recording of portions of the play just before commencement, complete with the scratchy fluting of a background piece by Paul Hindemith. The only entertaining part came when Mr. Crawford, who had but one line to speak, missed his cue and could be heard ejaculating a furious "Damn!")

I became very fond of Mr. Crawford during my last year, and kept up my friendship with him over the decades leading up to his retirement and the sudden death that followed it. We had a lot of fun getting drunk together, something that came very naturally to both of us, and shared a taste for gossip, the more outrageous the better. But whatever his virtues, and he had many, he was not a shrewd judge of character. He told Mother that he hoped I would become a comparative philologist. Mother hadn't the least idea what that might be but told him she was quite sure I wouldn't be interested in *that*. She was right. There is a vast difference between being a good student and being a scholar. The midnight oil was never for me. It occurred to me early in life that a thing isn't worth doing unless it can be done easily, i.e., gracefully, naturally, stylishly. That, I suppose, is the point of view of a gentleman, of an amateur. Is it appropriate in a professional world? And Mr. Crawford went even further astray in trying to influence Brosie's future (their paths crossed briefly the former's first year at Cate, which was Brosie's final year; I make a point of this because the Latin master obviously had little time to study the lad's character and interests). He told Brosie he had the makings of a man of the cloth and arranged a luncheon meeting at the then-fashionable El Paseo Restaurant in Santa Barbara with the rector of All Saints referred to in the last chapter, whose naughty proclivities were as yet unknown. (Come to think of it, so were Brosie's.) I would give thousands to charity to have an audiotape of that luncheon.

Chief among my intellectual discoveries in my last year was the poetry of Gerard Manley Hopkins, the self-tortured English Catholic convert who became a Jesuit priest. I found his experiments in meter that he called "sprung rhythm" extremely interesting, though I found his (to me) capricious use of stress marks to indicate those rhythms baffling. I was greatly moved by the alliterative power and the freshness of his language, not to mention the intensity of his religious feeling, which I admired without sharing. He remained my favorite poet for many years. And though I found him very hard to read in the original French, I developed a cult for Arthur Rimbaud, whose pre-surrealistic verse, all written by the time he was eighteen, not to mention his disordered way of life, suited my developing pose of *épater les bourgeois*. How *I* would have liked to be arrogant and contemptuous of everyone and everything! But it was not a role that suited me. In spite of my mantle of cosmic melancholy, I was irredeemably entertaining by nature, no matter how hard I tried to seem stand-offish and superior.

As my final year advanced, I prepared myself for another pose or role that I would try on at college where I could better get away with it since I would be for the most part among strangers. This was the "Nevill Coward" role in which I would emulate the brittle wit and sophistication of Noël Coward (dimmed somewhat by my lack of musical talent). Blasé, cynical, world-weary—I wanted to be thought of in those terms. But of course I couldn't really get away with it at Cate where people had known me since I was a wide-eyed little thirteen-year-old. Or was I ever wide-eyed?

I CALL TO MIND a few tidbits that were peculiar to this final year of my chronological reminiscences.... The great benefactor Max Fleischmann, before he moved away to Nevada, which advertised itself on huge billboards in the Tahoe region as a "storm cellar for the tax-weary," and made the University of Nevada the show-piece of his munificence, had recently presented Cate with a handsome gymnasium, complete with locker rooms, squash court, and basketball court. This became an important amenity in our lives. I took to squash right away, becoming the first school champion and going on to play on the freshman team at Harvard, where it was a very popular sport because of the long, brutal winters that kept one indoors for months. At Cate basketball was only recreational; there was no coach or interscholastic competition. I always supposed that Mr. Cate disapproved of basketball because of all those exposed armpits.... During our European summer just prior to senior year, Bosie and I had paid a visit to a London tailor on fabled Savile Row, a place recommended by our father; and I had had two very elegant but extremely British-looking suits made up. They required four fittings, excessive by American standards, as I was to learn at college, yet never fitted nearly so well as the custom-made clothes of J. Press in Cambridge, Mass., in spite of their vaunted English craftmanship. Mr. Cate thought they were the acme of good taste, and murmured to me one evening that I was the "best-dressed boy in school." I was delighted by the compliment but years later decided it was an odd thing for which to praise a boy at a school that emphasized achievement and character. But I have said on an earlier page that he had a strong sense of style, and I add now that at times his devotion to style seemed to overpower his other, more pedagogical values…. The summer before my final year he got it into his head (or, more likely, someone else put it there) that his boys should learn the rudiments of some trade that would bring them down to earth and provide them with practical skills in a harsh world. A program was developed to inculcate these skills. The whole school was divided into "work squads" nominally under the command of a master, but with sixth formers as foremen. I was named foreman of the once-a-week painting squad, a shrewd choice because painting is the one trade in which anyone, no matter how inept, can attain a reasonable proficiency. My mentor, Mr. Eric, showed me the basics of the trade and then pretty much left me alone to mix the paints, hand out, supervise, and take part in the assignments, and at the end of the afternoon see that the brushes were properly cleaned and the paints put away. To my astonishment, I found painting a bearable burden; I certainly didn't hate it as I hated making things. In fact, it was the only practical thing I learned at Cate, though the skill was dearly bought when one considers all the tuition money that lay behind it. And, as a house owner for nearly fifty years, I have had many a chance to put that one skill to good use. Why didn't they give me an apprenticeship in plumbing, too, and electricity?

SO FAR I have made no mention of girls. The reason is that they played an insignificant part in my life during my five years at Cate. Our lives were essentially monastic, though of course like monks we had our fantasies and relieved sexual tensions in immemorial and harmless ways. Now and then there would be a dance, with girls imported from private girls' schools in Los Angeles. The best girls were signed up in advance by boys who lived in L.A. and already knew them. The rest of us took potluck. I never got seriously interested in any of the girls that came my way during my Cate years. For one thing, I lacked sexual self-confidence; in a social context, I saw myself as an entertainer, not a lover, and as a mocking observer of mating rituals. I never even came close to falling in love at that point in my life. Obviously, young males mature in different ways and at different times. Many of my contemporaries became deeply involved with girls during their vacations, but quite a few like me did not. Of course I had dates and indulged in the usual necking.

The only girl that I found bewitching I met soon after graduation, staying with her family at the Biltmore. She was the archetypal Eastern debutante, complete with hot-potato-in-the-mouth boarding-school accent. Everything was "too, too divine"—pronounced "divahyn." She was magically pretty and spoiled and rich and lively and fun: everything I then thought a girl should be. Scott Fitzgerald would have gone wild over her. We spent a lot of time together and for quite a while exchanged letters; I even drove to see her at Foxcroft, her school in Virginia, when I was in Washington with my father and stepmother. A few years later I read of her marriage to the Marquess of Milford Haven, cousin, best friend, and best man of Prince Philip, the Queen's consort. And not so very long after that, I read of their divorce.

During my last summers before going off to college, my social life and that of my friends revolved around the Coral Casino. We gathered there in the afternoon, boys and girls, after a hard (!) morning spent on the tennis courts, and lolled about on the fine white sand between the pool and the cabanas, stubbing out our cigarettes languidly in the sand as we gossiped about the previous night's events—a private party, perhaps, given by a girl's parents in a lanterned garden, or a Saturday-night dance at the Casino itself where it was easy to order drinks, provided they were innocent-looking Bloody Marys that indulgent bartenders poured out (heavy on the vodka) while avoiding the eye of the strutting little British manager, Major Mouel-Fenton, who was death on teenage drinkers. The Casino parties were primarily for grownups, and it was great fun to observe their indecorous antics as the evening wore on. One of the sights was Brickie Conrad, middle-aged local tennis champion, as he worked his way genially through his daily training ration of eighteen gin-and-tonics—until, that is, he would fall off his bar stool onto the terrazzo floor. Also, one came across married people smooching with people they weren't married to. I must admit that, aglow with vodka (but only then), I felt very much at home in this world.

IN MY SIXTH-FORM YEAR I discovered drinking. Like many others before me, I was drawn to booze because it enabled me to enjoy things I avoided while sober—mostly parties, i.e., being sociable with people I didn't know well, including girls; and even dancing, sort of. Traveling in Ireland the summer before, I had been very censorious with Brosie, who loved quaffing Guinnesses with the local peasantry in the noisy, smelly pub that was invariably under our bedroom window. I was loudly scornful of his indiscriminate bonhomie and the (to me) foolish loquacity of the extrovert boozer. What a difference a few months made! During the Christmas vacation that followed, under his tutelage I discovered the carefree, fuzzy joy that liquor could bring to a shy introvert. Nobody ever questioned one's age in the Miramar bar of those days or in smoke-filled El Cortijo, a low-ceilinged roadhouse situated where today's Bank of Montecito branch stands elegantly, or in the empty bar of the moribund Samarkand Hotel; in all these havens I learned with Brosie or with groups of friends of both sexes to hold more than my share of the Old Taylor bourbon that my brother had started me on. Miserable drink, bourbon—the only one that has ever made me sick. Before long I switched to lovely, smoky scotch; and it had to be Cutty Sark as a tribute to Hart Crane, one of my favorite poets.

I was still faithful, however, to Old Taylor in the spring of sixth-form year. In fact, after a home-leave, I took a bottle of it back to school and stashed it in the dresser drawer of an empty bedroom in the dorm below my own. It was my goofy idea, as I recall it, to swig away at it before and during the upcoming spring dance, hoping it would work the same social magic for me there that it had proven itself capable of doing during Christmas vacation. Incredibly, it never occurred to me that my reeking breath, not to mention its concomitant, a lurching gait worthy of a sailor on a storm-tossed deck, would set me up for automatic, swift expulsion just a month before my graduation.

What saved me from this disaster was a fluke, pure and simple. The senior prefect and good friend of mine, Nion Tucker, took me into his confidence only a few days after I had secreted the bourbon. He told me that Tom Savage, the greatly respected Irish-born superintendent of grounds and general handy-man, had gone into the empty room to remove its dresser for use elsewhere and in emptying the drawers had of course come across the contraband bourbon. And what did I think of that? What, indeed? I could hardly believe my good luck. Of course, I was insulted to think that Tucker was so certain that I was not the guilty one that he had confided in me.

But if he had not been, I would have been a dead duck because Tom had been ordered by Mr. Cate himself to keep a watchful eye on the room where the crime had been committed and to nab anyone entering it. In the weeks that followed, I took pleasure in asking Tucker whether they had caught their man yet. No, and it appeared that the constant vigil he was keeping was preventing Tom from attending to his responsbilities in keeping the school's plant going. Tucker didn't know how much longer the school could afford to keep Tom on guard. I wondered aloud what had become of the whiskey. (I was mulling over whether to make a run for it; after all, it had cost me good money.) Apparently Mr. Cate had "confiscated" it. So I endured my last dance in dull sobriety and enjoyed it no more than those that had gone before.

But that wasn't quite the end of it. I had confided my role in this incident to Brosie; after all, he was my Bacchus and besides greatly enjoyed hearing anything about life at school, even though he was five years out of it. I've never been quite sure of his motivation (and I'd rather not speculate at this point), but I found out later that shortly after my graduation (we had to stay around an extra week to take College Boards) he either boasted, or complained, to Tucker of my involvement in the escapade. Tucker was an establishment boy through and through and reported what he had learned to Mr. Cate. It was too late for Mr. Cate to take disciplinary action, so no mention was made of the incident until during summer vacation when I was kayaking at Glenbrook just offshore in the clear waters of Lake Tahoe. Mr. Cate, who owned a summer place a hundred yards down the beach from ours, suddenly appeared at my elbow in his kayak and proceeded to confront the issue. I admitted my involvement, and he lectured me rather mildly on the evils of drink. I really don't remember what he said, because the spectacle of the two of us kayaking together was so unlikely that in my mind it blotted out any moral points he wished to make—not that I would have been in the least receptive no matter what the circumstances. I did refrain (but just barely) from asking him whether he had enjoyed the Old Taylor. *My* Old Taylor.

BEFORE WRITING about this rather discreditable incident, I spent some time trying to decide whether it really belonged in these—after all—highly selective memoirs. I concluded that it did because it seemed to me symbolic of the change that had come over me during my five years at Cate. I had arrived there barely pubertal in 1935, intoxicated with the challenges of my new world, a quietly but intensely competitive little boy, eager to please and anxious to leave his mark in every area he touched; and now here I was in 1940, seventeen—jaded, disillusioned, full of private pain and *Weltschmerz,* too. I was sick to death of being cooped up in that tiny world, tired of everybody and at the same time obsessively self-concerned. I knew one thing: my many victories were hollow, perhaps because they had come so easily. Success, victory in a world of my peers—these gave no real satisfaction. From now on I would not compete, overtly or covertly. I would do only what came naturally and even that only when I was in the mood.

Not long ago a good friend who had recently retired from many years of teaching at Cate asked me why it was that my brother has been so deeply and intimately involved with Cate as an Old Boy ever since he graduated whereas I have had virtually nothing to do with it though I live only ten miles away. "And how long has it been since you visited your high school?" I asked him. "I've never been back," he answered. "Well, there you are. We're introverts, you and I. My brother is an extrovert. It's that simple."

Brosie's years at Cate were the high point of his life, and he finds endless pleasure in reliving them as he returns year after year at reunion time to refresh and rejuvenate himself by giving speeches, slapping backs, and swapping memories with other extroverted oldtimers. My memories are just as vivid, I'm sure; I have forgotten nothing and no one from those long years. But all the people I knew then are dead now or unimaginably old. And I have no wish to revisit those scenes. Why should I? They exist only in my mind. Today's reality is a far different thing from the reality of 1940. It has nothing to do with me. Why should I intrude upon it?

What did I think lay before me as I drove down the steep hill from the Mesa for the last time? Harvard, of course, chosen semi-mischievously because there was a long family tradition on both sides of attending Yale. But that wasn't a very dramatic prospect, especially as it was just one more institution with silly rules. Unlike most American boys, I had already left home—left it five years ago. And leaving home, after all, is something one does only once. I had held my end up and more in a harsh environment; by now I took that for granted, but still it was no small accomplishment. In June 1940 the German *Wehrmacht* had just overrun France. What sort of future was there for my generation? Eat, drink, and be merry, said my inner voice.

If I made it through the war (as it turned out, many, many Cate boys, including d'Autremont and Tucker, didn't), I would be a writer. With one proviso: I wouldn't have to *write*. Somehow, that wouldn't matter. Everybody would accept me as a writer anyway because I was so special.

If a psychic had told me then that at some point in the murky future, say at the age of thirty or so, I would start to serve a quarter-century as an English teacher and counselor in a private day school, I would have hauled off and socked him in the eye. And if he had had the effrontery to add that it looked in the mystic ball as though after retiring in my mid-fifties, I would go on to spend the long years remaining as a community volunteer, a chronic do-gooder, I would have socked him in the other. *Sacré bleu,* what would Rimbaud think of me, or Baudelaire?

But there were no predictions. As I drove down the winding road after the week-long grind of four three-hour College Boards that followed my last Commencement*, with the back seat and

---

*This time Mr. Cate had decided to hold the closing exercises in the new Fleischmann Gym, of all places, probably to please its donor. De Mille and I had to stand up and recite some passages from Homer before the large crowd of students and their relatives. What foolishness! At least before, when we had acted Euripides in costume, those attending had known what they were getting in for. This time, our guests were unprepared and help-

trunk crammed full of boxes and suitcases containing what little I owned, and Mother in the passenger's seat, I knew that I had finished with my childhood. What I didn't know till I was old was that no period in the future would ever mean so much, would be so rich in variety and detail, as those first almost eighteen years. And that the memory of them would be an endless resource as my life wound slowly to its close.

---

less. On the bright side, I didn't have to wear a sheet but instead sported one of my elegant Savile Row suits, navy blue with a faint chalk stripe; and I won my usual string of awards. The guest speaker's topic was "Keep a Bright Lookout Ahead," not an easy thing to do when the Nazis had just completed the subjugation of Europe. Would we even have the chance to go to college?

BOOK II

The Families

CHAPTER SEVEN

The Meekers of Chicago

"Blessed are the Meekers, for they shall inherit the earth."
—old folk-saying

IN IMAGINATION, let us travel to the hospitable Thanksgiving dinner table of my grandparents, Arthur and Grace Meeker, in their large, comfortable, antique-filled apartment at 1100 Lake Shore Drive, overlooking Chicago's lakefront on the Gold Coast. The time is the late 1930s.

It is an enormous, rich, and delicious meal, shockingly caloric and cholesterol-laden by 1990s standards, prepared to perfection by Hungarian Alma and served by Rudge, the English butler, and his neatly uniformed waitresses. (Rudge has been into the gin and, as is his wont when under the influence, fails time and again to serve Mr. Arthur, the son of the house, to the latter's mounting irritation.) The host and hostess sit at opposite ends of the long, candle-lit table, whose numbers are rounded out by assorted relatives, all Meekers or Meeker in-laws. There are none to represent Grandmother's side of the family.

LITTLE AUNT LOUIE, Louise Meeker Walker, the elder and more foolish of Grandfather's two sisters, from her position at mid-table raises her wine glass to propose a toast. Her lower lip quivers, as it always does when she is about to make a pronouncement: "To our large and in-ter-est-ing family!" Grandmother, her sister-in-law, winces with displeasure and then asserts in her most cutting manner, used often to subdue rival Chicago society matrons, "Large, I grant you, Louise. But I take exception to your use of the word 'interesting.' It is out of place in its context." There is a brief and equivocal silence before the knives and forks go back to work and the chitchat resumes.

Was she right, my tart-tongued grandmother, who was much more prone to tear down than to build up? Let us examine some of the evidence. It's appropriate to consider Aunt Louie first, since she was the one who made the toast. By her lax and sentimental standards, all family members were *per se* interesting and every other good thing, too. It would be fair (and kind) to call her fey. Her world was as unreal and snug and cloying as a Victorian children's book. She had borne two sons, yet how could she have endured the sex act? The legendary prime minister's wife did it by closing her eyes and thinking of England; Aunt Louie would probably have thought of Stockbridge, Massachusetts, where she and Uncle Jamie Walker spent most of the year and brought up her children. Yet they fled the rigors of Berkshire winters and often came for a month or two to Montecito, where they would stay at the old brown-shingled Miramar. (Another favorite suntrap was Tucson, which Aunt Louie pronounced as though it were a French word, complete with French *u* and the nasal *on.*) As a little boy, I was very fond of my great-uncle and -aunt, and used to walk with my governess to visit them at their hotel cottage, usually with a handful of flowers, an offering I made to no one else.

It stimulated my curiosity that Aunt Louie always referred to her husband in his hearing and without protest as "your Uncle Jack." This was patently silly since his name was Uncle Jamie. Mother had no explanation when I pressed her for one. Nor did she know why he had one black tooth, right up front. These two elements alone combined to make the pair highly "interesting" to me, child that I was, to use the word that had irritated Grandmother. And years later I learned that the gentle and courtly Uncle Jamie, who never did a day's work in his life (for which I greatly admired him) or was heard to raise his voice in anger, used to slip away from their apartment at the Drake Hotel in Chicago and disappear for days on end to his wife's great discomfiture and puzzlement. Her brother, my grandfather, once had him tracked down by a detective, who discovered him and a friend in a little-known hotel on the outskirts of Chicago. There the two men had rented an entire floor and hired an orchestra that played for them night and day while they worked their way through cases of Dom Pérignon and bevies of chorus girls. Not interesting, indeed!

Their son Wirt would have been seated at the table, too. He ran Arcady Farms Milling Company, which Grandfather had founded as an outgrowth of his model farm in Lake Forest. Long after he had sold the farm, the company continued to market and distribute animal feed products throughout the Middle West, with Wirt in charge and Grandfather looking over his shoulder. I never met him. Mother used to come back from her infrequent visits to Chicago with detailed reports about whatever new wife he had taken unto himself, the piquant thing being that as he rose higher in the business world, his taste in wives appeared to deteriorate. Since there were many wives, this allowed for a good deal of deterioration over the years. His most recent (and final, as it turned out) had been the hostess in a night club; a dusky woman of Sicilian ancestry, she was profoundly disturbing in appearance and speech habits to the more conventional members of the family (i.e., everyone else). At family gatherings great pains were taken to position her at the table so that she could cause the least offense. In practice, that meant surrounding her with the Meekers' two grown children, Mary Cramer, who was kind-hearted and would make the best of the situation, and Arthur, Jr., who was not kind-hearted and would make the worst of the situation by later dining out, as the saying goes, on her indiscretions while at table.

THEN THERE WAS Grandfather's other sister, Margaret Meeker Cook. Though a pretty woman, she had been late to marry by Victorian standards, for a long while living with and tagging along after her mother. She was given to showing one her thick ankles and warning any family children in her hearing that they were the result of her childhood passion for jumping off roofs. This seemed like sound advice, but none of us, it turned out, was much given to jumping off roofs. In any case, we all had, and continued to have, shapely ankles. When she did marry, it was to a strikingly handsome man, David Cook. They lived in Montecito, probably because he was tubercular; and he died, sad to say, after only a few years of marriage. He was always referred to in reverent tones as "your

Uncle Dave," but he never seemed real to me until a few years ago, when I inherited a book of old family photographs. And there he was in a white linen suit, standing on a Miramar bluff, and just as good-looking as everyone had said he was. While in Santa Barbara as a young bride at the turn of the century, she established lifelong friendships with other young matrons, and she kept a warm place in her heart for Santa Barbara. She told me that she herself had planted the trees (already huge in my childhood) that line the first block of Miramar Avenue north of the highway. When in the '30s my grandparents began to spend their summers in their new house in Montecito, of which more later, Aunt Margaret loved to come out from Chicago for visits to her old stamping grounds. In one vignette, I remember her bending over the bed of my new little sister with a supremely sappy expression on her kindly old face and cooing endlessly as the baby blew bubbles, "Lit-tle Bub-ble, lit-tle Bub-ble!" Another memory from the '30s is of a Sunday luncheon at the Meekers', to which she had invited an old friend from her Santa Barbara days, a member of the Miramar Doulton family. The older generation knocked off the most prodigious meals in those days, with the result that they grew immoderately beamy. I remember following right behind the huge rumps of the two old ladies on our march to the dining room and thinking they were like two great Percherons. Under my breath I gee-hawed them and flicked imaginary reins as they heavy-footed it to the manger.

One could talk with Aunt Margaret in a way that one couldn't with Aunt Louie, who was just too goofy. The former was relentlessly sentimental, but she also liked to relate gossip, not always, bless her, of a kindly nature. And she was the family genealogist. She knew whatever there was to know about her (and therefore my, or at least half of my) forebears. I am reminded that when I was ten or so, she sent us a page from the Chicago *Tribune,* which evidently was doing genealogies of leading Chicago families. From this story I learned that we were collaterally descended from Aaron Burr—that was plausible enough since Aunt Margaret's father was Arthur Burr Meeker—and directly descended, of all things, from Robin Hood! I couldn't wait to share these two exciting tidbits with George Crane, who heard me out and then gave a double snort. The first snort was because he wondered why anybody would want to be connected with such a coward as Burr, who after all shot for the heart while Alexander Hamilton, gentleman that he was, fired into the air. The other, and louder, snort was followed by the assertion that there was no such person as Robin Hood, you fool. Well, I had been a little doubtful about the Robin bit, but surely a great big paper like the *Tribune* couldn't be wrong. "Oh yes, it could," said George, "and probably the whole article is one big lie."

Mary Cramer, my aunt/stepmother, was always of the opinion that Aunt Margaret was an interfering old busybody who couldn't be trusted an inch, whereas Mother said nothing but kindly, affectionate things about her. It was not too difficult for me, young as I was, to figure out that Aunt Margaret had taken sides in the Cramer/Meeker scandal that came to light very soon after my birth. Aunt Margaret's last years should have been romantic. Somehow, I suppose by letter, she was courted by an old beau from her youth, a recent widower, Sam Colt, head of the well-known firearms company. They were married, and she went to live at his big place near Springfield, Massachusetts. Her letters to Mother, far from expressing rapture over her resumption of the married state, were larded with complaints from beginning to end. The house was too big, the servants incompetent, she suffered a great deal from arthritis, and, worst of all, her grown stepchildren resented their father's having remarried and made life extremely unpleasant for her. Poor old lady; the situation had seemed to promise so much for one whose naturally affectionate nature had been deprived for so long of a worthy object. Her last years must have been a sore trial indeed, because she was not by nature a complainer.

And what did their hard-headed brother, my grandfather, think of his two sisters? Mother used to tell of a time when he was near death from double pneumonia long before the days of antibiotics. He was in the hospital nearly delirious, but still rational enough to give his nurses instructions not to let his sisters into his room *under any circumstances.* "They're good women," he said, "but I have nothing in common with them."

COUSINS JIM AND MARGARET FORGAN, ordinarily host

and hostess at their house in Lake Forest, might have been at table if their married daughters were not home for the holiday. (One of them had married a man whose allergies were so severe that he had to live aboard a houseboat in Florida, never setting foot on dry land. What a stylish solution to his problem! I admired the man greatly for this—but in absentia, as I never met him.) Cousin Margaret Forgan was Grandfather's niece, daughter of his brother George, who had died young. She was one of the most charming people I have ever met, incredibly warm and affectionate and kind-hearted, probably the nicest person in the family. In the '40s and '50s she and her husband used to spend part of each winter in a cottage at San Ysidro Ranch. That was their only connection with Santa Barbara, as they summered at their place in Vermont. Cousin Jim was a large man of Scottish blood, white-haired with a florid face, the vice-chairman of the huge First National Bank of Chicago; he served later as executor of Grandfather's estate. If I had been a businessman looking for a big loan, I think I would have by-passed Cousin Jim, whose appraising Scottish eye pierced right through one, and gone straight to his wife. It would have been a pleasure even to have been turned down by her.

MARY AND AMBROSE CRAMER must have been at the table; they lived nearby in a towering apartment building at 1120 Lake Shore Drive, and would have walked over to the Meekers'. I intend to devote a chapter to them and other Cramer relatives, so will not linger upon them here. Mary, the youngest of Grandfather and Grandmother's four children, bossed and scolded her parents, but in an attractive and light-hearted and loving way. None of the other children would have dared to scold them as she did; and the Meekers took it from her in a way that they wouldn't have tolerated from the three others. Father tended to be overwhelmed by Grandfather's massive presence and relentless self-satisfaction and was never at his best in his company, adopting a most unconvincing heartiness for protection or else withdrawing completely. They had absolutely nothing in common, for one thing. For another, I'm sure Father was never entirely forgiven for the scandal of casting aside one Meeker bride in order to claim a second. At heart, Father always considered himself superior to the Meekers and delighted in getting in little anti-Meeker digs from time to time (to me, by all means, because I greatly appreciated a good dig, and in time became effective myself at delivering them when appropriate—and sometimes when not; and to Mary, of course, who appreciated his sallies a great deal less than I did, and was apt to counter by rattling a few Cramer skeletons in Father's face.) But, as I have said, I intend to come to grips with their natures in a later chapter.

ARTHUR MEEKER, JR., to his nephews and nieces was known as "Unky." Who can have been responsible for that foolish name? I've never heard of any other self-respecting uncle who would put up with such an abomination, or of any other nephews and nieces who would be willing to use the term. But Brosie and I had other names for him, far too indelicate and pejorative to print here. Uncharitable, of course, but then he did not inspire charity.

Most literate people of a certain age have heard of the late Alice Roosevelt Longworth's celebrated pillow in her Georgetown drawing room, with its embroidered lettering: "If you can't say something nice about anyone, come over here and sit by me." Unky would have been exceedingly welcome at her side at any time of day or night. To him, the sole reason for the existence of a person's back was to give him an excuse to say something behind it; and he never, ever missed an opportunity.

In Chicago, he was a hostess's delight because he was so different from the stolid businessmen who largely made up its society and tended, for worldly hostesses at least, to spoil their more ambitious dinner parties with their dullness. There was nothing dull about Unky. Literary in his inclinations and extremely knowledgeable about concert music as well as opera and the theater, he convulsed dinner tables—the women, at least—with laughter over his uncharitable comments about absent members of the social set. And he did it with such apparent good cheer, throwing back his head to roar unashamedly over some mordant witticism he had just dropped at someone's expense, that people felt he must be a prince of good fellows himself. They failed to take note of the depths of malice that sparkled in his heavy-lidded eyes. And they tended to forget, in their enjoyment of his repartee, that their own turn to be ridiculed would come at the very next party that they weren't invited to but he was.

In the first chapter, I mentioned an item about a lost canary bird of Grandfather's that appeared as a filler in the *New Yorker.* An even more delicious one appeared around 1933, culled from a book of cocktail recipes published just after Prohibition was repealed. I forget why Unky was solicited for a contribution, but it was probably because he had written a couple of novels by then that had attracted attention in Chicago, if nowhere else. It should have read, "As a bachelor, I am often asked to mix cocktails in ladies' pantries," but the printer had dropped the *r* in the last word. During the many times that he angered me in his lifetime, I savored in my imagination what his feelings must have been when the book came out and he first came across that lethal little sentence. And then, weeks or months later, to have the grim jest replayed before a national readership in the magazine! He must have gone into hiding—probably in his beloved German Switzerland.

When he was a boy, he had suffered an illness that left him with a damaged heart, with the result that he was coddled by all around him until he grew up and was able to coddle himself, a duty he bravely carried out until his heart failed him at the age of sixty-nine. (His three sisters were made of far sterner stuff and lived on average to the age of ninety.)

Katharine and Grace, the first two Meeker children, remembered their parents as being very much a part of their young lives, but Arthur and Mary always complained that they were given short shrift because by the time they came along, their parents were so busy being rich and social that they had little time for the younger pair, for whom their Irish nurse, Minnie O'Connell, served and served supremely well as a surrogate mother. Occasionally the young Arthur would complain, but his mother would stop his lamentations with the flat reminder that "No children ever had such a mother!" What could one say to that? It always interested me as I grew up to note in this connection that Katharine and Grace viewed their parents as almost saintly beings, whereas the younger pair were very much aware of parental failings while still suitably affectionate.

Mary and Unky, being close in age, spent a lot of time together as children and remained good friends always, but it was very apparent to any observer that he bossed and bullied and generally took unrelenting advantage of her. Of course over the years this outraged my father, by then married to Mary, but his efforts to stiffen her backbone were fruitless.

I reminded her of this very recently, when I was asking Mary, aged ninety, to reminisce over the long-distance telephone. "Unky always took advantage of you, didn't he? I suppose it was because he was older."

"And he was a boy," she added.

"Well, almost," I said.

There was a pause, then a rich chuckle at the other end. "You're awful!"

"I know," I said. "I always have been."

"I *like* it."

I felt I'd scored one for Father, who couldn't abide his brother-in-law. He found him petty, bone-selfish, and treacherous. So did I.

Eventually the sheltered youth went on to Princeton, which he left for Harvard after a year or two in order to take the then-famous course in play writing, Professor George Baker's "47 Workshop." Then he returned to Chicago and through family connections secured a job as reporter on Col. Bertie McCormick's *Tribune*, where he specialized in interviewing celebrities. He always claimed that this experience gave him confidence and a degree of poise.

Then he decided to be a novelist, a goal he had set for himself while still very young. Unfortunately his literary tastes were formed by childhood stories and genteel novels written before the turn of the century. His characters were for the most part two-dimensional, the language cliché-ridden and the stories insipid and sentimental. His protagonists tended to be young American women husband-hunting in Europe. The novels might indeed have been written by Henry James—but Henry James at the age of twelve. In order to find the peace and quiet he needed to flesh out these pallid romances, for a part of each year he fled from Grandmother's demands upon him as an extra man at her dinner parties (living at home to save money, he was altogether too accessible) to havens in Switzerland, where the surroundings were right out of his beloved childhood fairy tales.

So year after year this portly, balding man with his two fat dachshunds steamed back and forth across the Atlantic, enjoying his winter role as one of Chicago Society's favorite extra-men while living rent-free with his parents, bickering with his mother and avoiding his father as much as possible (since they had nothing to say to each other), as well as his summer role as the industrious novelist in a fairy-tale chalet near Luzern, cosseted and clucked over by Swiss maids and driven about the postcard countryside in his Mercedes by Divino, the chauffeur. His novels attracted no attention whatever, but he had an agent and publishers who apparently believed in him.

When war broke out in Europe in 1939, he high-tailed it for home and spent the war years plaintively immured in a charming farmhouse that he had remodeled in the Illinois countryside some miles outside of Chicago. In the fall of 1940 he published a massive and well-researched historical novel called *The Ivory Mischief* (he was thoroughly at home in French history and classic French literature) about two beautiful women of noble birth during the reign of Louis XIV. It was chosen by the Book of the Month Club and became a best seller to his parents' utter astonishment. Even his father began to look at him with a measure of respect, though he felt strongly that spinning tales was not what men were put on earth for.

The novel was highly readable; I did the whole of it while crossing the country by train during Christmas vacation in my freshman year. It would stand up well today, I think, except for the absence of sex, the depiction of which he very wisely, it seems to me, did not try to fabricate. As a result of the book's popular success, his personality blossomed forth, if by that one means that instead of tittle-tattling amusingly about others, he chattered far less amusingly about himself. After years of being put down by his parents because of his modest accomplishments, he now felt himself to be their equal, and even superior; and from now on he no longer lived at home, nor did he accept many of his mother's dinner invitations. He was too busy being lionized. And, like other successful writers of those days, he went on the lecture circuit, which increased his feeling of self-worth.

I remember hearing of an entertaining incident that took place one day when he was lecturing close to home in a prosperous but unfashionable suburb of Chicago. When his lecture was over, he was accosted by a stout, elderly clubwoman (my contemporaries will know exactly what I mean when I refer to her as a Helen Hokinson type), who complimented him on his lecture and especially on *The Ivory Mischief,* which she had enjoyed greatly. "My son is a writer," she confessed. "I do wish he could write like you."

"What's his name?" asked Unky in a patronizing way, thinking he was probably someone on the local literary scene who hadn't yet achieved Unky's kind of success. "Perhaps I know him."

"Ernest Hemingway." Ouch.

A few years later he ground out another French costume drama, this one selected by the Literary Guild, fierce rival of the Book of the Month Club. And of course self-esteem rose higher still.

But this was the climax of his career. His later novels were period pieces about Old Chicago, and in his home town, at least, they were well received in spite of being vapid and trite. Then, years after his first successes, he wrote another French historical novel that was pronounced unpublishable even though it was exactly similar in tone to the earlier pair. By now the reading public demanded redder meat than he was able to provide.

He wrote one last book before putting away his typewriter. In 1955 he published *Chicago, with Love,* described on its jacket as "Warmhearted memories of Chicago and Chicago Society—its life, leaders, and sensational events, its activities and peculiarities—glowing recollections of a past greatly enjoyed." True enough, I would say. The book is highly readable today, even for those without Chicago connections. He was an excellent memoirist. And his memories were for the most part "warmhearted," as the blurb put it, without being sentimental. I especially enjoy remembering, perhaps because warmheartedness is not my long suit, in a chapter on Harold McCormick, some ruminations on his lady-love, Ganna Walska, who created Montecito's extraordinary "Lotusland." (Remember that Unky was a man who took his music very seriously.)

He concludes his section on McCormick and Mme Walska (whose singing efforts he had derided earlier in the chapter, along with all others who had ever heard her) with these remarks: "After their divorce Ganna settled herself and her loot in an enormous house in Santa Barbara, not very far from that occupied by another retired prima donna, Lotte Lehmann: curious that the world's *best* soprano should have chosen the same spot as—but why belabor the comparison?" Find the book if you can in a second-hand book-store. It's delightful.... We'll meet Unky again, though in a minor role, in the next chapter about the Meekers in Montecito.

IT IS TIME NOW to have a look at the tribal elders, Arthur and Grace Meeker. First, a word about Grandfather's origins before I deal with his Chicago years. His father, Arthur Burr Meeker, grew up in Utica, New York, in what is surely the most delightful Victorian house I have ever seen—a carpenter's jewel, rich with intricate scrollwork and totally lacking in the heavy pomposity one associates with Victorian domestic architecture. The house, which I saw for myself when Brosie was married to a Utica girl in 1941, sat on an entire city block and was rightly considered at that time an historical treasure; it belonged to a relative of ours, ancient beyond imagining, on whom we paid a call. I believe it has been preserved as part of the city's heritage. But Arthur B. left Utica for Chicago—exactly when, I don't know, but probably in the late '50s, well before the time when Mrs. O'Leary's cow kicked over the lantern that started the great fire that all but demolished the city. In Chicago he married a young woman named Bentley who had emigrated with her family from upstate New York via the Erie Canal. Their union produced two sons and two daughters, all of whom I have referred to above. What I know of my great-grandfather is scanty and sad. He became an iron manufacturer and prospered. He was able to send his son Arthur, my grandfather, born in 1866, to Yale as a member of the class of '88, but after the young man's sophomore year his business collapsed in one of the "panics" so common in those unregulated days (what we would call a recession today), and young Arthur was called home because there was no more money for his tuition. Yale was Grandfather's idea of paradise, and he was bitter over having to leave it.

The ruined businessman went into a decline and became an alcoholic. His wife turned against him and so did his son, who apparently despised him for his weakness. An American tragedy, and not an uncommon one. Mary blames her grandmother for not standing by her husband and has nothing good to say of her. Apparently his unfeeling wife gave him a very cold shoulder for the rest of his life, which was not a long one. The young Arthur, too, seems to have been lacking in compassion, but that would not have been his long suit.

So the young man had to go to work instead of returning as an upper-classman to manly carousals in New Haven. Through family connections, he secured a job with the flourishing meat packer, Armour and Co., and soon began impressing the company's founder and president, Philip Danforth Armour, with his abilities. He was a tireless worker, for one thing; for another, people liked and trusted him. Because of these qualities and because he was a natural leader, he was rapidly promoted to positions of responsibility. Extremely gregarious and sociable by nature, he became very popular on the Chicago social scene as an eligible bachelor. (He used to tell of dancing all night at balls and then, without any sleep at all, showing up for work at dawn in the stockyards, still in white tie and tails.... I trust he kept a business suit in the closet of his office.)

Mr. Armour thought so highly of him that while Arthur was still in his twenties, he sent him to London to take charge of Armour's substantial European operations. In London Grandfather acquired a taste for the way British gentlemen led their elegant, moneyed lives. He fell hard for club life and bespoke tailoring, champagne, and beautiful women. When I knew him years later, he still peppered his conversation with such late Victorianisms as "doncha know" (also a favorite of Max Beerbohm's) and always spoke of "stopping" at hotels. But no trace of an accent; he was no mimic. Unlike me, he was too content with being himself to want to copy anyone else. While still in England, he sent for his fiancée, Grace Murray, a childhood friend from Chicago, and they were married in Paris. Not long after, the young couple were summoned to return to Chicago, where Grandfather continued his rise in the company's ranks.

They lived for many years on Prairie Avenue, the most fashionable street in those days, in what is today's highly unfashionable

South Side. (Many years later, Unky gave the title of *Prairie Avenue* to one of his Chicago historical novels.) Their children had the happiest possible memories of growing up in spacious Victorian town houses with a full panoply of European servants, chiefly Irish, and horses and carriages with their attendant coachmen and grooms.

They spent most of their summers when the children were growing up just outside Chicago's premier suburb, Lake Forest, about thirty miles north of the city. There they built a large, rambling country house supposedly in the French provincial style and designed by Arthur Heun, a well-known architect of the day. It was named "Arcady Farms," which was not a misnomer as Grandfather had the Midwesterner's keen interest in farming and soon developed a model working farm complete with every known species of barnyard animals. Mary and Grace fell in love with the bucolic life, while Katharine and Arthur could hardly wait for summer's end to return to the sophisticated pleasures of the city.

Grandfather got richer and richer as he rose to the top of the company. P.D. Armour's son Ogden became titular head of the company after his father's death, but as he was a man of limited abilities, Grandfather was soon in charge of the day-to-day operations of the firm. It's hard for us now to realize the significance of the meat packers in the economy of the early part of the century. A few years ago when I read about Armour and Co. in the business pages of a newspaper, it was referred to as a subsidiary of Greyhound; and more recently, of the giant conglomerate Conagra. But a short while ago, I read a piece somewhere informing readers in a "Would you believe it?" tone that of the four largest U.S. corporations at the end of the Great War, the top two were railroads, and the third and fourth were two meat packers, Swift and Armour. So it is no wonder that in those days top meat-packing executives were able to feather their nests with brilliant plumage.

And Grandfather did love plumage. Before World War I, he indulged himself with a 120-foot yacht named the *Arcady* after his farm in Lake Forest. Mother had agreeable memories of cruises aboard this vessel, which she considered an ideal size. I infer from that that she must have cruised in quiet waters at the calmest time of the year. Then, flush with business successes, Grandfather bought a 220-foot monster called the *Victoria,* one of the largest in the world (the tenth largest or thereabouts, a fact he was not unwilling to reveal). Mother didn't like her size and elegance and lack of coziness. Once they cruised to Alaska in her, but mostly it was up and down the Eastern seaboard. When the Meekers carried a full load of society guests, as they often did, the children were left behind, usually in a rented house in Manchester-by-the-Sea on Boston's North Shore, where the sea breezes were more welcome than the steaming airs of Arcady Farms at home. One summer they were unable to rent their usual seaside mansion, but Grandmother scouted about in advance of their planned cruise and found a house on Marblehead Neck not too far away from Manchester. She wrote to her husband in Chicago that she had found a place that was "cheap and nasty, but it will do for the children." Unky came across this regrettable document, read it of course, though he had no right to, and added the quotation to his permanent list of grievances against his mother. He got back at her for this and other slights by telling everyone in his mature years that his "real mother" was Minnie O'Connell, his nannie.

One summer in Montecito, Grandfather held me captive, as he often did for want of a better audience, in the study of his house while he related the story of a memorable cruise in New England waters aboard the *Victoria,* presumably before Prohibition. To prepare for the comfort and pleasure of his many guests-to-be, he laid in what he told me was "$10,000 worth of champagne" (he didn't need to call it French; there wasn't any other kind in those days). Imagine what that might translate to in today's money. Their cruise started out pleasantly enough in Boston, but in a dense Maine fog the captain managed to run the ship aground off Mt. Desert, very near that Eastern millionaires' paradise, Bar Harbor. Far from daunted, Grandfather took over a hotel, had his champagne brought ashore (he must have had to swallow heavy corkage charges), and turned his yachting party into a land-based gala.

Another appurtenance of the millionaire of those days was a private railroad car. Here Grandfather showed an unwonted thrift. He never bought one because he was on such friendly terms with railroad presidents that he could borrow one any time he liked. Mother greatly enjoyed one journey aboard a borrowed car through the scenic wilds of western Canada. She remembered that her father would occasionally disengage the car from the train for a few days while the men in his party would disappear into the forest to take pot shots at elk and grizzlies and whatever else moved freely and fearlessly in the Canadian wilderness.... Once in Montecito at one of her dinner parties, Grandmother, making conversation with a notably stuffy bachelor of Eastern origins, remarked fatuously that she wished her family had emigrated to the West in a covered wagon. He slapped her down: "I thank God, Mrs. Meeker, that my forebears came to California in a private railroad car!" My sentiments, exactly; and almost certainly, if she had told the truth, Grandmother's as well.

After the Great War Grandfather could no longer resist the pull towards the now-fashionable northside of Chicago. He and his wife commissioned a highly regarded Eastern architect named Charles Platt, I believe, to design them an enormous three-storied Georgian house in the remote northern extremity of the Gold Coast that soon came to be called Meekerville. Mother felt about this house as she had felt about the yacht *Victoria*: too big, too formal, too *ungemütlich*. In memory she always harked back to the Victorian houses in Prairie Avenue as representing a halcyon time. Her parents, however, were supremely happy with their enormous new toy, and outdid themselves in the frequency and lavishness of their entertaining for which the house had been designed. It provided a perfect setting for Mary's coming-out ball in the early '20s.

Grandfather liked to tell this story on himself: He was talking to a telephone operator one day and upon her noting with surprise that both his new street address on Lake Shore Drive and his telephone number featured the digits 3030, he couldn't resist adding, "And not only that, but my license plate is 3030, too." "Whew!" she ejaculated. "Aren't you the Charley Cheese!" That's just what he was, and what's more, he wanted the world to know it.

And then around 1922, the fortunes of Armour and Co. crashed—spectacularly. Family tradition has an explanation for it, and points the finger at extraordinarily unwise speculations on the part of Grandfather's boss, the titular head of the company. It's no business of mine to rake over those particular old coals, so I will limit myself to saying that, according to my brother, Grandfather

was called upon to testify before a Senate committee and was ad-
judged to have acted honorably in connection with the company's
collapse. His name was cleared of any possible taint. (The Ogden
Armours were wiped out, but their creditors, I have been told by
reliable people, allowed them to retain substantial but in those days
"worthless" blocks of stock in two obscure companies. Those corporations were United Air Lines and Schlumberger, one of today's
premier oil-drilling companies. The descendants have reason to
bless the subsequent performance of those two corporations.)

But of course Grandfather was no longer the Charley Cheese.
The big house went (it became a convent ultimately), and they
moved to 1100 Lake Shore Drive, where he bought a whole floor
in a handsome building facing the lake. This apartment was to be
home to them for the rest of their lives except for their summers
spent in Montecito (starting in about 1930, as we shall learn in the
next chapter). And what became of this unusually vigorous, active
man, apparently beached in his mid-fifties by a tempest that left
him high and dry?

Some of what I have to say now is conjecture, but I am reasonably sure that it is accurate in the main. He lost his job and his salary, but he undoubtedly had substantial investments in the stock
market, which he followed with great avidity for the rest of his life.
I suppose they came crashing down in the Wall Steet debacle of
1929; and then in 1932 he suffered another grievous blow when
Samuel Insull's Chicago-based Midwestern utilities empire collapsed
(I remember a newspaper photo of that unloved magnate in Athens,
to which he had fled to escape the disgrace of his fall, which ruined many a widow). So Grandfather lost three fortunes, as I see it,
in the course of ten years. Yet I never heard him complain, though
I came to know him as well as a young boy is likely to know an old
man during his Montecito summers from 1930 to about 1943. The
tolerant attitude of his descendants has always been that it was quite
all right for him to lose three fortunes since he died possessed of a
fourth.

How did he keep going after such severe reverses? He had an
office downtown that served as the hub for his business activities,
and he spent much of every day there. From it he ran his Arcady
Farms Milling Company for years, making it into an important

provider of feed to Midwestern farmers before turning its operation over to a nephew near the end of his life. He lunched every weekday at the Chicago Club, the nerve center of his life, repairing there for long multi-martini lunches with business executive friends, the presidents and chairmen of all the important Chicago corporations. There of course he must have received many a tip on the stock and grain markets that he took full advantage of. His mixture of business shrewdness and jovial extroversion made him very popular in his world. There wasn't anyone of consequence in the Chicago of those days who didn't know Arthur Meeker, and very few indeed who didn't like him.

He was named a regent of the University of Illinois. And he it was who was expected to entertain visiting dignitaries, as a sort of permanent "Mr. Chicago." In this role I see him as looking like the cartoon image that Russian Communists propagated in the 1920s and '30s of the Bloated Capitalist, with top hat, large stomach barely covered by a cutaway, striped trousers, and spats. He had a particularly good time, I remember, with Queen Marie of Rumania, who took the country by storm in those innocent days. In his drawing room there were many autographed pictures of the celebrated visitors who had passed through his hands. He was very fond of visiting military men; both of the top generals, French of course, of the Great War, the Marshals Joffre and Foch, ended up in silver frames on Grandmother's Steinway; and you may remember from the first chapter that the Fascist Air Marshal Italo Balbo, namesake of the lost canary, enjoyed the bountiful Meeker hospitality. Once the Meekers gave a large dinner party for the celebrated London hostess Lady Colefax. She was known for being one of the first London hostesses of her day to mix the upper classes with figures from the artistic world and the intelligentsia. In that connection, many years ago I came across the following tidbit in a book by the sociologist Dixon Wecter, who was making the point that the same word might mean quite different things in England and the States. Thinking to honor his Chicago guest, Grandfather had apparently proposed a toast to "the Queen of Bohemia!" Lady Colefax paused a moment and then responded tartly with this zinger: "Yes, wherever she may be." A propos bohemians, Grandmother had once been inveigled into giving what was called a "bohemian" party. Guests were asked to sit on the floor of her elegant drawing room and eat spaghetti on their laps and drink red wine. The picture is delightfully preposterous. For one thing, how could Grandfather possibly have risen to his feet? He had a hard enough time getting up from an easy chair. Unky said the party was not a success.

I remember, snob that I was, the elation I felt one year at Cate, probably around 1938, when there was a story about Chicago in *Life,* then at the apex of its popularity as the leading exponent of weekly photojournalism. One picture showed Grandfather in white tie, seated at a table during a party; the caption read, "Absolute dictator of Chicago society, Arthur Meeker annually blue-pencils the list of people to be invited to the Assembly ball." That was pretty heady stuff. I loved the "absolute social dictator" bit, though I couldn't imagine why anyone would want to be invited to a ball. One of my good Cate friends, a year ahead of me and very sophisticated, sniffed that it was only Chicago, after all. True, but my friend's family had originated in Pittsburgh, "of all places," as I put it. And nobody had ever suggested *they* were social dictators, even of the smokiest city in America, as it then was. They had to settle for being the Parks of Park Lane in Montecito, and I didn't think that amounted to very much—at least not in 1938.

Of far greater interest to his family, especially to his descendants in the years to come, is the fact that in his 60s Grandfather founded a new company that started very small and then grew mightily, especially after his death. One day he was approached by a man who had developed a product that would do an excellent job of softening water for use in the steam-driven locomotives of those days. What he needed, and what Grandfather amply provided, was access to the heads of railroads. So Grandfather founded a company, named the National Aluminate Corporation, and as chairman appointed a board of directors from among his friends in the business world of Chicago, and proceeded to market its wares to the big railroads of the day. Over the years, in the hands of very capable industrial chemists, the company grew and prospered, changing as its original market disappeared to manufacturing other products, astutely keeping up with the times and their particular needs. For many years it has been known as Nalco Chemical Company, Nalco for short, manufacturer of specialty chemicals with an emphasis on pollution control. Considered an environmental stock, at the moment it concentrates on water purification, and operates plants and sells its products in dozens of foreign countries as well as throughout the United States. Its stock, which has split many times and grown hugely in value over the years, is in the portfolio of many large institutional investors. I think even Arthur Meeker, that natural optimist, would be astonished at just how far his "baby" has come. Astonished, and proud.

AND WHAT OF HIS WIFE, Grace Murray Meeker? What manner of woman was he married to?

As to her provenance, her children knew little of their mother's parents because the latter died before their grandchildren were born. Grandmother's father, William Murray, was a Scot (or of Scottish extraction) described by a Meeker family member as "an old curmudgeon," an epithet that has a somewhat chilling effect on any desire to research him back to life. I've heard he was a heavy drinker, like so many of the forebears and relatives that dangle thirstily from my family tree. It is said he was a compulsive speculator on the grain market with the result that his little family of three ate very high on the hog for long stretches only to be reduced to gnawing on bones (figuratively speaking) when his speculations went awry. When things were going well, they travelled for long periods in Europe, staying in the most expensive hotels in capital cities and fashionable spas and then fleeing in the dead of night when creditors were on his trail. Unnerving, to say the least. It's no wonder their daughter, my grandmother, had her neurotic side.

Her early travels gave the young Grace, and indeed the old Grace, a pleasing and worldly sophistication as well as a taste for music and literature. They gave her, too, a familiarity with French and German in direct contrast with her husband's inability to formulate a sentence in any foreign language. (To make up for this deficiency, when in France, for instance, Grandfather simply spoke his English sentences louder and louder till he was convinced that it was only the Frenchmen's fabled contrariness that prevented them from understanding.)

Her mother, too, died too young to have left memories with her grandchildren. Born a Schwartz and of German extraction, she was a handsome woman. Her brother, Gustavus Adolphus Schwartz, "Uncle Gus," his nieces remember as a noted "swell," to use their word, in Victorian Chicago, with particularly handsome horses drawing his carriage and its elegant occupant smartly along the city streets. In addition, there were two little-old-lady Schwartz cousins, very genteel, living in La Jolla when I was a child, one of whom, as I related in an earlier chapter, sent me a book of her devising; and in Santa Barbara, in the next chapter, I'll introduce you to Grace Meeker's first cousin, Irene (Mrs. Bernhard) Hoffmann, who with her husband had a profound and enduring effect upon that town after the earthquake of 1925.

Grandmother Meeker's inclinations and instincts were primarily social, and she must have served her husband well as she planned and supervised their entertaining, a matter of immense concern in her world.

She adored her husband—there was no question about that. But she must often have been a trial to him. Once, when one of her children was criticising her sibling Gracie (my mother) for complaining too much, Grandmother silenced her by saying, "Leave her alone. That's just her way of expressing herself." But Mother actually complained no more than the average; complaining was in fact Grandmother's long suit. She was relentless; nothing ever suited her. Nor did she keep her dissatisfactions to herself. (In the next chapter, when we meet her in Montecito, I'll be able to relate some examples of this side of her nature.) In Chicago she kept a "distressed gentlewoman," to use a British expression that I have always enjoyed, as a sort of companion to vent her spleen on. Once this poor woman, who showed occasional little flickers of independence, was so rash as to assert herself by some action or other. Grandmother countered with an opposing move that quickly "brought her to heel," as Grandmother cheerfully put it at the time. Mary Cramer, when I pumped her just the other day about this relationship to see if I had got it right, commented, "I'm afraid poor Helen was 'brought to heel' many, many times."

She had strong feelings about politics—Republican, of course. In fact, she was a delegate to one of the national presidential conventions in the days when delegates actually chose the nominee. I think it must have been the Coolidge one in 1924. Once she said disconsolately in my hearing, probably about 1940, "I haven't felt I had a friend in the White House since the day Mr. Roosevelt moved in." Many of his predecessors had been personal friends of hers and her husband's, but I suppose she was really thinking of political congeniality.

Her passion for opera was a very real thing to her. Samuel Insull before the collapse of his empire had brought opera on the grand scale to Chicago, and the Chicago Opera Company's productions, along with its glamorous stars, added greatly to Grandmother's enjoyment of life. She befriended many of them with her warm hospitality and helped them, almost all foreign-born, to feel at home in her city. She and her son were both enthralled by the opera and its temperamental performers. They hardly ever missed an opera. And they even dragged poor Grandfather to opening nights, where he was a fixture in his prominent box, snoozing away in full dress, his huge hands encased like great sausages in white gloves, martinis and champagne having done their magic trick of dulling the pain for him.

She was not quick to forget slights. I have heard her called "vindictive" by one outside the family, and I daresay she was. But she was quick to recognize quality and intelligence in people, and excellence in the arts. She set high standards for herself and her family. She had no use for the mediocre. She struck me as a *grande dame*, but one with an approachable, cozy side. I liked and admired that combination in her.

CHAPTER EIGHT

🏵 The Meekers in Montecito

FOR YEARS I ASKED LITTLE JESUS in my prayers to bless "Bon Papa et Bonne Maman" without being entirely sure who they were. My first memories of my grandparents place them in the beautiful house they built in Montecito in 1929. As it always did, before the days of air conditioning, it had seemed a good idea to clear out of the insufferable heat of Chicago in summertime, and since their daughter Grace Lloyd had lived in Montecito year round since the breakup of her marriage to my father, and since their daughter Katharine Gray came down from San Francisco to spend the summers there with her family, the pull of Santa Barbara with its ocean-cooled air was irresistible.

By the time they had settled in, I was well over my French-speaking phase, and so they at once became "Grandfather" and "Grandmother" to me, replacing the mysterious characters in my prayer with their own very solid flesh and blood. It soon became evident that they were to loom very large in our lives. Mother was atttentive and deferential and adoring with them. And I noticed that people in general kowtowed to them. This was attractive to me in itself, and besides I found that a tiny bit of their glamor rubbed off on me when I trailed along with them, as I often did for one reason or another. To a certain kind of child there is something very heady about being ferried around in a shiny limousine driven by a deferential chauffeur in a black whipcord uniform.

Since cars have been a lifelong passion with me, I'm going to indulge myself right now with some memories of Grandfather's limousines. That word had noble associations in those days, right up to World War II. The cars were coachbuilt to the design of artists with taste and flair. Not for them the dachshund proportions of today's monstrosities, lined with wretched plush and decked out with unspeakable plastic wood, the darlings of rock stars and teenage promgoers. At first the Meeker limousines, when their owners started to summer in Montecito, were antiquities from the 1920s: lofty monsters that Grandfather could enter in Chicago on the way to a ball or the opera without removing his top hat or, in California, the Teddy Roosevelt sort of hat that he affected, gray I think, with a perfectly round, stiff brim and a circular crown with four pinched-in indentations—a sort of glorified forest ranger's hat. Perhaps he got the idea from Montecito's number-one rich man, Maximilian Fleischmann, who wore one very similar that overwhelmed his very small and very round person. The first of Grandfather's cars that I remember was a Rolls-Royce of a nondescript green, a model built for the American trade in Springfield, Massachusetts. (This model had a very brief life because the potential customers wanted the real thing, not an American cousin that they perceived as a poor relation.) Grandfather, extravagant in most ways, was on the thrifty side when it came to buying these elegant conveyances. He often bought them second-hand with very low mileage and, since after the Crash there was little demand for them, at very favorable prices. The next car that I remember was a glorious Belgian Excelsior that I referred to in an earlier chapter, sky blue with black fenders, very square and upright, with only four (gigantic) cylinders that throbbed imperiously, scaring peasants from its aristocratic path and sending me into raptures as I sat next to the chauffeur on his black leather seat, open to the sky. I wonder whether parts were available for such a rare and exotic beast. Probably Grandfather had to throw the car away when the transmission first gave trouble.

It was followed by the most luxurious one of all, a square-rigged but curiously delicate Rolls painted a glorious midnight blue, shiny beyond imagining. Can the tires have had white sidewalls? I seem to see them in my mind. All the fittings in the owner's compartment were gold-plated. It was the sort of car that in the depressed early '30s might easily have started a riot. But who in Montecito would have rioted, since the locals profited mightily from the out-of-town rich folk? I must say it looked out of place in rural Montecito but must have cast a long shadow in Chicago. As a matter of fact, it had been built for Edith Rockefeller McCormick, daughter of the original John D. and wife (till they divorced) of Harold, the McCormick who later became enamoured of Montecito's Ganna Walska. Grandmother said she would not ride in the car because it had "belonged to my dear friend." And in fact, though she did ride in it, many times, they didn't keep it very long.

Many of the limousines overlapped and crowded one another for elbow room in the five-car garage (with chauffeur's flat above) near the entrance gate to the Meeker estate. I suspect that, though they were very easy to buy, Grandfather found they were hard to dispose of in a depressed economy, so they gleamed in idleness, pampered and polished by the chauffeur, providing seats of honor for one dreamy grandson, imagining triumphal parades before cheering throngs.

Presently everyone in the family began to put pressure on Grandfather to move with the times and get rid of his tall monsters. He was stubborn because, for one thing, he resented taking off his hat and stooping his way into and out of the back seat. Once, years later in Chicago, his case was pretty well proved one night as we were alighting in the rain from a new, much lower limousine in front of a theater—to see my first ballet, put on by Colonel de Basil's Ballet Russe de Monte Carlo—when my courtly father tried to help his mother-in-law out of the limousine by standing on the sidewalk and opening up an umbrella to shield her. But most regrettably he caught the point of the umbrella in her—as it turned out—wig, which lifted skyward as the umbrella snapped open. What consternation all round! Of course one had to pretend that nothing whatever had happened, which was very difficult indeed for me, as I was convulsed with inner laughter. I am afraid that incident made the evening for me; certainly *Swan Lake* did not. So if Grandfather had not bowed to the pressures that propelled him towards low-slung modernity, Grandmother's wig would have remained the secret that God meant it to be.

A "halfway" car in the direction of modernity was a black Lincoln. I remember a leaping Greyhound hood ornament, a split V-shaped windshield, and a powerful engine. Grandfather, bored with the sybaritic summertime life in Santa Barbara, would mount the Chief or Superchief in Pasadena in August to see how things were going at his Chicago office—totally unnecessary since all he needed to know could be found out by a phone call or two. But he greatly enjoyed getting away from domestic life and batching it at the Chicago Club, which served him as a base for convivial drinking; his avowed cure for hangovers was a Turkish bath, I suppose to steam the poisons out. Presumably the womanizing that I'm quite sure he indulged in took place outside the Club's dignified portals. (He once said to me with a twinkle in his eye after his wife had said something displeasing to his ear, "There's such a thing as being married to the same woman too long!" At least I *think* there was a twinkle.) And what does all this have to do with the Lincoln? Just this. One year when he left, Grandmother was lonely, so she planned a scenic, educational trip to the Yosemite Valley with Mother, Brosie, and me. The new local-boy chauffeur, a young man from nearby Summerland, was at the wheel of the Lincoln. Brosie and I were crazy about him, as he was a knowledgeable and enthusiastic baseball fan, not like the pompous old Chicago chauffeur whose wife hated Montecito. But we cared not a fig for the beauty of "majestic old Half-Dome" or the "delicate tracery" of Bridal Veil Falls. Instead we played endlessly with the young man at three-cornered catch under the Sequoias while exchanging major-league gossip. As punishment for slighting Yosemite's wondrous beauties, we were forced at dusk to hike quite some distance and gather round a folksy campfire to listen to bits of nature lore narrated robotically by forest rangers who would rather, like us, have been doing something else.... In other, more modern Meeker limousines, there were many delightful jaunts to Hollywood, of which more later, but the Lincoln was the only one that we took a long excursion in. It was a fine car. And Yosemite was a fine place—for three-cornered catch.

Finally we all succeeded in persuading Grandfather that his cars were prehistoric monsters, reeking of the '20s, and that we were by now embarrassed to be seen in them. I don't know who would have had the courage to say this, but we certainly felt it. It must have been Grandmother, and it was probably her way of getting rid of the Rockefellermccormickmobile, which I think was sold to MGM for period films. So one day in the mid-1930s Grandfather showed up with a long maroon Packard limousine, low and slinky by Rolls standards, a gorgeous thing. I enjoyed many a drive in it, seated, as always when the owners were aboard, on one of the small folding jump seats positioned ahead of their richly upholstered seat. Sometimes I was allowed to give orders to the chauffeur through the speaking tube. I remember a fur lap robe redolent of sybaritic luxury, though I never had the chance to snuggle under it, since it was for the grownups in the rear seat. I wonder why lap robes were necessary or at least desirable. Can it be that cars had no heaters? Or just that the rear seat was so far removed from the heater outlets in the dashboard? The final car that I remember was a Buick Limited, dark green and extraordinarily long. One day the Meekers arrived at Cate in it, and its sleek, expensive bulk made my stock soar. (But I was horribly worried over the prospect of this visit, which was to include dinner. Had they invited themselves, hoping with two free dinners to get some small return on the tuition they were helping to pay? Or had Mr. Cate invited them, hoping for a new soccer field? Would Grandfather "entertain" with long, tedious, and boastful anecdotes? And worst of all, would he fall asleep and snore while Mr. Cate was reading aloud to the boys in the McIntosh Room after dinner? Bless him, he committed neither of these barbarities, and the memory of the gigantic Buick remained as a large plus on my personal ledger at the school.)

As I look back, I realize to my surprise that the Meekers' summers in Montecito covered no more than a dozen or so years. And yet see how many cars Grandfather crammed into that short span. Before this very moment, I had never thought of this. Can it be the hidden inspiration of my own notorious infidelity to the cars I profess to love? I have had ninety-one in my seventy-two years. (Golfers who boast of "shooting their age" can't touch me in this respect. And of course there were many years of relative poverty when I couldn't indulge myself, not to mention the first eighteen when I owned no car at all. I pass on to all who may be interested in automotive research that I have proven scientifically to myself that six months is the ideal period of ownership. That is, if one doesn't count depreciation.) But a sturdy self-respect prompts me to state that of the ninety-one, thirty-two were bought by me over the years as presents for loved ones. But perhaps I shouldn't have made that point at all, as the ratio is not a generous one.

❀

IT'S TIME NOW to tell about Constantia, the house the Meekers built in Montecito. Once the decision to build had been made and an ample site found featuring glorious mountain and ancillary Channel views, Grandmother had a third and final chance in her married life to choose an architect and an appropriate style. For architect, her obvious choice was her two-time (two-timing?) son-in-law, my father, Ambrose Cramer, trained at the Beaux Arts in Paris and apprenticed to the great Midwest eclectic architect, David Adler. Grandmother had strong dislikes in architecture (indeed in everything), which she of course communicated to her architect. She was "uncomfortable" in what she called Montecito's "pseudo-Spanish houses, with their uneven, tiled floors, different floor levels, and small windows, nor do I hold with those who like a large plate-glass window focussed on a view, which seems to let a mountain into the house and destroys that intangible thing the French call *intérieur*." (Trust Grandmother to keep a pushy mountain in its place.)

Father, after due research, gave her a book on the Dutch architecture of the Cape of Good Hope, which John Ruskin in late-Victorian times had called "the only real contribution to architecture in the last few centuries." She fell in love at once with the pictures of beautiful farmhouses, charmed by the great baroque gables and many-mullioned windows with their paneled shutters. And she noted the "striking similarity of the scenery, the climate, and the flora" to those of Montecito. In time my father produced a set of plans that she found exactly to her taste. He replaced the traditional thatched roof with one made of slates and flouted tradition by adding second-storey dormer windows to the steeply sloping roof. Then he laid out a basic landscaping plan featuring a large reflection pool on a lower level than the house, which sat on a ridge, the pool serving to reflect the magnificent mountains nearby to the north. Grandmother engaged that most delightful of men, the landscape architect Lockwood "Lock" de Forest, to design the planting throughout the grounds, with special attention to choosing flora indigenous to South Africa. She worked closely with him on the project.

Grandmother wrote, in the speech that accompanied a slide

show about South African houses and gardens that she presented to the Fortnightly Club in Chicago in the '30s:

> I cannot resist telling you about a visit paid us in Santa Barbara by [the internationally famous mining engineer] Mr. John Hays Hammond. He was very much surprised to find we had built a South African house. We were tremendously anxious for Mr. Hammond's opinion of our Constantia because he had spent so many years of his life in South Africa. He looked at everything very carefully and, as he was leaving, said to us, "Your house has been wonderfully carried out, with great fidelity to detail, but—" and here my heart sank, for *buts* are so ominous, "I can assure you that there is no house in South Africa so lovely as yours."

The place was sold in the late '40s by the Meekers' children, none of whom had the inclination to staff and maintain it, and has passed through many hands since. Succeeding owners have been kind enough to allow the public to view it—often in recent years as the setting for large parties given for charitable purposes. For the last decade or so it has been painted an unusual color that I would liken to tomato soup. In the Meekers' day it was off-white, with the paneled shutters in two contrasting shades of green. The five-car garage (near the reflection pool) with living quarters above was turned into a house some years ago, with its own one-acre plot. It sold for ten times what the heirs had sold the whole estate for. Well-meaning but misinformed owners of the big house have let it be known that Constantia is a copy of Cecil Rhodes's house. Not so. Rhodes's house was called Groote Schuur, or Great Barn. The name Constantia belonged to a famous house built by a seventeenth-century Dutch governor. The Meeker house was not a "copy" of any South African house, but rather my father's distillation of all that he found most attractive in that style, with the happy result that found expression in Hammond's pronouncement quoted above.

I FELT ON HALLOWED GROUND whenever we visited the house. My earliest memories of it were of Sunday luncheons with all available Lloyds and Cramers and Grays in attendance. I greatly enjoyed the formality of these occasions, beginning with the butler's announcement of our arrival, and the swift, silent, dextrous service of the waitresses in the dining room as we sat, on our best behavior, in the very formal dining room and worked our way through an enormous midday meal, course after artery-clogging course. I always seemed to be close enough to Grandmother for her to point out that I hadn't done a thorough job of cutting up my chicken, so that my plate had to be handed to her for further attacks upon the carcass while my distended stomach cried out, "No more, no more!" After luncheon, with my belt undone, I would join the others in strolling about outdoors, admiring the view of Montecito Peak and its reflection in the great pool below us, or walking through the sunken garden, with its beds of exotic, multi-hued succulents. And then we would sit in the long, graceful, high-ceilinged drawing room, a furniture grouping at each end, one set clustered in front of a fireplace faced with blue-and-white Delft tiles and the other featuring an enormous and superb Dutch *armoire,* whose brown wood gleamed richly in the midday light and whose curves echoed the baroque Dutch gables of the roof.

Grandfather was a genial host, one of those born to function in that role. People gathered about him by instinct. He loved to talk about himself and his exploits, and of course grandsons were ideal for that purpose as they matured. But I often saw him with adults and had many chances to observe how he liked to draw them out with endless questions, some shockingly personal. For instance, to an attractive youngish woman guest he was overheard to say,—and he was so obviously interested that no one ever took such questioning amiss—"Tell me, m'dear, why did you leave your husband?" In a moment he had her telling the story of her life and thoroughly enjoying his attentive ear. (A woman contemporary of his in Chicago once gave him a diamond stickpin for his tie in the shape of a question mark.)

On some occasions Mother and I would be the only guests for luncheon or perhaps dinner. We would meet the Meekers in the small walnut-paneled library off the front hall where they spent much of their leisure time, Grandfather doing busy-work at his desk or sitting in a haze of Melachrino cigarette smoke in his favorite leather wing chair while Grandmother took her ease on a downy sofa with Mother's second-best Sealyham, a regular summer boarder, snoozing in her lap. The two women would indulge in feminine chit-chat while Grandfather took advantage of my presence to dictate some very basic business correspondence, the sort he couldn't be bothered to get a secretary for. My southpaw handwriting was (and is) displeasing to the eye but was positively calligraphic compared with his illegible scrawl. Clearly, I had inherited his inability to control the small muscles that determine manual dexterity. It was a comfort to realize there was a genetic reason for my awkwardness and to be able to pin it on him. As I look back on his open, aggressive, gregarious, sociable, confident, and tough nature, so utterly different from my own, I realize that manual indexterity was the only thing I did inherit from him—with one vastly important exception: my fair share, eventually, of his trust funds. He died when I was a very young man, and at the time part of me was selfishly relieved because he would have tried to push me into a business career, the only one he thought suitable for a man in the modern world. But instead with a modicum of family backing after his death, I was able to lead exactly the life I wanted to lead. Not that I didn't make mistakes, but they were my mistakes, and I had no one to blame but myself. I proposed a toast during the family dinner that followed my mother's death in 1983: "Here's to Grandfather. He would have disapproved of everything I have done with my life, but he made it possible for me to live that life."

Unky told me that one day in Chicago his father, now retired, was looking over his family tree as he toyed with the idea of writing his memoirs. He was silent for quite a while as he pored over the tree's complexities right down to the generation of his grandchildren; then for a while he seemed to be indulging in reveries. At last he gave his highly individual and contemptuous grunt of disapproval (a violent "eugh" sound that spelling can't hope to reproduce) followed by this explosion: "God, how we've fizzled out!" And poor man, by his standards of course he was right; perhaps by any standards. In any case, it's long been a favorite story of mine.

Still, I can't resist adding that after a week sequestered in his office with his secretary and old documents, he called for his chauffeur and was driven home in the middle of the day. His son asked him how he was coming along with his book. "Sonny," he sighed, "there's more to writing a book than I'd thought." The memoirs were never referred to again. And Unky felt that his own life's work had been to a degree validated.

ON OTHER OCCASIONS Grandfather was more or less silent and preoccupied. This would give Grandmother a chance to do what she did best—complain and criticize. Come to think of it, it was probably her stream of complaints that accounted for his occasional silence and preoccupation. Even Mother, who loved her dearly, saw her complaining as a flaw, especially, as Mother pointed out, since she had been greatly indulged throughout her life and had nothing that she could see to complain *about*. And Grandmother liked to have a different preoccupation each summer.

One that I remember in particular centered on the extremely pretty daughter of a close friend of Aunt Katharine's from her early married days in Boston. This girl, eighteen or so, was Boston's number-one "glamour girl," to use the term common in those days for unusually attractive debutantes, at least those that "came out" in cities that were considered to be socially worthwhile. They received, for a year or two, tremendous publicity almost equal to what a rock or film star reaps today, and some of them made good money, even though they didn't need it, by appearing in advertisements for luxury products. The most celebrated example of the type was Brenda Frazier of New York, who thrilled Montecitans by appearing for several weeks at the Coral Casino and Biltmore Hotel when I was seventeen or eighteen, modeling the jewelry of New Yorker Paul Flato. I was greatly taken by her black hair and dead-white makeup, not to mention her world-weary poise; it was for me the acme of sophistication to be sitting in a group with her, sipping daiquiris. Later I was disillusioned when she married one "Shipwreck" Kelly, who didn't sound nearly good enough for her. But then who would have?

The Boston deb, whom I'll call "Queenie," was equally beautiful in a blonde way. But she was a madcap exhibitionist and seemed at all times to be having a great deal more fun than Grandmother thought appropriate. The latter was horrified, as she lunched with her rich, elderly friends beside the Casino's pool, to see Queenie in a skimpy swimsuit rush across her field of vision and fling herself onto the lap of a nearly naked youth. Whenever Grandmother lunched at the Casino, Queenie managed to outrage her sense of dignity and propriety; and any family member lunching or dining with the old lady at Constantia had to pay a heavy price by lending an ear to her story of the latest outrage. One day the complaint was especially acerbic because Queenie had planted a very loud and public wet kiss, accompanied by screams of affectionate recognition, upon the cheeks of Aunt Katharine, her embarrassed godmother, who was seated next to Grandmother. Such matters were gone over in obsessive detail before, during, and after lunch or dinner for the whole of one summer. Why couldn't Katharine make her own god-daughter behave? What were godmothers for, in fact, if not to instill notions of seemly conduct? I daresay Aunt Katharine tried, because she was pretty good at telling young people, especially her own children, how to lead their lives. But she was daunted by the thought of trying to reform Queenie. "She has a mouth like a shark's," said Grandmother with relish, as if in final judgment.... And next summer she was on to something else.

Which was even harder for Mother and Aunt Katharine to handle. Fortunately, because of the intimate nature of the problem, Grandmother talked on this new subject in an undertone when I was about, and of course not at all when her husband was.... She was positive there was another woman. This "other woman" was a middle-aged, happily married interior decorator that he saw daily when he bathed in the ocean. They sat together under an umbrella on the sands of East Beach, which Grandfather, public though it was, considered the best swimming beach (he would have nothing to do with the Coral Casino's thin strip, though he entertained frequently at the Casino's mouth-watering buffet lunch, all the while audibly disgusted by the hairy Hollywood-producer types that he saw sunning themselves across the pool). I joined the two of them at East Beach a number of times. I daresay he was attracted by her; why wouldn't he be? After all, she was a handsome forty or so with hair coiled over her ears, and Grace Meeker was in her seventies with the regal beauty of her prime long gone. I seriously doubt that anything untoward went on, though he may have been generous with gifts, and there was talk of how hard the poor woman and her husband had to struggle to make ends meet. For one thing, Grandmother knew where he was every moment of the day. Where and when could he have "done it"? In the back seat of the limousine? But for a long time Grandmother talked of nothing else, obsessively, and even my mother's sturdy patience occasionally snapped.

Another summer she complained continually that she was being asked to her friends' "second-best parties," as she put it. She seemed to believe there was a first tier of *soirées* distinguished by a profusion of swan-necked beauties with be-ribboned ambassadorial types hovering over them, bowing and kissing hands and clicking heels, and that she was being excluded from these entertainments by malign hostesses. I remember one hostess in particular that she would often inveigh against, who bore the superb name of Mrs. Hobart Chatfield Chatfield-Taylor—Estelle to her friends. And she and her husband were from Chicago, too, though they had long since outgrown it. Perhaps she felt that Grandmother had not.

Grandmother was not given to compliments, at least with regard to her grandchildren. Whenever one of them, stopping over for a visit in Chicago on the way to or from college, had left her bed and board, she would write to her daughter, the youth's mother, that they had found young so-and-so "much improved." That was as far in a positive direction as she would ever go, and the remark gave little satisfaction to the sensitive mother since it was regularly repeated. For how could there be that much room for improvement? Once she complained that one of her grandsons, named Arthur after her husband, had been met at the railroad station in Chicago at considerable personal inconvenience and turned out to be displaying, to her great discomfiture, a three-days' growth of beard, as she put it. Unky, listening to her with less than his full attention some time later as she recounted the incident, thought she had said not "Arthur" but "Margaret," the name of her sister-in-law, and sought to account for this apparent lapse by adding soothingly, "She must have misplaced her depilatory." One can imagine that there was a good deal of confusion while this misunderstanding sorted itself out.

Another time she took the trouble to go to the boarding-school graduation exercises of one of her grandchildren hundreds of miles away, but all that she cared to say about it after she had returned was that everyone in the school seemed to have received an award except her offspring. "They gave prizes for improvement, and she didn't even win one of those!" I got my comeuppance one day when I was bedded at La Vereda Road, aged sixteen or so, with a rather severe case of mumps. She made the grand effort of walking upstairs to visit me and eased herself down into my armchair that had never been honored by so august a figure. She told me she had just been to a luncheon during which her hostess had sung the praises of her own grandchildren, boasting that she was enjoying them much more than she had ever enjoyed her own children. I was purring with pleasure as I waited for Grandmother to expand upon this affectionate theme, intended to cheer me in my sickbed, as I thought. "I told her in no uncertain terms," Grandmother briskly added, "that I didn't agree with her the least bit. I said I greatly preferred my children." Well, honesty has it charms.... I wondered occasionally what she thought of me. I know she appreciated my literary interests and respected my academic reputation. To her son she once referred to me, when I was about college-freshman age, as "that inscrutable young man." I took that as a compliment of sorts, because in those days the last thing I wanted to be was scrutable.

She had a gift for self-pity that I suppose went along with her complaining. One day in my hearing she announced, for no reason that I could discern, that her three daughters had all married aristocrats—and that none of them liked her! And once when we were on a jaunt to the Santa Ynez Valley, after luncheon at Mattei's Tavern, the only restaurant in the Valley in those days, we drove about Solvang, hoping, I suppose, to see the Danes being Danish. In those days the Danes had not figured out how to make money out of their Danishness, and the little town, though exceptionally well swept, had none of today's Disneyland/fairytale quality. Grandmother spied a neat little stucco cottage, in no way unusual, that proclaimed itself to be the home and office of the local dentist.

Grandmother had the car stopped so that she could feast her eyes on the little house. After a few moments, she said, "If only I could live in that little house, I'd be a happy woman." Mother, astonished, said, "Oh, Mother dear, you know you'd hate it after two hours." "No, I wouldn't. I could be happy there." And whenever she went on an outing to the Valley, she asked to be driven by the little house, "my house," as she called it. And Mother, who was on to her self-deception, never failed to pooh-pooh the idea of her living there. It apparently was not to Mother an acceptable fantasy.

I MENTIONED in the last chapter that Grandmother had a passion for music, especially opera, and she very much enjoyed treating the younger singers in the Chicago Opera as protégés. One of these, a tenor named Michael Bartlett, appeared one summer in Santa Barbara and enlivened many a weekend at Constantia with his glamorous presence. He flattered her relentlessly and took to calling her "darling Amie," which he pronounced to rhyme with *balmy*. A Princetonian with a Barrymore profile who had played leading roles in Triangle Club productions while at college, he had had some success in grand opera and now well into his thirties, with receding hairline more or less balanced by expanding waistline, found himself under contract to Columbia Studios, a fact that accounted for his recurring presence in Montecito. He came up often that summer, usually with enough friends to fill the house, their voices shrill with merriment.

One time in particular I remember. Bartlett had just finished making a movie, an operatic story with the soprano Marian Talley, and the whole company had come up to Santa Barbara for a sneak preview of it. He and several friends were staying with the Meekers. I can see him now, in the empty little study (everyone else was in the drawing room at the time, in celebratory mood) as I happen to walk by. He is standing up, waving a telephone about and exulting to his mother. "It was a triumph, darling, a triumph! And I carried the whole show!"

Well, he didn't, and soon his contract lapsed and he was seen no longer in Montecito. But not until after we had been his guests in Hollywood, where he showed us about the Columbia studios, and we stood raptly as we saw scenes being filmed. (The only figure I can bring to mind after all these years is Peter Lorre, acting suitably sinister.) Later we lunched at the famous Brown Derby, at Hollywood and Vine, where I was agog trying to match the faces of nearby diners with the caricatures on the walls. Grandfather had checked his big Max Fleischmann hat, and I retrieved it for him as our entourage made its way out. As I held it out to him, I couldn't help noting that the hatcheck girl (presumably) had scribbled in crayon on the sweat band, "You big bloat!" First Charley Cheese, and now this indignity! I daresay William, his irreverent Irish valet, rubbed it out before Grandfather had a chance to see it, but not before having a good laugh over it. Were the masses seething, I wondered, or was this just natural cheekiness?

Grandmother had noticed that Michael was always accompanied by chattering males and seemed not to care, in Montecito at least, about meeting local women. "Do you think he might be a lesbian?" she asked her worldly son one day out of the blue. I never heard what his answer was. I suppose "No" would have done the job.

Unky, who was sharply envious of him and lost no chance of belittling him, ran into Bartlett in London not long after the war. He was as irrepressibly ebullient as ever, predicting a great future for himself in the new medium, television. "I have the looks, I have the voice, I have the personality!" he crowed. (Tenors are like that.) I wonder what he did with the rest of his life. But whatever he may have done, he didn't do it on television.

GRANDMOTHER'S FIRST COUSIN, Irene Hoffmann (their mothers had been sisters), and her husband were Meekers-by-marriage only, but they left a far more enduring impression on Santa Barbara than did anyone else in the family, including, in later years, Aunt Katharine and my mother, both of them outstandingly civic-minded. They came out originally, the Hoffmanns did, to have their very ill daughter benefit from the research that the famous Dr. Sansum was doing into the causes and treatment of diabetes. They built a large Spanish house behind the Mission overlooking Mission Canyon that eventually was absorbed into the St. Anthony's

Seminary property. Soon after their arrival, the famous earthquake of 1925 struck, killing twelve people and devastating a good deal of downtown Santa Barbara. Cousin Bernhard (in spite of its Germanic look, he pronounced his name BERNerd, in the English manner), already drawn to the Spanish style of architecture, formed a group of people under his leadership to rebuild the commercial part of the city in the Spanish mode. (Before the earthquake, the downtown lacked any real character and would not have been out of place in Grand Island, Nebraska.) And it was Cousin Bernhard who conceived the idea of El Paseo, the Spanish shopping center-cum-restaurant, and commissioned the young Scottish architect James Osborne Craig to design it around the historic old de la Guerra adobe, a job he carried out to perfection. The Hoffmanns owned El Paseo for many years. Meanwhile, Cousin Irene, an executive sort of woman with deep pockets, interested herself in promoting the arts, acting as a moving force in the 1920s behind the Community Arts Association, founded to stimulate local art and music and drama. It accomplished a lot of good while it lasted but fell victim, like so many good causes, to the Depression in the 1930s. Unky was imported from Chicago in the late 1920s, after he had resigned from his briefly held reporter's job on the Chicago *Tribune,* to handle publicity for the Community Arts in Santa Barbara. He lived, he told me years later (I was too young at the time to be aware of it), in an upstairs apartment with an outside staircase that rose steeply out of the Paseo's central patio. He didn't stay with the job very long because he found Cousin Irene domineering to a degree he professed to find intolerable.

I always liked her. She had a red face with a large beak, windblown hair, and burning eyes, and looked as though she had just stepped off a Scottish moor on a blustery day. She had real character and was born to command. In the years when I remember her, I never saw her with Grandfather or Grandmother because while they were in Montecito, she was summering in the charming town of Stockbridge in Massachusetts' Berkshires, where she had an iron grip on the local Garden Club. And of course while she wintered in Santa Barbara, the Meekers were in Chicago. When I was little, I thought her name was Cousin Marine, which I thought charming. I never liked her quite so well after I learned her real name.

Cousin B., as we called him, was deceptively mild looking, with a bland smile and rimless glasses. He used the word *joyous* a good deal, the only person I've ever known who did that. (I used to wonder if perhaps he wrote greeting cards on the side.) He was said to be an engineer, though no one in the family knew, or cared to know, what sort. It was enough to know that he controlled his wife's money, even though it was murmured that he had lost a million dollars of it in the Crash.

He had relatives in Santa Barbara. His brother Ralph, the much-admired and beloved first director of the Museum of Natural History, died an untimely death by falling off a cliff on Santa Cruz Island while reaching out for a bird's egg. His spunky widow, Gertrude Wesselhoeft Hoffmann, turned later to an acting career and without abandoning her home in Mission Canyon played many character roles in Hollywood under her maiden name, carrying on well into extreme old age. And their daughter, Eleanor Hoffmann, though severely crippled by rheumatoid arthritis, wrote attractive children's books, many of them set in Morocco, of all places. She once told me during a party in her old age that, in spite of all the millions of dollars spent on arthritis research, there were only two things that had ever helped her pain and discomfort: alcohol and aspirin. Well, the former has been my friend and companion (sometimes a treacherous one) since youth, and the latter has played an important part in keeping me alive in my Medicare years. Bless them both. I'm glad they helped Eleanor, too.

DURING THE YEARS covered by these memoirs, Unky hardly came to Santa Barbara at all, because it was his habit, as I have indicated, to spend his summers in Luzern, in Switzerland. What memories I have of him in Montecito must date from the very early 1940s, because he had had to leave Europe when war broke out in the fall of 1939. He complained bitterly about being in Montecito because his mother was merciless in using him as an extra man at her parties and he couldn't find the quiet he craved to spin his tales. I was a witness one day to a very Unkyish way of paying her back, though I daresay what I saw him do grew out of a long-standing irritation with her. Or was it pure instinct? In any case, one day we were walking into the noble drawing room after a characteristically enormous luncheon when an earthquake struck. At the age of eighteen, I had lived through enough shakers to pay very little heed to them. By now, in her early seventies, Grandmother was tottery on her legs and suffered from cataracts that limited her vision, so she always walked arm-in-arm with her resident nurse, Miss Barker, a large Canadian woman with a fixed but meaningless smile. When the quake struck, Miss Barker let out a piercing shriek and propelled her patient towards the French doors that would let the two of them escape to the outside. However, Unky's reflexes, unimpeded by concern for the old lady, were far quicker than Miss Barker's. In a flash, he interposed himself between the women and the door and by dint of some sharp elbowing managed to scuttle out to safety in first place without so much as a glance behind, let alone a helping hand. It was an extraordinary performance on Unky's part, of the sort that is known today as a "defining" moment.

I have always been grateful to that same Miss Barker for adding a delightful phrase to my working vocabulary. One afternoon, not long after the earthquake incident, Mother was showing her mother and Miss Barker (and I happened to be along) over her small ranch in Santa Ynez. There were forty acres of farmland on a plateau considerably higher than the house and the horse pasture, so Mother decided to drive us up the steepish hill to show off her cropland. There being no road, Mother chose what looked like an easy diagonal ascent to where she wanted to go. But she evidently miscalculated, or perhaps a wheel of the big station wagon fell into a gopher hole. The wagon suddenly listed a bit to port—and I heard once more Miss Barker's unforgettable shriek. "Stop the car!" she shouted. "I want *out!*" She flung open the massive door of Mother's "woodie" and stumbled off across the dusty hillside. Mother muttered, "Silly woman," and, nettled, plowed her way to the upper level. She and I both laughed for years over that earthily vivid "I want out," an expression neither of us had ever heard before.

I HAVE MENTIONED that during the late 1930s Mother spent a

large part of every summer at Lake Tahoe, where she rented a cottage on the magnificent Glenbrook Inn property on the Nevada shore. In retrospect, it seems very odd to me that she was willing to turn her back so resolutely on her parents, whom she professed to love. After all, they were in Montecito for just those very months that Mother chose to be away. There must have been overlapping at least in early June and late September, or perhaps the Meekers came earlier and left later than I remember. I enjoyed Glenbrook and the lake for about a month, no more; after that, I was restless, especially as I grew older, to get back to the fleshpots of Montecito. Mother, if she felt hard up, rented her big Montecito house to someone from Pasadena for a pretty penny; if not, it was "put away" for the summer and locked up tight. So it was arranged that I would be a guest at Constantia during most of July and August during the years 1936-1940 when I was fourteen, fifteen, and seventeen (in 1939 I spent the entire summer in Europe with Brosie and Cousin Joanie).... A horrid thought has just come to me. Grandfather paid for our round-trip steamer fares; that I have always known. Could it be that he was willing to buy those tickets for all three of us just to get rid of me for one whole summer?

In actuality we got along very well, my grandparents and I. I don't remember any friction, and I am not aware that I caused them any unhappiness. I would like to think that each summer they found me "improved," but I doubt that they did because young males as they climb more deeply into their teens grow harder and harder to endure. But I was bookish and had polished manners, and that would have pleased Grandmother; and I was a willing listener to tales of Grandfather's exploits, and that must have made me on the whole acceptable to him, though he would have looked in vain for any signs of youthful entrepreneurship on my part. I had no intention of soiling my hands with the brutalities of *laissez-faire* capitalism; that was for him to do, while I of course was free to reap the rewards. Now and again he would stop in the telling of an adventure, perhaps set in the inner sanctum of some very posh New York club of which he was the only member from Chicago, and look at me over the tops of his reading spectacles.

"Of course," he was likely to say, "you're going to have to earn your own living."

"Of course," I would answer. But not now, I would think. And not soon. And maybe, just maybe, not *ever*. (In actuality, I was able to stave off the evil day till just after my thirty-first birthday; and I retired at fifty-six. These are both commendable ages, and of course it was Grandfather, after his death, that made them possible.)

To tell the truth, living at Constantia suited me down to the ground, as the English say. I liked everything about it. Everything. The intoxicating smell, the opulent fragrances of sweet oils and polishes and perfumes and pot-pourri and bay rum and Melachrino cigarettes. The immaculate cleanliness of everything. Servants tip-toeing about their business, addressing me as "Master Nevill" and ready to carry out any request, no matter how whimsical.

If there were other house guests, I would be assigned one of the upstairs bedrooms with their old-world dormered windows and hand-decorated furniture from a small town in Holland (I've owned one of these bedroom sets ever since Grandmother died nearly fifty years ago). One, the more spacious, gave one a view of the channel and its islands while the other overlooked the romantic sunken garden. In each I felt magically cut off from the subdued bustle of the ground floor, as though I were living in a tower that freed me to inhabit a world of my own imagining. And when I descended from my "tower," it was as a dreaming prince that I would return to my earthly burdens, such as ordering a menu for a luncheon party of my friends that Grandmother had encouraged me to arrange, since she and Grandfather had an engagement. I tried to carry out my hostly duties with utmost suavity, as though I had been entertaining formally for all of my seventeen years. (Perhaps in my mind I had been.) And after lunch I would give my friends the full tour of house and grounds if they seemed interested, and they always did. Special favorites were two large, arched panels surfaced with Delft tiles. These were in a wide and bright hallway that led to the dining room, and what delighted my friends was that if one pushed hard against one of these panels, it gave way to reveal—who knew what mysterious, cobwebbed cell from a tale by Edgar Allan Poe—but in actuality a surgically clean and fragrant lavatory. Grandmother's bathroom was another favorite because featured in the tour was what I described as the only *bidet* west of the Mississippi, which squatted low and proud in a prominent position in the room. Another source of pleasure for my guests was to stroll around the large reflection pond carrying loaves of bread provided by the kitchen staff to feed to the fish. The hungry fish followed one around, avid for the bread scraps, snapping at the air. Many of them were gold-fish, but a foot or more long. It seemed, according to someone who knew, that a goldfish's size is determined by the size of the container it lives in. But if this was what the Meeker pond did for them, I couldn't help wondering what size they might attain to in the broad reaches of the tropical Pacific or wherever it is they come from. (My ichthyological curiosity burns with such a low flame that I have never moved to solve that question.)

More often than not I was the only guest in the house, and in that case I was allowed to stay in a large and beautiful bedroom on the ground floor furnished with French antiques and featuring rose-and-white *toile de Jouy*, looking downwards to the pond and upwards to the majesty of Montecito Peak. Here I felt more a member of the family and was greatly pleased to come under the ministrations of not only the chambermaid, as was the case upstairs, but now also of William, Grandfather's valet, who besides taking care of my clothes was an excellent source of backstairs gossip. One summer he kept me abreast of the efforts of Emil, the Japanese but-ler, to seduce the remarkably pretty Austrian waitress, Marie. He would catch her in narrow servant hallways and force kisses upon her while she squealed in protest. Then, unwilling to admit defeat, he would write her love letters to try to sweet-talk her into sub-mission, signing them "Emil Nizeboy." Emil's reign was short be-cause Marie found the courage to complain, and Grandmother sent Emil packing, to be succeeded by the impassively proper, though frequently tipsy, Rudge, an enigmatic and unlovable Englishman. His weakness was not pretty waitresses, according to William, but Beefeaters gin, or really anything in that line that he could get hold of.

To keep the bachelor William happy in what must have seemed a dull, provincial community after Chicago, Grandfather bought him a little Ford V-8. In the advertising of those days, I remember that William's model was called a "Tudor," and of course the larger model was a "Fordor." I mention the car because since William was free to use it only on Thursdays and alternate Sundays, Grandfather thought it would be wasteful for it to be idle the rest of the week and with characteristic generosity offered me, aged fifteen, the use of it. What fun I had, savoring my independence, racking up mile after mile in the country. It was the zippy 85 horsepower model, not the 60 horsepower one that would have shamed me among my friends, but the noise and vibration were fierce and helped me to keep speeds more or less legal. Of course Brosie, at the time a college man, had his own car, a handsome Plymouth convertible (all the college boys one knew had convertibles, except for the very serious-minded ones); it was much smoother to drive than the Ford, but when one stepped on the gas pedal, very little happened, a grave drawback, it seemed to me. Mother had forced him into a Plymouth because she said Plymouths were safer and besides the dealer had been a Valley Club friend of "poor, dear Pop's." Typical maternal reasoning; I wonder why Brosie succumbed to it since he was a relentless arguer, at his most dogged with Mother. When my time came for a car of my own, at the end of freshman year in college, I sweet-talked Mother into letting me have a Buick convertible, white with red leather, a dream of a car that I picked up at the factory in Flint, Michigan (of course there were no foreign cars for sale in those days, or I would have wanted one). Brosie was hopping mad since, by now married and on the lower rungs of management at Lockheed, he had just climbed his way up to a Pontiac, which was a clear step below my new car; and besides his was a drearily practical club coupe, emblematic of his self-imposed slavery to domesticity and the workplace.

Self-imposed? His marriage certainly was, to a delightful girl from Utica, where the Meekers had come from. But, as for his job: well, that was not his idea at all. When he graduated from Yale in 1939 with his Phi Beta Kappa key, he announced that he wanted to do graduate work in English at Berkeley. Commendable, the family thought; he had earned that right. As the year wore on, it became apparent that he was there to have fun, and that, cheerful extrovert that he was, he had found plenty of people of both sexes to have fun with. In fact, he was making no progress at all towards his M.A. Grandfather in Montecito called him on the carpet and asked him what he wanted to do with his life.

"I want to be a poet," he answered in a small voice.

Grandfather gave his famous snort of disgust. "Eugh! I never heard of such damned nonsense. I know the second-best poet in America and he earns $8,000 a year.... Forget it, m'boy!"

Brosie forgot it—and went to work. It took a while for us to figure out just who the "second-best poet in America" might be, but with Unky's help the mystery was solved. A good friend of Unky's was a poet named George Dillon who at that time was editor of the then-famous *Poetry, A Magazine of Verse,* published in Chicago. The $8,000 was his salary, subsidized by generous patrons of poetry. (I'm sure Grandfather didn't realize that the to-him despicable sum represented riches for a poet in those days.) Dillon was friend and lover of Edna St. Vincent Millay, whom Grandfather had heard of; ergo, she must be the best poet, and since he hadn't heard of any other contemporary versifier, Dillon must be the second best.... Lest it be thought that Grandfather had no respect for poetry, I remember that one of his favorite parlor tricks was to recite from memory the beginning of Chaucer's *Canterbury Tales,* I suppose bludgeoned into him in freshman English at Yale. His round eyes twinkled as he wrapped his tongue around the Middle English sounds that he had learned some fifty years before. Implicit in his recitation was the thought, "Can you imagine making any one learn such foolishness?"

Well, as he said to me when I had my bags packed for Harvard, "When you go to college, it's not what you learn that matters; it's the friends you make." I silently took great exception to this remark and reminded myself of the vastness of the space between the old man and his grandson. I knew he was wrong, but it wasn't long before I concluded he was a good deal better off than I because when I got to college, I discovered I didn't even care about the learning part.

To his grandchildren he was wonderfully generous, even though I doubt that he was very fond of us as individuals. After all, we were the generation that had "fizzled out," in his words. Still, we were all that was available to carry his genes into the future, and so he tried to ignore the obvious deficiencies of his Cramer and Gray grandsons. One could hardly ever be in his presence without his peeling off a large bill from his fat wallet. Blizzards of Nalco stock certificates were directed our way as the years, and Nalco, rolled on. (Mine transformed themselves magically in the 1950s into MGs, Porsches, Aston Martins, Bentleys, and Mercedes gullwing coupes, and I blessed his memory even though I was fitfully plagued by the high-pitched hum of his body whirling in its Chicago grave.) He was of course even more generous to his children, for whom he bought houses and provided large allowances that turned into four fat trust funds when he died in 1944.

I remember an incident when I was twelve or so that neatly differentiated my two grandparents in their attitudes towards people and perhaps life itself. There was a plague of snails that flourished on the grass and shrubbery surrounding the big pond. The gardeners had no constructive ideas, so Grandfather offered Brosie and me a penny apiece for any we could catch and kill. We decided to give it a try since we had trouble keeping within our allowances. It turned out to be an extremely profitable, though disgusting, occupation. We made twenty dollars each night we went hunting, and that was good money in those days for a couple of hours' work. Grandfather shelled out bills with no questions asked. After all, this was the closest either one of us had ever come to having a job; perhaps he thought we'd start up a little business in Montecito as exterminators. But Grandmother grew sourer and sourer as we reported for our money after our task was done. One night she could stand it no longer and demanded that the next time we show her the evidence to justify our rewards. We were happy to oblige, and accordingly entered the study where they were sitting after dinner, each of us carrying two buckets filled to the brim with snails, steaming and hissing in their death throes from the boiling water we had poured over them moments before in the kitchen. Grandmother gave a cry and turned her face aside in revulsion, waving us away while Grandfather smiled indulgently. Our integrity was never questioned again. But finally there were no more snails to be had, and we reverted to relative poverty. Brosie had to cut back sharply on his dating.

NO ONE EVER PICKED UP a restaurant check in Arthur Meeker's presence. On the other hand, I suffered agonies of shame whenever I dined with him in a restaurant because he never failed to complain angrily that the particular dish he had ordered wasn't fit to eat. Of course this always created a great commotion with agitated waiters and headwaiters, chefs, and sous-chefs scurrying back and forth between kitchen and dining room, waving arms and mouthing flustered, abject apologies in French and Italian. Grandfather of course remained serene throughout, thoroughly pleased with all the excitement he had occasioned while I shriveled with humiliation as the other patrons stared at the source of the disruption. The upshot was that there was no charge for Grandfather's dinner, which was always acceptable the second time around, and that he received extraordinarily attentive service if he deigned to patronize the restaurant again. I think he saw it as "keeping them up to the mark." The same with his employees. I was in the room with him once when he sent for the head gardener, a mild and obsequious Dutchman who stopped just short of pulling his forelock, and proceeded to show him the rough side of his tongue. The poor man shuffled miserably, close to tears, his vocal cords paralyzed from the lashing. Grandfather's criticisms were most likely valid, but his treatment of a vulnerable underling was most certainly not. In those days, it seemed to me that the high and mighty had one set of behavior for their families and social equals and quite another for those who existed, presumably devoid of personal feelings, to serve their betters. This was probably a result of the corrupting influence of power, but it may also have been due to the American tendency in the nineteenth century (and on into the twentieth for as long as Great Britain retained its power) to ape English class-ridden customs and behavior. Grandfather's longtime business secretary in Chicago, one Charlie Hubler, who was thought to be the soul of loyalty and probity, robbed Grandfather's children blind for a year or two after the old man's death before he was caught out. Who knows how much he had had to endure at the hands of his employer, who simply took him for granted? (Not many years ago, my cousin Art Gray told me that he was present in Chicago when Grandfather one day turned down Hubler's request to attend his daughter's wedding in a far-off state because he was needed in the office.) Hubler must have had a field day when he eventually found himself alone with the checkbook and no one to countersign. I am happy to say that Grandfather's children declined to prosecute, but I don't think they ever made the connection between the thieving and the treatment that had for so many years preceded it. They just put it down to the perversity of human nature and looked the other way.

One of Grandfather's harshest criticisms of people of his class was the flat and final "They don't know how to live!" This was a fearful condemnation in his eyes. It applied chiefly, as I remember, to the quality of food served in the miscreants' house but referred also to a laxity in living standards in general. If one had money, one should set a good table and entertain frequently. One should live in a large house and one's wife should be idle. A "lady" was a woman who did nothing for herself, who must be waited on hand and foot; again, this curious standard was borrowed from the English and was pretty generally accepted by the moneyed right up to World War II. One must remember, too, that Grandfather lived the first half of his life in the Victorian era and, being a conformist, accepted its values and customs with a whole heart.

Another group of people that he had it in for was "dirtyrottenstinkers." (I write it that way because he said it as though it were one word.) These were people, usually Chicagoans, of non-WASP background whose sin was, I surmised, that they had outsmarted him in business deals, though he didn't put it that way. I wondered why he would have had dealings with them in the first place. In spite of his condemnation, he wasn't above trying to use them to advantage, as I found out when I was eighteen or so. I had been so rash as to say, when pinned down, that I could (barely) see myself as a scriptwriter for the movies. He immediately dashed off a letter to two of these "dirtyrottenstinkers" who happened to be joint owners of Paramount Studios at the time, asking them to find a place for me on the lot, no matter how modest. To my great relief and joy, they were never heard from on this matter. I daresay they thought him a stinker, too.

When Grandfather wanted to know what a man he had recently met or perhaps just heard of "did," his question was invariably phrased as "What's his excuse for living?" This could be rather daunting if one wasn't ready for it, especially when he applied it to the fathers of many of my friends who, when I was backed to the wall, really didn't seem to have any apparent "excuse." Obviously it wasn't my place to lecture him on the difference in mores between Chicago and Montecito. Or between Chicago and London, for that matter. Here was one area where the newer culture did not borrow from the older one. And when one came right down to it, what exactly was *my* "excuse for living"? Or at least, what would it be after college?

IN THE SUMMER OF 1938, the Lord Tennyson of those days came to Montecito with his new bride, an attractive divorcée of Chicago origin. The parents of the bride were friends of the Meekers', and so it was quite natural that my cousin Joan Gray and I were made available to help entertain the baron's son and heir, the Honorable Harold, known as Harry. Direct descendant of the great poet laureate, he had inherited none of his ancestor's darkly romantic good looks. Harry looked like my idea of an English bank teller, short and slender with thick-lensed tortoiseshell glasses and usually dressed in a pin-striped suit. I liked him because he was highly responsive and had a delightful sense of humor. I don't think I ever met his father, but he was pointed out to me one day as he was about to enter the doorway of the Coral Casino. I was struck by his elegant appearance but even more struck because he looked as though someone had hung a mouse on his left eye. I made inquiries in an appropriate quarter and discovered that that was exactly what had happened. I was told that at a recent Montecito party he had made a less-than-gallant remark about a local woman, and one of his American fellow guests had let fly. (I will add here that the transatlantic marriage did not last very long.)

Our Harry was cut out of different cloth, however. Someone in our family (probably Aunt Katharine, who would have liked nothing better than to marry her Joanie off to an English peer-to-be) had arranged an expedition to Los Angeles that would include Joanie and her very pretty schoolmate-houseguest, named M.L., as well as Harry and me. We were to travel in the Meekers' maroon Packard limousine, and our twin destinations, taking into acount our precarious balance of sophistication and childishness, and our differing ages, ranging from my fifteen to Harry's pre-Cambridge seventeen, were the Huntington Library and Gallery in San Marino and the Venice amusement pier on the Pacific. We all got along splendidly. I filled Harry in on the drive down with amusing anecdotes about Grandfather, whom I could imitate pretty well; I told Harry and M.L. enough about him to make him seem larger than life, as indeed he was, and Harry soaked it all in. The four of us stayed together for quite a while in the Library, which fascinated me as I was in the midst of my brief period as a bibliophile. But enough was enough, and Joanie and I had never seen the English eighteenth-century portraits in the Gallery. We persuaded Harry that the portraits would be coals to his Newcastle and that instead he owed it to himself to get permission to have a private look at the Library's Tennyson holdings. Shy though he was and loath to put himself forward, he nevertheless went along with our suggestion, and we parted company for an hour or so.

When we met again at the car, we asked him if everything had gone well.

"Oh, yes, they were most welcoming and I had a good look. Lots of interesting things there."

"And did you tell them who you are?" asked Joan, purring vicariously at the thought of the curator's pleasure in having a live descendant of the Bard in his precious library.

"Of course."

"What did you say?"

A pause. Then, "I told them I was Arthur Meeker's grandson."

The three of us collapsed. It was such a marvelously unexpected thing to say and yet perfectly in tune with the anecdotes that I had been feeding him in the car. I could have hugged him.

And then I thought how glad I was that I could make the same pronouncement—and what's more, in my case it would be true. For it's all well and good to have a legendary poet among your forebears, but for downright, everyday come-in-handiness, it's awfully hard to beat a millionaire. I wouldn't have traded Grandfather for anyone.

CHAPTER NINE

✿ The Grays

THE ENGLISH WRITER HUGH KINGSMILL, cursed with a family he could not abide, declared that "friends are God's apology for relatives." I never felt that way when I was growing up; in fact, it wasn't till I was an adult that friends began to play a significant part in my life. As a boy, I considered blood relatives infinitely precious. They were like an extension of oneself, and their existence added richness and texture to one's life. Far and away the most important relatives, apart from my immediate family, were the Grays.

The Montecito Grays, the ones I considered part of my family, consisted of Uncle Horace and Aunt Katharine (Mother's slightly older sister) and their three children: Horace, Jr., a little older than my brother Brosie; Artie, a little younger than Brosie; and bringing up the rear, the red-haired Joanie, a year older than I. Horace and Brosie tended to pair off, as did Joanie and I (but only because she was a tomboy; if she had been a girlish girl, I'd have had nothing to do with her), with Artie in the middle, shifting allegiances as required.

UNCLE HORACE (Horace Gray, M.D.) was strongly introverted, somewhat withdrawn, and every inch a Boston Brahmin, though he hated Boston. After graduation from Harvard, where the Gray name was old and honored, he had attended and received his degree from Harvard Medical School, after which he went to Munich to pursue his medical studies. While in Munich, he met Katharine Meeker, who was there studying singing, a suitable sort of "finishing" experience in those days before the Great War, when it was only the determinedly intellectual young ladies of the upper classes who went on to college, and women's colleges at that. The serious medical student and the lighthearted young post-deb fell in love in Munich, became engaged, and were married in Chicago, and then went to live in Boston where Uncle Horace served his residency at Peter Bent Brigham Hospital. Grandfather Meeker, rising to the occasion, bought the couple a handsome house near the hospital. Uncle Horace's mother (of whom more later), a fearsome old tartar who was none too happy over the Chicago connection, delighted in speaking of Katharine to her friends as "my porkpacking daughter-in-law."

Aunt Katharine told her mother, "I want to have six boys, and I want them all to look exactly like Horace." She promptly had two, neither of whom looked at all like their father, followed by a girl. (Uncle Horace, who could be garrulous on a favorite topic, wasted no words when they cost him money. His Meeker in-laws had insisted that he wire them about the birth of their third child, and he agreed, somewhat reluctantly, to do so. The message came through in due time: "GIRL.[signed] GRAY." After all, what more was there to be said?) She loved her children passionately and undertook to bring them up with no interference, as she saw it, from her husband. He made a few half-hearted efforts to correct the boys' savagery and then resigned himself to indulging his little girl while more or less pretending that the unruly boys didn't exist. Grandfather Meeker, visiting Boston one day from Chicago, was so outraged by young Horace's rudeness to his mother that within twenty-four hours he had packed him off, aged eight, to board at a pre-prep school, Fessenden in Massachusetts, a place that specialized in trying to civilize the very young, a quixotic goal if there ever was one.

Uncle Horace was trained as an endocrinologist, seeking a cure for diabetes. Yet when his residency was over, the family moved to Chicago, where he busied himself, God knows why, in measuring the "sitting heights" of private school children. Joanie and I came across a sheaf of grim photographs, rather like mug shots in a police station, of depressed boys in their underpants, sitting in profile with a level piece of wood atop their little heads and their sitting height clearly marked on the photograph. Joanie and I were perplexed to discover this cache and did not know what to make of it. I took it as a piece of harmless lunacy, and I was not about to rattle my uncle by asking questions about it. When we found it, the Grays had already migrated to Santa Barbara, where they had bought a delightful, rambling old California redwood bungalow named "Hope Lodge" on Miramar Avenue in Montecito, less than a block north of the highway, which in those days carried only a thin stream of cars. Uncle Horace soon established himself with the Santa Barbara Clinic, recently founded, and pursued, among other things, the hopeless task of trying to help the obese to lose weight.

AUNT KATHARINE inherited the executive ability and extroversion of her father, Arthur Meeker. She was a leader, a manager; perhaps a little on the bossy side. She was not one to let her young grow up without the benefit of her counsel, which she dispensed freely. Lest that conjure up a false picture, let me add that she was one of the most feminine of women, and relied heavily on her very real charm to get what she wanted out of life. At first, she was concerned with "society" because she had been brought up to be; but before long she branched out into causes of real importance, society in the other, superior sense. During the time I am writing of, as a young matron in the 1920s, she founded the Santa Barbara branch of the Junior League. In the 1930s, when the Gray family had moved to San Francisco because Uncle Horace had accepted an appointment to the faculty of the Stanford Medical School, she was named a Commissioner of Public Housing in that city and became an authority in her field, flying to conferences all over the country and the world on behalf of the cause.

In the late 1940s, when she and her husband moved back to Montecito and built a handsome modern house on Olive Mill Lane, she looked about her and decided Santa Barbara needed a lot of things that it then lacked, and over the decades that followed set herself to correct some of those omissions. She was instrumental, with a few others, in starting the Citizens' Planning Association, which has worked against reckless development. Later, inspired by her friendship with Margaret Sanger, she helped to establish Planned Parenthood in Santa Barbara, and after seeing the Hospice idea in practice in England, she applied herself to helping found one of the first hospices in the country. She energized the local chapter of the League of Women Voters, accepting responsibility for its growth and development during the years she was its president. She had many other involvements, but these are the most significant ones. In 1957, she became the second person to be named "Woman of the Year," following on the heels of the local conservation icon Pearl Chase, whose gifts and interests were very different from Aunt Katharine's.

Unlike my aunt, who ruled by persuasion, flattery, and charm, the famous Miss Chase simply bulldozed her opposition. Brusque, forceful, and often extremely rude, she won all her battles but left many a bruised and bleeding ego along the way. My mother, Grace Lloyd, for example, couldn't stand her, though of course she admired her accomplishments in helping to make Santa Barbara the beautiful place it is. I'm sure Mother had suffered at her hands and, no good at hand-to-hand fighting, retaliated by running her down to friends at the Little Town Club, that formidable redoubt on East Carrillo Street for WASP women of gentle birth, founded for the purpose of serving them rich lunches and at the same time providing them with a central clearing house for what men refer to contemptuously as "gossip," something of course they never practice in their own bastions! I never met Miss Chase, but I was pleased for Mother's sake a few years ago, not long after the latter's death, to read in a newspaper interview with Miss Chase's secretary that her employer had not been (as the secretary so tactfully but so obviously understated the matter) an easy person to get along with.

That could have been said of many people of accomplishment, but it could not properly have been said of Katharine Gray—nor of my mother, who was the fifth recipient of the "Woman of the Year" award for all *her* many good works, and who maintained a genial composure throughout most, if not all, of her long and honorable involvement with the boards of non-profits. Though Mother put in much time with "do-good" boards, I think she was happiest with ones that promoted some special interest of hers, such as the Music Academy and the Botanic Garden and the Garden Club. This predisposition led to occasional conflict with Katharine over any activity on Grace's part that, in the elder sister's sometimes censorious mind, smacked of self-indulgence.

This mild conflict carried over into their private lives in a comical way. One year, when they were in their sixties, Mother was bubbling over with excitement over a trip she was planning to Greece and the Aegean Islands. Aunt Katharine was deeply, visibly shocked.

"Gracie, I don't see how you can take pleasure in going on a trip that has no purpose behind it. In these times, how can you possibly justify it? I only go to Europe if there's an important conference scheduled and I can contribute in some small way."

Mother was incensed. "I'm going because I want to go. And I don't like conferences." Then she began her tuneless hum that signified extreme irritation and served to block any further discussion.

She was never effective with her sister in fighting back. The subservient role of younger sibling (don't I know it) is formed very early in life and leaves one effectively without defenses against the older one. All she could do was fuss and fume when she got home, and she did a lot of that. "I don't know what's come over my sister. You won't believe what she said to me today. And she's getting worse as she gets older."

But they were devoted to each other all their lives, and for the most part to each other's children, though of course there was sisterly rivalry in that connection; it was not unendurable for one aunt to hear of some misadventure of a nephew or niece. And, since we all had feet of clay, these misadventures were not uncommon. (That phrase reminds me of a delightful remark made by Winston Churchill, near the end of the war, when Greece was in ferment and the British, charged with restoring order, were leery of dealing with the Greek General Plastiras, pronounced to rhyme with "master class." "I hope he doesn't turn out to have feet of clay," said the prime minister.)

One evening, during a pause at a large family dinner at the Meekers', Mother dropped a ball into the conversational roulette wheel. "Isn't it nice that Artie [her absent college-age Gray nephew] has a new girl friend?" Grandmother's interest was instantly piqued. "Who is she? What's her name?" "I don't know her real one, but Brosie says she's known as 'State Street Jenny.' Isn't that an odd name?" Choking sounds were heard along both sides of the table, and Aunt K. flushed scarlet from her neck to her forehead.... Artful bitchery or stunning naiveté? Mother was a hard one to figure out. But Sister K. came out on top more often than not.

Hope Lodge was my second home in childhood. Even after their move to San Francisco, the Grays continued to spend their summers in it, and hardly a day went by in the long vacation without my biking over to see what might be going on there. It was built on a small lot, as was the case with most of the early cottages in what has now come to be called "hedgerow" Montecito, but the lot was well arranged for pickup games, especially baseball played with a tennis ball to avoid breaking windows or scoring unfieldable home runs over the hedges. The front side of the lot was almost entirely paved—good for base-running—except for a plot of grassy earth that nourished an enormous tangerine tree, the fruit of which was very satisfying while one waited for one's turn at bat. The paved drive led to a three-car garage, where the closed doors provided a fine carom effect to line drives down the middle, making them tricky to field. I can see white-haired, stone-deaf old Nora, the Gray cook, lounging outside her back door that gave onto the "field" as she shouted encouragement to whichever team she favored that afternoon. "C'mon, Arthur, swat that sphere!" she would bellow with the flat intonation of the very deaf. I became celebrated in the family for what I must admit was a superb imitation of her voice; Artie in particular used to urge me to "do Nora," and I never failed to oblige, improvising routines with him as straight man that had him rolling helplessly on the floor.

COUSIN ARTIE, who was four years older than I and about two heads taller, was a most engaging fellow, sweet-tempered almost all the time and charming even when he was angry, like a huge and utterly harmless teddy bear gone temporarily amok. Often I would ride him while he careened around the room on all fours. I never knew anyone so delightfully open and guileless, in other words so unlike me, and playing with him was an endless source of pleasure. We had a game exclusively ours that we enjoyed by the hour both in his house and in ours, in which I played the role of a fresh brat named "Candylamb" while he threatened me with chastisement that he was far too tenderhearted to administer.

Some years later while I was visiting the Grays in San Francisco, when I was perhaps fourteen and he was at home on vacation from college and very serious about his studies in Romance languages, I remember pestering him affectionately in our old traditional way to such an extent that, instead of beating me up, as anyone else would have done, he locked himself in his cramped little bathroom that looked out upon a lightshaft, and there he sat on the toilet (where else?) by the hour, hunched over his college texts, but at least secure from interruption. He repaired to that unsavory privacy daily because he knew I was ready to pounce if he let down his defenses. And all in vain, too, as he later changed his major.

His brother Horace, like my brother when he was with the Grays, considered himself too mature to bother with Joanie and me. But as he was the eldest of us five cousins, it was he who was the first to earn a driver's license, obtainable at fourteen in those days. To the great joy of all our parents, it became his duty, and of course his heady pleasure, too, to drive us every day to play tennis at the Montecito Country Club. I see us now bowling along in the Grays' vast light-gray Packard touring car, with the huge top folded down, all the boys dressed in white shirts and white ducks, and Joanie in a white skirt and blouse. Horace drove very capably, as I remember—not such an easy job in those days of non-assisted steering and probably no synchromesh, either. The gearshift sprouted up, immensely tall, from the floor.

Artie boarded with us during one winter, I suppose at the time when his family lived briefly in Chicago. He was thought to have a weak something or other and so was sent out to his aunt's care in salubrious Santa Barbara. Mother, in reminiscing happily years later about his winter with us, enjoyed recalling how, on his way home from the little Howard School a couple of blocks away, he would knock at the back doors of our neighbors that lay upon his route and, pleading starvation, play upon the mercies of the various cooks, most of whom could be counted on for cookies or a slab of cake. Mother professed to be mortified, but it all went to add to the legend of Artie's appetite for sweet things. Another favorite story of hers concerned a visit to a *patisserie* in Paris with various members of the family. A waiter came by periodically with a tray heavy with flaky delights, which he offered to his customers in turn. Eventually it was time for the *addition* to be reckoned, and the waiter discreetly asked each member of the party how many good-ies he or she had consumed. I think *deux* was the standard answer until the waiter came to Artie. There was a discernible pause, and then out came the muffled, guilty (but oh so honest) answer: *onze!* And everyone turned around to stare at this extraordinary American child.

At a later time, during summer vacation, he came frequently to our house on La Vereda Road and always brought with him a thirst that apparently could not be slaked at home. He did great damage to Brosie's and my supply of soda pop, the generic name then for soft drinks. Mother bought the stuff for us by the case, a mixed bag of ginger ale, root beer, creme soda, and Delaware Punch. She dis-approved of Coca-Cola, and so we never had that. Can she have heard that it contained cocaine, as indeed it did in its earliest form? 7-Up hadn't been invented, and sarsaparilla belonged to an earlier generation. Of course there were no sugar substitutes in those days, nor were people aware of the connection between sugar and dental problems. We wallowed in the stuff. The trouble was, so did Artie, more than was fitting for a visitor, even if he was our first cousin. So one day we mixed up a vile brew drawn chiefly, as I remember, from roots and leaves and even dirt that had steeped together for many hours to achieve the dark, rich hue of root beer. We poured it into an empty root beer bottle and offered it to our dear cousin as an example of old-world Cramer hospitality. Bless him, he drank a hearty swig. I need say no more. Brosie told him why we had done it, so that the experience would not have been in vain.

THE COUSIN I WAS CLOSEST TO was Joanie, because she was only nine months older than I and something of a tomboy, as I have indicated. At the Edgecliffe Athletic Club, which occupied a great deal of our leisure time in our pre-pubertal summers, we were known as "Carrot Top" and "Cotton Top." Her hair color soft-ened a little as she grew older but retained till her death at the age of sixty-nine a distinctive and pleasing golden redness. (Mine, on the other hand, went from white to yellow to dirty blond to brown to grey to—what's left of it—white again. Perhaps the reason men don't dye their hair frivolously is that they don't need to since they are likely to experience naturally the whole gamut of color changes.)

We competed against each other, usually in friendly fashion, in almost every conceivable way, spurred on about equally by our natures and by our elder brothers, especially Horace and Brosie. I remember that they established a formal competition for us, perhaps a decathlon, with (besides other events lost to memory) swimming and running and tennis and one strange event in which we were timed while we held our faces under water in a bathroom sink. I don't remember which one was crowned overall winner; Joanie must have won the swimming competitions, and probably I did better in most of the other things. She was a good head taller than I because of the earlier growth natural to a girl, so that gave her an advantage in some areas. However, my quickness and nimbleness were usually more than a match for her strength. She had a crush on the great tennis champion Helen Wills Moody, so it was important to her to excel in that sport, and indeed she had a strong serve and handsome ground strokes, but like most girls in those days, she couldn't cover the court worth a damn, and I delighted in moving her around to her great vexation. I see her on the court, hot and flushed and angry because I had just executed a neat little drop shot that she couldn't get her racket on. Very satisfying.

Throughout our long and affectionate relationship that lasted until her death just a few years ago, I must admit that I enjoyed teasing her. Just a little; she couldn't take much. (That's not true. I teased her a lot.) I especially enjoy teasing around with those who are my equals in that particular pastime, but there is also a naughty pleasure to be found in teasing people one can dependably get a nice, fat rise out of. Joanie fell heavily into that category. Just a few years ago my wife, Pat, and I were at a sizable birthday party given for Joan by a good friend of hers and ours. She had chosen to wear some very elegant pale-blue silk pyjamas, oriental in appearance and more appropriate, it seemed to me, to the boudoir than the drawing room. To make a point, when I looked at her I yawned extravagantly. "I feel exhausted just looking at you," I said. No response other than a look of extreme irritation. This was not at all the effect she had sought. A few minutes later, I couldn't resist yawning at her once more, this time silently. She set her jaw and glared, and there was a lull in the general conversation. Then she struck, addressing her remark to all in the room. "Now you know," she said with great satisfaction, "why I don't invite him to my *good* parties!" I was much amused, whereas the other guests, embarrassed, pretended not to hear her remark. But I still am wondering why she felt it would be more acceptable to be teased at a bad party than at a good one. Indeed, how did she know in advance she was going to have a bad party, bad enough to justify inviting Cousin Nev to it?

We spent a great deal of time in each other's company during our growing-up years, and of course during some of that time we egged each other on in doing mischievous things behind grownups' backs. One summer, in between our beach and tennis activities, when I was about eight, we decided we would become shoplifters. I wanted Tootsie-toys for my car collection, and Joanie felt her dolls were inadequately outfitted, so we determined, almost like young entrepreneurs, to do something constructive about filling our needs. Hitting up our mothers was just too easy; we wanted to taste forbidden fruit. So, over a period of a couple of months, we plied our trade, as it were, in the two downtown toy stores, the Children's Shop downstairs in the 800 block of State Street and the Western Book and Toy in the block where the Arlington Theatre now stands. Did we carry bags or just stuff our pockets? I don't remember. One day, while she did errands with son Horace, Aunt Katharine left Joanie and me to while away the time browsing in the Children's Shop. We moved openly from counter to counter, filling our pockets to capacity. When they returned, Horace said in the aggressively harsh voice that he sometimes used, "We'd better search their pockets." We shriveled, but Aunt Katharine looked shocked and said, "What a horrid thing to say, Hossie!" That was our only close call. That is, until the jig was up.

I came to feel that stealing at kiddy stores was just too easy (didn't the owners know that children are instinctive thieves?) and decided to strike at a store for grownups. I chose Lewis's in the old Orena adobe, part of the El Paseo complex, at the corner of Anacapa and de la Guerra—a charming and tasteful gift shop and an excellent hunting ground because it contained a number of rooms, only two of which were staffed. I remember stealing a pretty ceramic ashtray from Portugal and other smallish things of that ilk. How did I get them out? No idea; some sort of sleight of hand, I suppose. And I struck again at dear old Fanny Brown-Browne's little lending library-cum-gift shoppe in Montecito off what is now South Jameson Lane. (She was Mother's friend who, with me, had enjoyed the Christmas tree hung with wieners at La Villetta while Mother was in Chicago getting a divorce.) I was fond of her, but that counted for nothing when my shoplifting blood was coursing through my veins. Besides, it never occurred to me that stealing did anyone any harm. It was simply a test of one's nerve and resolve and in our opinion was most certainly not for sissies. While Mother and she chatted in the store, I dropped several of Mrs. Brown-Browne's choicest bibelots into a bag and later deposited them in our cache of stolen goods, the bottom drawer of a dresser in Joanie's bedroom.

We were found out by our damned brothers. We never knew what led to the discovery of our hoard; some sort of dishonorable snooping must have gone on. We were a little shocked by their lack of faith in us. And they were very sanctimonious when they lectured us on our delinquency. (Why would they have been so suspicious if they hadn't been shoplifters themselves, we wondered?) They made us tell them where all the goodies had come from, and then, pompous and self-righteous, proceeded methodically to return them, of course all the while blaming their wicked little siblings.

Some years later they admitted that they had been received with disbelief and hostility by shopkeepers who made it plain that they despised them for not having the guts to 'fess up! This of course was music to our ears. We hoped they had learned their lesson.

We were up to other mischief, too, a few years later. Hope Lodge, which had five bedrooms in the main house, had several other bedrooms and storerooms as well in the outlying buildings that, along with garages, used up most of the small lot. (California bungalows were surprisingly spacious because people had large families in the early part of the century, besides a household staff to provide quarters for.) The storerooms were of great interest to the Grays, Artie and Joanie in particular. Methodical and meticulous, they were a tribe given to hoarding and classifying. Unless I teased her too much about her addiction to her storeroom, Joanie would occasionally allow me in to watch her at work on a classifying project while I tried to lure her outdoors to play catch. One day, however, it occurred to both of us that the windowless room provided a remarkable degree of privacy; it was even possible to lock the door from inside. When this fact dawned upon us, like a light bulb turning on in a cartoon character's mind, we stripped off our clothes and began a wordless but precise examination of each other's bodies, rather like monkeys looking for fleas. What a lot there was to discover, for me at any rate! Joanie had reached puberty well before me, as was natural given her age and sex, and her particular version of puberty centered in the mammary region, to my great delight.

It was a while before I had much to offer in return, though my time came. My feeling in the beginning stages of our fooling around could be well summed up by the anecdote concerning the little girl who found herself naked in a bathroom with her naked mother: "How come I'm so plain and you're so fancy?" Odd, I thought; but after all better than the other way around. I must say that Joanie never made me feel inadequate, and over several years we had a great deal of good, clean fun (as we saw it) in that storeroom before we boldly took our little act indoors—to the main house, that is, hers or mine. I have one vivid recollection of Joanie's spending the night at our house on La Vereda. She was taking a bath in my bathroom, and I thought to slip in and squeeze my way into the tub beside, or perhaps on top of, her. Such consternation when I found the door locked! Nor would she open it in spite of my angry whispers and fierce rattling of the doorknob. I learned at that moment the hard truth that females are not always in heat when males are in rut. Mother Nature handles these things better in the wild.

We continued to let off sexual steam with each other for a number of years. We were never in love, but we had genuine affection for each other throughout our lives in spite of the great differences in our natures, Joanie's being slow-moving, stubborn, intensely thorough, and sincere, and mine being the reverse of all those things. We used to say, when we were twenty or so, that we might end up marrying each other if nothing better turned up. But it did, for both of us.

One of my last memories of her is set in the San Ysidro Coffee Shop, where we lunched together every month or two when we were in our sixties. After the death of her companion, Dr. Helen Hart, she became a restless world-traveler, specializing in camera safaris in Africa, not a part of the world or an activity close to my heart. (She had done every inch of Europe with Helen.) On the occasion that I am remembering, she had just come back from her first around-the-world trip. She was one who liked to talk about her travels, and ordinarily I am a good listener, but my heart sank with dismay at the prospect of hearing about the entire trip, even in "digest" format. I tried to shorten the monologue that I knew was coming by interrupting after the first few minutes to ask what were the high spots. "Don't distract me, Nev. I know just what I want to say, and it upsets me if you interfere with the sequence." I was a good boy, and held my tongue, but it was a long, long luncheon. You will have some idea of it if I tell you that when the snapshots from her trip were later developed, she had to write a check for $720.... Could I have been paying her back when I kept yawning at those blue silk pyjamas?

I ADORED AUNT KATHARINE. I can't say she was like a second mother to me because I already had two, counting my stepmother/aunt, Mary Cramer. I'll say instead that she was everything an aunt should be, and that is saying a good deal. When I entered her house, she made me feel there was no one in the world she would rather see at that particular moment, even though she might be busily engaged—perhaps paying bills at her desk in her study or accompanying herself on the piano in the living room while she sang *Zwei Herzen in Drei-Viertel Takt*. In those faroff times she spent a great deal of time warbling and trilling—and very prettily. And I seem now to hear, if it happened to be late in the afternoon, the tinkle of ice in a glass teapot as she swirls her beloved martinis (called "Hope Lodge tonic" by her husband) round and round to chill them to her taste. A swallow, and then more warbling. How she loved those martinis! And didn't in the least mind being teased about them. She had the ability, as I discovered later in life, to absorb very large quantities of them without going through the offensive stages common to most of us. Her face flushed, and her neck a little too, and her voice tinkled like the ice cubes, and perhaps she became a little arch—but always charming, even though she downed enough in the evening as the years went by to fell a rhinoceros. I observed, when I was old enough to be interested in such matters, that the moment it was time for dinner, she stopped cold. Not another swallow; not even a glass of wine or a sip of a liqueur. And so she was able to face the challenges of the next day with a clear head and an active will unlike those (Cramers among them) who like to carouse through the night.

Her habit (and it was a habit; for example, she would never sit down in a restaurant that didn't serve liquor even when those with her might want nothing but a sandwich or scrambled eggs) and the militant activism that went with it resulted in the overturning of a rule that had stood for decades at the Little Town Club prohibiting the use of liquor at the club, which served only lunch in those days. The rule had been established in the 1920s because one of Montecito's finest had gotten into a face-slapping match over the bridge table with one of Hope Ranch's finest, and the governing board had blamed the fracas on gin. When Aunt K. came back after the War from her years of exile in San Francisco and resumed her membership at the LTC, she couldn't believe that that "silly old rule" was still on the books. A lesser woman would have done some grousing and let it go at that, but not Katharine Meeker Gray. She proselytized right and left, marched her disciples to the ballot box, and overthrew the offending by-law with a smashing victory. I wish whoever wrote her long obituary in the local paper had included that triumph among all her more generally known ones. I have not heard of any face-slappings at the LTC since alcohol was reintroduced by her almost fifty years ago now, and I would like to think that it may have been that detestable game bridge, and not gin, that had caused the trouble in the first place.

I can blame her, in a way, for my first alcoholic disaster. When I was seventeen, the summer between Cate and Harvard, she gave a biggish cocktail party for her children, which of course I attended. Because of her predilection, martinis were the staple offering, though of course I might have ordered whiskey—but I hated Brosie's bourbon and hadn't yet discovered the smoky charm of scotch. (I really had very little to go on in choosing. At home Mother hated the taste of liquor but would occasionally indulge in a dry sherry, which she professed to like, but she grimaced comically as the nasty stuff went down.) So I drink one chilled glass.... Revolting; this is supposed to give pleasure? A few minutes later I take another from the waitress's proferred tray. Nasty; but not quite so nasty as the first one. Then number three goes down. Hmmm. The bartender's really got the recipe down pat now. Wonder why he didn't make the others like this. And aren't cocktail parties fun. I don't say no when the fourth comes my way. What I do, though, is fall forward, like a pine tree in a forest scorched by lightning.

But that's not the end. The Gray boys and Brosie, choreographed by Aunt K., carry me out to a guestroom in an outbuilding and put me to bed, out of harm's way. Or so they must have thought. An hour later, woozy and dry-mouthed, I come to life, dress, and drive back to Constantia, a couple of miles away, where I have been staying. I let myself in with my latchkey, fumbling like a movie drunk to find the keyhole. I cross the entrance hall and sneak a look into the study as I hope to pass it by, but drat it, there's Grandmother, looking up at me through her spectacles from her seat on the sofa. "How was the party, dear?" Before I can mumble an answer, Susie, Mother's little Sealyham that summered with Grandmother, leaps off the sofa and runs to greet her old friend. Of course I bend over to pat her. "Hi, Susie, good old Susie." Can a stately pine fall twice? This one does, with a slow, rolling motion, right down to the carpeted floor. I pick myself up as best I can. No one speaks, for what is there to say?

There were no recriminations, then or later, nor even any reference to the incident. That is, not in my hearing. But Grandmother was not one to stay silent long. "I'm afraid he's just like his father. Oh dear, isn't it dreadful? It's Ambrose all over again." That would have been the refrain.

Years after the incident, Aunt K., bubbling with laughter, reminded me (if that's the right word, since I have no memory of having said it) of my words to her while she was putting me gently to bed in her guest room at Hope Lodge. "If you tell anybody about this, Auntie K., I'll *kill* you!" It doesn't ring true because I am not fierce by nature, but then it's not the kind of thing an aunt would invent. Is there truth in the old adage *in vino veritas?* I've never been able to decide.

I always found her great fun to be with. She was candid in saying she had no sense of humor, but I think what she meant was that she didn't know how to make others laugh—quite another matter. Responsive laughter was always close to her lips. I see her and Mother and myself in Pasadena, probably after dropping Horace and Brosie off at the Pasadena station to catch the Chief, starting their long journey back to college after a vacation. We stopped for an early dinner at the Rose Tree Tea Room, a Pasadena institution. I've no memory of what we saw or said that set us off, but we started to laugh, all three of us, wildly, uncontrollably, weeping into our entrees. Perhaps it's just as well I can't remember what it was all about because I'm sure it would fall flat in the retelling. The pleasure comes simply from remembering the intensity of the laughter, and the happiness that the three of us felt in each other's company, those two dear, good-hearted women and the young boy who was so happy to be laughing with them over some foolishness, there in the noisy tea room.

I remember, too, what a fine hostess she was when she put Mother and me up in San Francisco over a long—but not long enough—weekend when I was ten or eleven years old. I had never been to the City before. We took the night train up, were met by Aunt Katharine and Joanie at the station, and went on to enjoy the endless pleasures available for children in that (I thought then; I don't now) glorious place. Of all the things we did, I remember most happily some of the simplest: riding an elevator up and down and up and down, to and from the Grays' flat on Gough Street with its panoramic view of the bay; a huge escalator (my first) at the Emporium (my first department store); the fashionable stores on Maiden Lane, Gump's and V.C. Morris and Ransohoff's; the little electric boat that I piloted round and round the island in Stow Lake in Golden Gate Park; the animals at the zoo; the Bay ferry. It was all entrancing for a smalltown boy, and it is Aunt Katharine's glowing face as she proudly showed off the wonders of her new home that comes to my mind now, the most charming and gracious of hostesses.... I sobbed for a long time in my Pullman berth as the Lark on Monday night inexorably returned me to Santa Barbara and the familiar burdens of the Crane School and daily life.

(A propos the Fleischacker Zoo, I have a memory of visiting again some fifteen years later, this time with Mother, my wife, and my sister Nancy with a young friend of hers, who had been sprung from their Marin boarding school for a weekend in the City. We found ourselves in front of the monkeys' cage. Mother was far too innocent and recklessly sentimental about animals to realize the danger she was exposing the girls to. "Look, children," she cooed. "See how the dear mother is picking fleas out of her child's fur. Isn't that sweet?" Then, to her horror, the "mother" proceeded to commit what the British term "a gross indecency" upon the child. Mother whirled around 180 degrees and thrust out a pointing forefinger. "Oh girls, do look over there at the pond! Nancy, I'm almost sure that bird ruffling its feathers is a crested grebe. Don't you agree?" And the girls, being well brought up, turned as they were bidden without so much as a smile. Whether they knew it or not, it was a fine example of practical etymology: as good an account as any of the origin of the term "monkey business.")

Aunt Katharine possessed other qualities than those I have stressed, ones that served to round out her powerful character. She was extremely adept, for one thing, at hitting up her father for substantial sums, far more so than her siblings, who, less aggressive than their older sister, tended to let come what might as far as money was concerned. They ruefully admitted her supremacy in that area as well as in virtually all others. She was unfailingly successful in playing the eldest-sister card, reducing the other three to ineffectual grumblings behind her back.

Unky related that he could always tell when a frontal financial attack was about to be made upon their father. First, she would fly to Chicago on some pretext, usually, I think, that her husband was being difficult, i.e., he didn't want to disburse money for some purpose close to her heart. Unky said that once in Chicago, as the critical moment drew near, she would become extremely affectionate with her father, approaching nearer and nearer until she could put her arm around him and kiss the top of his bald head. This gesture apparently softened whatever small amount of resistance he had at his disposal and caused him to reach for his checkbook. Brosie and I used to do a little skit that involved Aunt Katharine's supposedly warbling and trilling out, "Oh, Daddy dear, I wouldn't dream of accepting your check for a new roof that just happens to be in the amount of $3,415.89." Whether we were close to the mark or not, she always managed to return to San Francisco in triumph.

Once, in the darkest years of the Depression, when her husband was being neurotic, to her mind, about finances, she told her father that she simply had to have more money and that she proposed to wipe out her shortfall by starting up a diaper delivery business, of all things, in San Francisco. Grandfather, when approached, of course lost no time in quashing that disgraceful venture and provided the healing balm of a large check, but Brosie and I then and later had fun with the notion of a fleet of milk-white vans with bells a-jingle cruising the streets of San Francisco, their flat sides painted with the enormous, shameful rubric, KAY GRAY'S DI-DEE WASH. A capable woman, she would probably have made a success of it, but she would certainly have been drummed out of the San Francisco Social Register and the Francisca Club, and that she would have found intolerable; besides, I'm certain the project was just a ploy.

When Grandfather died in 1944, her younger siblings were delighted to discover that his will took into account moneys already disbursed to his children, at least with regard to such major things as the purchase of houses (as to roofs I don't know), and that by and large economic justice in the end was done.

My three cousins, Aunt Katharine's children, though of course they loved their mother, had to contend with an aspect of her nature that I was spared, at least to any significant degree. She "managed" people—with persuasion, with charm, with all her natural feminine wiles, so that the relentless bossiness lay hidden in a nosegay of sweet-smelling posies. But it was there, indomitably there. Horace Jr. opposed her as soon as he found a tongue to speak with and never let down his defenses as long as she lived. Artie and Joan enjoyed the role of obedient, loving children until in their twenties they turned on her and for some years after would have nothing to do with her. They found her loving but smothering intrusions could be repelled only by a degree of rejection that might have seemed harsh to an outsider. But by taking stern measures, and by calling upon their limitless reserves of Gray stubbornness, they were able as they matured and defined their own identities to resume loving relationships that brought great happiness to all concerned.

In small ways she tried to impress her will upon Brosie and me. He would have none of it, flaring up resentfully when he caught her at it, no matter how smooth her performance. She had a habit, after presenting a course of action that she wanted one to adopt, of asking, "Does that make sense to you?" It never seemed to make sense to Brosie, and he made no bones about it. Once, when he was not long out of Yale and working at Douglas Aircraft in El Segundo, he appeared at La Vereda Road with a dog in tow. Then he went back to El Segundo without the dog, leaving it behind to board for a time with Mother while he made arrangements for keeping it with him. In any case, he had every intention of reclaiming it, and soon. Somehow, Auntie K. came into the picture and persuaded Mother, who made only the feeblest of protests, that it "made no sense" for Brosie to have a dog at this stage in his life; and in the winking of an eye she had found another home for it. He was enraged when he returned the next weekend, but the dirty deed had been done and could not, I forget why, be undone. He never ceased to hold the incident against his aunt, seeing it as an unforgivable example of gratuitous meddling, which of course it was. And yet, from her point of view, it probably did "make sense." She had decided that he was not in a position to have a dog. Therefore, something should be done. (And perhaps it was payback time for "State Street Jenny.") Brosie never forgave her. Decades later, when her name came up, he would mutter darkly, "She gave away my dog!"

I was made of more pliant and complaisant stuff, and when Auntie K. would suggest a course of action and follow it up with the inevitable "Does that make sense to you?" it seemed to me that it always did, and I was happy enough to take her advice. She seemed a reasonable woman to me, in fact in my youth a far more reasonable person than I was, and so I was glad to bow to her superior wisdom. I perceived her as a warm, sweet-tempered, and loving person who made a marvelous aunt, but I was also extremely glad that she was not my mother because I think she would have sucked the life out of me. In truth, I wouldn't have traded my own mother for anyone else. My mother, like her mother before her, was very judgmental about others, but not about her children, who were of course perfect: she took that for granted; it didn't need saying, and she never said it. In fact, she rarely complimented us to our faces. We were free, Brosie and I, to make mistakes both great and petty, without fear of censure. We learned our own lessons from our mistakes; there was no one to rub them in and make us squirm. And if one chose not to profit from one's mistakes, well, that was all right, too. Eventually one would see the light. Eventually. Is all this what people mean when they speak of spoiling a child? I don't know. Whatever it was, I liked it.

Not long ago, while rummaging among some old papers, I came across a card from Mother written on my birthday in 1974. "For fifty-two years," she wrote, "you have been a source of comfort and joy to your devoted mother." Not strictly true; but she felt it, she wrote it. As for me, I could not have had a finer mother. Not much given to expressions of sentiment, nonetheless I told her so a few months before she died; she was lying still in a darkened room, and I can't be sure she heard me. It didn't really need saying anyway, because I'm pretty sure she knew it.

UNCLE HORACE was a different kettle of fish. Where his wife was emotional, sentimental, intuitive, and extroverted, he was rational, unemotional, neurotic, reserved, and strongly introverted. Their differences, which had very likely seemed charming and provocative in the early days of their marriage, caused predictable problems in their later life together, but their marriage held fast through the years. Because they were so very different and because he wouldn't follow where she led, she found emotional stimulation and satisfaction in relations with other men that I am pretty sure involved the heart rather than the body. But there is no question that she did have these intense relationships; in fact, they were essential to her nature. I imagine she saw herself as having outgrown her husband in many important ways, and I am sure that his rigidity and limited range of interests from her point of view and his unwillingness to share to any degree her involvements and activities must have been a disappointment and frustration for her. But his love for her flamed steadily, in spite of the mutual conflict that might have served to quench it, and provided for her a sort of glow and comfort that she could always turn to and rely on.

Born a Proper Bostonian, a product of Groton and Harvard, he must have had a depressing upbringing, though I know very little about it. Grays were prominent in early Boston. A seagoing forebear, Captain Billy Gray of the good ship *Grand Turk,* was said to have owned more vessels at the time of the War of 1812 than did the fledgling United States. Grays founded a Boston law firm—Ropes, Gray—that is still very highly regarded. A Gray became a justice of the U.S. Supreme Court. A large Victorian building in the Harvard Yard is named after the family.

I know nothing really about his father. Unky remembered him as sporting an Adam's apple bristling with red whiskers that protruded from his stiff collar. That hardly does justice to the man's nature, but I'm sure he was forbidding. I *know* his wife was. Helen Howe, author and daughter of the genial Boston biographer M.A. de Wolfe Howe, wrote of a summer weekend that her father and mother spent with the Grays at their cottage on the North Shore in Nahant. The Howes were younger than their host and hostess and as native Rhode Islanders very much in awe of these distinguished Bostonians. Well into the weekend, Mrs. Gray indicated that she wished to have a private word with Mrs. Howe. Later she was summoned to a sparse New England boudoir and offered a seat. Mrs. Howe was greatly alarmed. What frightful *gaucherie* could she be guilty of? Mrs. Gray leaned forward and murmured conspiratorially, "There is something I want to tell you." A pregnant silence. Then the glorious anti-climax: "Mr. Gray thinks you and your husband are quite nice." Helen Howe also mentioned the tidbit that while a child, Uncle Horace, son of the above-mentioned Mrs. Gray, and his younger brother Augustine (pronounced with the stress on the second syllable) were referred to by their peers as "Horrid and Disgusting." One hopes that the simple Boston pleasure in having fun with words was the reason for the appellations because I suspect the boys must have been exceedingly well behaved.

His mother, Amy Heard Gray, daughter of Augustine Heard of

Ipswich, north of Boston, came from a family that had prospered in the China trade, but the family fortune had pretty well disappeared by the time Amy came of marriageable age. While traveling with her parents in Europe, the young woman had fallen in love with a Spaniard of noble family who reciprocated her love. But the affair came to nothing when the Spaniard's family learned that there was no dowry to speak of. Back again in Boston, Amy was married off by her parents to a prosperous older man, Russell Gray.

And by producing two sons, she fulfilled her duty to him. Soon thereafter, however, I surmise to repel any further connubial assaults, she moved to a separate room and took to her bed in a serious way, rarely leaving it again. She became known to her segment of high Brahmin society as "the wounded eagle of Marlborough Street." Her eyesight failed her, but she prevailed upon friends to take turns, in unvarying sequence, reading aloud to her. Aunt Katharine, belittled, as I have mentioned, as "my pork packing daughter-in-law" during her Boston period, was added to the rotation and proved very faithful in spite of a notable lack of gratitude from her mother-in-law.

Mrs. Gray had a long widowhood. In the 1930s, rather surprisingly, she took to coming out to Montecito for the summer, renting a French provincial house with a small tower on Mimosa Lane. Aunt Katharine was obliged to continue her reading-aloud bondage. It was only a short distance from our house on La Vereda Road, and frequently as we drove along that blindest of all roads, with its tall, dense, overhanging hedges on both sides, we would come upon her walking slowly right in the path of our car, dressed in her eternal widow's weeds, holding up a black parasol against the harsh western light. These perambulations seemed to give the lie to her bed-ridden Boston existence. Did she forget that the Montecito woods teemed with Bostonian exiles who might report on her deception?

I learned only recently from her grandson Arthur that Uncle Horace was terrified of his mother, and that she never failed to treat him as an inferior being, belittling him with all the acid her sharp tongue was capable of spitting out. And yet she apparently treated her second son, the naval officer Augustine, with unfailing respect. What lay behind this great injustice no one today knows, but the fact of it can't have failed to affect Uncle Horace's nature.

In the late 1930s there was a palm-reading fortune teller at the Restaurante del Paseo. Many people had a high opinion of her, including Aunt Katharine, who thought to inject a little spice into the life of her grim old mother-in-law by engaging the palmist to join them for a reading while the two had luncheon. I've no idea what truths, palatable or unpalatable, were revealed, but I do know that at the end of the session the palmist turned to the old lady, draped in her shapeless black garments, and said, "Honey, there isn't anything wrong with you that I can see. What you need is to go out and get yourself some new duds." Enchanted by the glorious incongruity of the word, Brosie and I re-christened her "Dudsie" Gray, and we have never thought of her by any other name from that day to this.

A frightened but dutiful son, Uncle Horace regularly visited his mother in Boston to endure who knew what humiliations. One of these visits took place while I was a freshman at Harvard. He paid me a ceremonial call in Cambridge, and we dined together very happily before repairing to my rooms. He showed no signs of leaving, and of course now I know that he couldn't face going back to the old gorgon on Marlborough Street. I needed to get rid of him because I had a paper due early the next morning that I had foolishly put off, and I became almost frantic as the clock ticked on. Then, knowing he was due to leave for California the next day, I asked him what time his train was to depart. Surely, I thought, this would start a useful line of thought. Far from it. For the next two hours he held forth, in his precise and oh-so-thorough way, on every conceivable aspect of train schedules and departures. My heart sank as he lit a cigar, which was his habit as he settled down (or "in" in this case) after a good dinner, and gave himself over to this apparently engrossing subject with its endless possibilities and permutations. It was a virtuoso performance, but I was in no condition to enjoy it. He took the last train home from Harvard Square. I stayed up till dawn working on my paper. (Now you can see why I tried—and failed—to head off his daughter at lunch that day not so long ago while she plodded on about her trip around the world. It is hard to deflect a Gray from his or her goal.)

In other circumstances, I loved to watch him drawing on a cigar with the placid but intense satisfaction that he brought to the performance. I used to get goose pimples, my symptom of thralldom, as I watched him in the living room at Hope Lodge while he went through all his ritualistic motions and procedures. No man seemed more contented, and some of his tranquil bliss always rubbed off on me. He was a man of real charm when it suited him to display it. And as I grew older, I greatly enjoyed his conversation, which, as it tended to deal with ideas and abstractions, was a heady change from the trivialities of a Meeker dinner table. He especially held my interest when, during the last years of his San Francisco period, he became passionately interested in the theories of Carl Jung, so much so, in fact, that he changed his medical specialty to psychoanalysis of the Jungian persuasion. Through him I became fascinated and underwent an analysis myself in San Francisco with his good friend Dr. Joseph Henderson, considered by many to be Dr. Jung's heir. For the last twenty years of his life, including his semi-retirement in Santa Barbara, Jung's theories were almost obsessively at the center of Uncle Horace's life.

But whatever he learned from his studies about the working of the human mind semed to have little effect upon his own quirky nature. When at home (I'm thinking now of the postwar years in Montecito, in the handsome house that his wife built on Olive Mill Lane—in leaner times he used to lie awake at night wondering if they were headed for the poorhouse), he would immure himself in his private library and read and study endlessly, carefully annotating the margins in pencil. If he heard a car enter the forecourt, he would move swiftly to a tiny peephole in his door that gave on the drive and squint at its occupant. Almost always it was someone he wanted no truck with, with the result that he would bolt the door that separated his quarters from the more public part of the house before returning to his annotating. He never attended his wife's frequent parties, nor would he accept invitations to other parties. This is not to say he had no friends. He had quite a number, but he chose not to share them with his wife or his children. He liked to pay prearranged calls on them, especially if they were attractive women, as they often were. He could be quite skittish with and about these women, but they had to pass muster with regard to both charm and intellect. His little coterie were devoted to him and liked to exchange stories about him with each other, stories emphasizing his endearing eccentricities. He was a very stimulating companion, provided one didn't ask him about train schedules.

The things that gave most people pleasure pained him, and he made no effort to conform. When I was young, there were lots of joint family picnics. He would have nothing to do with them, as he complained that sand or dirt always spoiled his food and the proper place to eat was a dining room. I don't think he ever took part in anything his boys did by way of recreation, nor do I remember any signs of affection directed their way. With his daughter he was much warmer. I don't believe I ever spent a Christmas with him, and I can't imagine him Christmas shopping. A friend of mine told me the other day that years ago she had run into him in early December and had remarked casually that she was suffering from a pre-Christmas headache. He replied, "Yes, my dear. Christmas is a very black time of the year." She relished the memory of that wonderfully characteristic remark. Who else could have expressed so neatly and succinctly his opposition to received opinion?

He was said to be frail and suffered from various ailments that were disagreeable but by no means life-threatening. He was his mother's son in that he took to his bed when things went wrong. Why don't more men do this? It thoroughly frustrates wives, at least for a while; I'm sure it unsettled Aunt Katharine when he arrived home in San Francisco from one of his Boston trips to find that she had had their apartment re-decorated by someone she knew he couldn't abide. He glared in furious silence at his wife and, knowing he was sure to lose in an emotional verbal battle, went immediately to bed for two weeks.... The sight of anything purple made him sick to his stomach. (His wife, on the other hand, when it came to colors was passionately anti-red. Once, lunching at El Paseo, she became incensed to discover that her table was set with bright red napery and refused to order her meal until the offending linen was stripped off and replaced with white.) Once he and Aunt K. visited us in Lake Tahoe: her idea, not his. And she drove him, knowing he suffered from vertigo, up the twistiest of all the approaches, the one that winds up from Placerville to the south end of the lake. Once in the safety of our cottage, he collapsed upon his bed and never rose till their stay came to an end a few days later. Aunt Katharine was a very strong-willed woman, and clearly he had to resort to innovative means to resist her. He simply didn't have the equipment to slug it out, so his way was to withdraw temporarily from life. When the going gets tough, the untough get going, too...to bed.

One day something happened that shattered the calm of the Meeker-Gray connection. I would say that the fault lay primarily with Aunt K. for constantly complaining to her father about her husband's alleged deficiencies, but he bore responsibility, too, because of his often neurotic behavior. As I reconstruct the incident from what my mother told me at the time, Aunt K. must have complained to Daddy once too often, and he sat down forthwith to dictate a letter that, as Grandfather put it in a favorite phrase, would "straighten him out." That phrase may sound harmless enough, but it invariably meant a brutally honest assessment of the victim's nature and comportment. In this case, I'm sure he gave his son-in-law hell, using intemperate language that expressed decades of irritation and resentment over his perceived parsimony.

From what I know of it, the letter was unforgivable, and Uncle Horace never forgave him for it. The only direct quotation that I can remember hearing at the time was, "Nobody's ever eaten a good meal in your house!" That was probably the strongest condemnation Grandfather was capable of uttering. It was false, too; what it meant was that the Meekers' meals were rich and heavy, while the Grays' were simpler but delicious, as I well knew. I suspect Grandfather also used his scornful old standby, "You don't know how to live!" But in Uncle Horace's typically Bostonian "plain-living-and-high-thinking" view of life, Grandfather as a rank materialist didn't "know how to live." Of course Uncle Horace was too much of a gentleman to answer in kind. His response was simply to tell his wife that he would never see or speak to his parents-in-law again. And he never did.

AFTER HER HUSBAND'S DEATH a good many years later, Aunt Katharine was disconsolate. Then someone told her about a wonderful woman medium on Coast Village Road who had had extraordinary success in bringing mourners together with their dear departed ones in the spirit world.

"Do you think there could be anything to it, Gracie?" she asked my mother.

"I certainly don't," said Mother, bracingly pragmatic as always. "It's all perfect nonsense. And you know it'll just upset you if you go ahead with it."

But Aunt K. was avid to test the medium's power and made an appointment. When her first session was over, she rushed to phone her sister.

"I had the most wonderful experience!... Come right over. I don't want to talk about it over the phone."

Mother told me about it afterward, snorting derisively. "The woman told K. that both her parents and her husband were standing there in heaven, smiling down at her with their arms around one another. I told her that just proves the whole thing is a fraud. I said, 'You know Horace would never put his arms around Father and Mother!' "

When I told my wife Pat about this comical interchange between the two old ladies, Pat in her outspoken way pointed out the fallacy in Mother's thinking. "That doesn't prove a thing. After all, negative feelings are supposed to be left behind when people get to heaven."

Myself, I hope Pat's wrong. But if she's right and all animosities in heaven are burned off as so much dross, then I'm going to opt out and head for the other place.... They say it's a dry heat and one soon becomes accustomed to it. Like Arizona.

Above: My maternal grandparents, Arthur and Grace Meeker,
in their Chicago heyday.
Below: The Meekers' fiftieth wedding anniversary, Chicago.

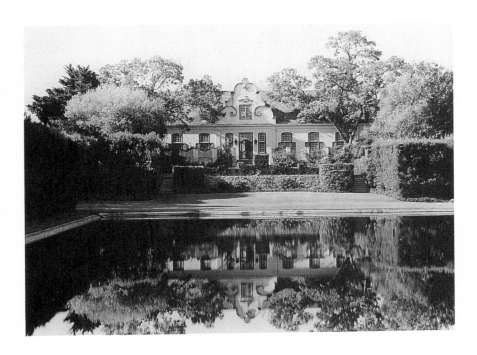

Constantia, Montecito.
Above: North elevation (Wayne McCall).
Below: View from the north terrace.

Constantia luncheon party.
Back row: Artie Gray, Grandfather with his California hat, Horace Gray, Jr.
Middle row: Mrs. Russell ("Dudsie" to Brosie and me) Gray, Grandmother,
Mother, Aunt Katharine Gray.
Front row: Joanie Gray, Brosie, Nevie.

Above: Mother, Unky (Arthur Meeker, Jr.), Aunt Katharine.
Unky said of them, "They have the most talked-about wigs in Santa
Barbara." His sister, Mary Cramer, when I repeated this remark, retorted,
"Yes, and who do you suppose is doing the talking?"
From the look of things, he would have been smart to
shut up and get one for himself.

Below: The three Meeker sisters in old age—
Katharine Gray, Mary Cramer, Grace Lloyd.

Above:
Uncle Horace Gray, M.D.

Below:
Artie Gray in Fiesta regalia.
Could he be looking forward to
a rendezvous with "State Street
Jennie"?

Above: My paternal grandfather, Ambrose Cramer of Chicago.

Middle: My father, Ambrose Cramer, in Camden, Maine.

Below: Aunt Katharine and my father. Father to his wife, Mary: "I had such a good time with Katharine that I think I'll marry her, and then I'll have had all three of you."

CHAPTER TEN

❧ The Cramers

SEVEN YEARS OLD, I STAND TENSELY AT THE WINDOW
in our house in Green Lane, waiting for the sound of a car climb-
ing the short rise to the graveled forecourt. I wait for quite a while
because as Mother has told me, Daddy is always late—at least he
was in her day, she says. She keeps me company for a while, but at
the sound of tires on gravel she bolts from the room. On my own
now, I run to the big front door and open it timidly, waiting for
Him to step out of the car. This is to be my first meeting with my
father since Mother and her entourage left him behind in Paris six
years earlier, in 1923, when I was a baby in the care of a French
nurse, too young to speak, too young to understand, too young to
register memories.

The car opens and the stranger steps out, his arms outstretched
towards me. Why, how wonderful, he's half the size of Pop, that
vast, hulking tyrant! And what a warm, welcoming, *gleaming* smile!
But what's that strange, big, dark-brown spot on his neck, only partially hidden by his collar? (Mother forgot to tell me about his birth
mark, and of course that's the one thing I can't take my eyes off.)
But how pleasant he is, and how young compared with Pop! How
glad he is to see me! Brosie *must* have been wrong when he
crowed, "Daddy didn't want you!" over and over. Daddy says he
wants to buy me a toy, and would I direct him to the proper place?
At the Children's Shop downtown I guide him without hesitation
to the thing I most covet in all the world, a wooden model of an
America's Cup sloop: huge white sail, white hull, and everything
green below the waterline. Half as big as I am. And built to sail, not
just look at. What a beauty! I know it costs a lot, $75 in fact, be-
cause Mother has already refused to buy it for me: "You children
must think I'm *made* of money." How often have we heard that

irritable response, and how often are we to hear it in the years to come! Never mind, I have a *father* now. He'll give me anything I want. He'll love me to pieces.

I have no other memory of that marvelous outing, except that Daddy seemed to have a lot of thick, blondish-brown hair, but there was a big empty spot in the middle, like a clearing in a forest. Oh well, Pop was much worse than that; his bald head was all middle. Once I had the sailboat in my hands, doing anything else together would have fallen flat, so I wasn't sorry when he dropped me off at Green Lane. I doubt we'd been gone more than an hour in all. (It probably seemed endless to him as children made him uncomfortable, I learned later. And the reason for his presence in Montecito was not to see his little darlings, but to speak with the contractors, engagingly named Snook and Kenyon, who were starting construction on the Meekers' new house.)

Who was this man, this newfound father of mine? I knew the Meekers, Meekers galore, a rich variety. What did the other side of my family have to offer? Who on earth were the Cramers, and was it good or bad to be one? Over the years I strove to find satisfactory answers to these questions.

I THINK THERE IS NOTHING MORE TIRESOME than hearing in detail about someone's dream, even the dream of somebody one loves, but a close second would surely be a thorough exposure to another family's genealogy. Mindful that my Cramer relatives already have abundant genealogical material in their possession, I intend to spare the general reader that sort of discomfort by providing only minimal background information, at least until we reach my paternal grandfather.

In brief, then, the Cramers orginated in Germany, in Swabia. Our ancestor, Tobias Cramer, a well-born younger son, left his homeland to pursue a military career under William of Orange, William III of England. He fought successfully in Ireland in the Williamite wars against King James and some years later retired as a colonel. He married into the Anglo-Irish aristocracy (known in Ireland as the "Ascendancy" and resented for centuries by the old Irish stock), and his offspring settled happily into their new country, living for many generations as landed gentry or serving as high-ranking jurists or officers in the Royal Navy and Army.

Our first American ancestor was Ambrose Cramer (there are thirteen of this name in the family tree), born in Ireland in 1754. In 1797 there was an abortive revolution in Ireland, in which some members of the Ascendancy rose up against their English masters. Many patriots lost their lives, two of the famous martyrs from that period being Robert Emmet and Wolfe Tone, whose names still bring tears to the eyes of all bibulous Irishmen (i.e., to all Irishmen), and when the uprising was put down, my grandfather's great-grandfather found it expedient to flee to the new world, where he settled in Virginia.

He and his heirs prospered as plantation owners and slaveholders, taking pains to marry well. Until, that is, the Civil War, which my grandfather, born in 1857, witnessed at first hand as his family's multi-columned plantation house came into the line of fire. Grandfather, in a handwritten memoir of his early days, says the family were driven out of their home by the Union troops and fled to Cumberland, Maryland, where they were obliged to live in a more modest style. Grandfather was Navy-minded and managed to secure an appointment to Annapolis in 1874, where of course he received a free education from Uncle Sam and thoroughly enjoyed himself, being apparently a scrappy little extrovert, outdoorsy, jovial, and (to me) dishearteningly low-browed. In his memoir he proudly records the following: "A negro named Baker had been appointed to Annapolis, a disagreeable, nasty-smelling brute. My friend Hood and I resented taking any commands and hammered him, for which we were sent home. I remained out a year, then was reappointed. Came back, entering the next class—quite a hero for my misdemeanor. Got lectured by the Admiral good and plenty, but stood this easily. Afterwards the Admiral asked me to dinner." Though I never met my grandfather, I doubt that I missed very much. I have long since ceded all of my descendant's rights to him to his namesake, my brother, who resembles him in many significant ways while adding, thank goodness, significant dollops of intelligence and humor.

Much of his memoir concerns a voyage he took to Japan as a naval officer. It would have been most interesting to read about the

Japan of those days, but there is nothing of the sort in the manu-script—only bits describing shenanigans afloat and ashore with his fellow officers. In his old age he was the victim of what Mother, then married to his son, described as "softening of the brain," evi-dently a term of the 1920s for senile dementia or perhaps even Alzheimer's. A lifelong friend of Mother's, a woman who was part of her Lake Forest childhood and known for possessing the sharpest tongue in the Prairie States, always insisted that his degeneration was the final stage of syphilis, possibly contracted during his Japa-nese tour of duty. Nonsense; he produced two healthy and highly intelligent children from his first marriage and a third, though far less capable, from his second marriage.

I don't think he ever had much of a brain to start with. Mother remembered her former father-in-law as a soft-spoken gentleman with merrily twinkling blue eyes. No quotable remark of his has survived. He was short and handsome, I would say; I have several photographs of him. His features seem not to have been passed on; a pity. But then neither has his "softened" brain—Brosie and I like to think.

Crossing the country by train as a young naval officer, he fan-cied the look of Chicago beside its lake and promised himself to re-turn to live when his tour of duty was over. In due time he settled there and entered the business world. Before long he wooed and won the hand of the charming and witty Susan Skinner, whose fa-ther, Judge Mark Skinner, was a very highly regarded and prosper-ous judge in early Chicago. Of early Puritan stock, pointing his horse westward towards Chicago, he had left his roots in the idyllic New England town of Manchester, Vermont, where his father, whose house is one of the ornaments of its main street, had been the first governor of the state and where today, set among the graceful old white clapboard houses, stands the Mark Skinner Me-morial Library, erected by a reverent descendant. The graveyard, a particularly pleasing one on the outskirts of the little town, contains many Skinner headstones, including one over the remains of the Judge's brother, who died at a young age in the Civil War.

In that connection, it is said that there was quite a flapping of indignant wings in the Chicago household of the Skinners when Susan, one of three Skinner daughters, became engaged to Ambrose

Cramer, a son of the Rebel South. Nonetheless, the marriage took place and two children were soon born of it, Elizabeth (known as Siddy) and Ambrose, my father. I know next to nothing of their childhood, whose presumably happy innocence was shattered by the death of their mother from a burst appendix when Father was seven and Siddy a year or two older.

After a decent mourning, my grandfather married again, this time to a widow with a daughter named Isabelle, a little older than the two Cramer children. The three became very good friends and maintained the warmest relations throughout their lives. Later a son, Corwith, was born to the couple, providing my father with a half-brother to add to his existing sister and stepsister. Father had to adjust to life with a stepmother, and from things he told me late in his life, I would say that that adjustment was never very well made. Throughout my childhood, he spoke either affectionately or at the worst noncommittally about this stepmother, whom we were instructed to call Amama (stress on the first syllable), but his true feelings came out years later when he branded her to me as a scheming little woman who had diddled him out of money rightfully his and who, in his opinion, grossly favored her own son, Corwith, over him.

An early settler in Lake Forest, Grandfather built a large, handsome, Southern-mansion kind of house that he called "Rathmore" (after a rumored Cramer manor house in Ireland) on a bluff overlooking Lake Michigan, probably with money left him by his Skinner wife, and lived there in considerable state for many years, Amama lingering on till after World War II. Amama was never a favorite of Brosie's and mine; in fact, she came into our consciousness only once a year, on December 25th, and we judged her (how else, as there was never any other communication during the year?) by her offerings at that time. They were a dreary lot indeed. I remember two presents in particular. One was a soft yellow "scarf," I was told. I had no idea what that meant and had to ask. When I learned what it was for, I buried it under sweaters in a drawer, and there it lay, hidden, until the moths ate it up years later. A Montecito boy wearing such a thing: crazy! But the next Christmas she outdid the scarf. Brosie and I each received a small, flimsy-looking box containing—an assortment of colored rubber bands.

We were furious. Even she knew she was getting by very, very cheaply because instead of signing her card "Amama," she wrote, "from the Tree." That only made it worse, as far as we were concerned. Her name was mud in our house from then on.

I met her only once, during Christmas vacation of my freshman year at college, which I was spending with my father and step-mother in Chicago. We drove out to Lake Forest for a family re-union at Rathmore. Amama turned out to be extremely sweet in manner, in fact unconvincingly so, but the atmosphere seemed to be affectionate, with hugs and kisses all around, and Father effu-sively greeting and being greeted by his stepsister, Isabelle Ryerson, whom he loved, as well as by his half-brother Corwith and his handsome wife, visiting from Maryland. One would have thought it was a model get-together of loving family members, all using pet names that spoke of happy childhood intimacy. Only later did I learn that Father couldn't stand his stepmother, and as for his half-brother Corwith, well, I've never seen two grown men greet each other with more effusive and apparently genuine warmth—but wait.

When I went upstairs to bed, I counted twelve other bedrooms besides mine. It seemed to my eighteen-year-old mind that "the Tree" might have done better by us than two little boxes of rubber bands.

But the truth about the relationship between the two brothers came out twenty years later in a notable example of the hypocrisy my generation has always ascribed to the one before. Father and Mary were wintering in Scottsdale, and Uncle Corwith and Aunt Laura went to a hotel nearby, traveling from their home in Annapolis to enjoy some winter sun. Of course there was a jolly family get-together at Father and Mary's house during which Uncle Corwith drank too much and then out of the blue proceeded to tell his brother how much he had always resented him, in fact hated him. He felt he had always been compared to his discredit with his brother Ambrose. Too inept in his studies to get into Yale, he was a man without a respectable profession, eking out a living in the De-pression as a yacht broker on the Annapolis waterfront, bringing up his son aboard a cabin cruiser instead of a pillared mansion. "Why can't you be like Ambrose? What's the matter with you?" This recurrent cry of his parents had ruined his life, he wailed with mounting rage. In fact, he took a drunken swing at Father as the discussion grew in intensity. Father and Mary were astonished and dismayed by this washing of ancient dirty linen, but as Father brooded over it the next day, he realized *he* had for years resented and hated Corwith because his stepmother (Corwith's mother, our Amama) always favored her own son outrageously over him, and as he continued to brood, came to wish that *he* had taken a good poke at *Corwith*. Soon the two men were spilling out their resentments to their respective psychiatrists but pointedly avoided each other till Corwith, still burning with resentment, died a few years later.

I have only one other anecdote concerning my Cramer uncle, related to me by Mary, who let it slip absent-mindedly one day in connection with something else. Corwith and his attractive wife were on an outing in New York City, staying in a hotel, when once again his passions were inflamed by liquor. This time he had no one to be furious with but his wife. Finding his accusatory sentences thickened and blurred by alcohol, in a rage of frustration he raided his wife's closet, wrenched all her dresses and coats off their hangers, and hurled them out the window, from which his wife could see them fluttering softly down eight floors to land in an ungainly heap by the hotel entrance on East 54th Street. "Then what happened?" I asked Mary, but she didn't know.... Alas, people tend to be weak on the follow-up questions.

I KNOW LITTLE OF FATHER'S CHILDHOOD AND YOUTH because as we never lived together, I wasn't exposed to the bits and pieces of reminiscence that parents ordinarily pass on to their children during the easy give and take of everyday life. He had two "aunties" who survived their sister, his late mother, and he spent a good deal of time with them at their large Victorian house in Chicago. Though one of them was said to be a forbidding Calvinist type, they both indulged him over a long period of time with, I suppose, an ultimately deplorable effect on his character. It was understood that he and his sister Siddy would be the heirs to the very substantial estates left to the maiden ladies by their father, Judge Mark Skinner.

At an appropriate time he was sent off to the Hill School in Pennsylvania to prepare for Yale. The only tidbit I have concerning his time there is a most unseemly one, though to me singularly pleasing. It had to do with a chamber pot being emptied from Father's second-storey dormitory window onto a spot below that was daringly close to the heads of the headmaster and several important guests as they passed by on a tour of the school. The upshot of it was that Father was ordered to take a term off to think things over. Instead of meditating upon his sins in disgrace, he allowed himself to be packed off for a new beginning to the Florida/Adirondack School, which shifted between its two handsome campuses according to the season. He began his lifelong passion for sailing while at the Florida campus.

He entered Yale in 1909 as a member of the Class of 1913 and spent four very happy years there, making many friends and indulging his fondness for English literature while becoming increasingly attracted to the study of architecture and French civilization. A propos English, many years later he told me that the luminous star of English letters during his time at Yale was George Meredith, who had just died when Father matriculated. He asked me around 1960 whether Meredith was still held in such high regard. This quaint question made me realize that, unlike mine, Father's affair with English lit was only a college flirtation, whereas his attraction to architecture was nourishing and long-lived. His scholarly abilities, like Brosie's a generation later, earned him membership in the Phi Beta Kappa Society.

Father in later life waxed sentimental about his college, I suppose. He took me to New Haven near the end of my school days, feeling sure that what I already envisioned as its Gothic glooms would serve to entrance me. I had long since decided that any campus that had been home to Grandfather Meeker, Father, and Brosie in turn would not see my shadow on its stately paths and had decided on Harvard. After all, I thought with the arrogance of my youth, if number one is available, what's the point of wasting time on number two? But to please Father, I pretended to keep an open mind. I was under the faery spell of Ireland at the time, and I saw that this passion could provide me with a tactful way out of committing myself to Yale. I knew from studying their catalogs at Cate that only Harvard offered courses in Gaelic, so I was able in my interview with Yale's dean of admissions to ask the man point blank just how many courses in Gaelic he could offer me. What, none? (Harvard, I knew, had several, perhaps as a sop to the large Irish population of the Boston environs.) I explained to Father that therefore Yale was of course out of the question. He was both angry and amused, and made a good story out of the incident that he relished telling and retelling for years. At least I didn't hurt his feelings; he just marveled at my eccentricity. But he paid me back the evening following the visit with the dean by taking me to Morey's, the famous undergraduate hangout, and proceeding to get pie-eyed. That was bad enough, but after a while he was overcome with sentimentality and began to weep into his drink. Still a virgin when it came to alcohol, I was hideously embarrassed. And the worst of it for him was that the poor, decrepit old waiter had no recollection of anyone named Ambrose Cramer that he had served a mere twenty-five years before, no memory whatever of his long-gone cronies and their musty old high jinks.

After graduation, Father went to work as an intern in the Chicago office of the great eclectic architect David Adler. He became one of the aesthetic young men surrounding Adler, and learned as they did to laugh through their noses (according to Mother) in the manner of their master while at the same time absorbing a great deal about the theory and practice of formal architecture.

Not long after his graduation, the young architectural apprentice, on vacation in the West, met his bride-to-be, Grace Meeker, for the first time at a house on Channel Drive in Montecito belonging to Chicago friends they had in common. I have photographs showing a very formal Father in well-cut three-piece suits (and one, to show his sporting side, in tweedy knickerbockers) and a languid, doe-eyed Mother in very long skirts. I suppose the reason they had never met in Chicago was that Father was several years older than Mother, though it seems odd that they hadn't run into each other. They were married in 1915, I think, and soon moved into a very smart Regency house that Father designed for them in a small square in Chicago.

My brother was born in 1917 in Chicago. By that time Father must have been in service as a naval officer. Soon he was sent to France, where his assignment was to design hangars and the like at our air stations. He enjoyed his time with the Navy, having been spared the horrors of actual warfare, and fell in love with French culture and civilization—so much so that when the Armistice was signed, he chose to stay on in France and pursue his architectural studies in Paris at the Ecole des Beaux-Arts, whose international prestige was at its height. While there, he was made a member of the *Légion d'Honneur* for his wartime services to France.

Mother and little Brosie were sent for, and Father and Mother set up housekeeping in a well-staffed flat near the Parc Monceau. Father studied hard at the Beaux-Arts while Mother, who was a born sightseer, familiarized herself with the charms of Paris.

Upon her graduation from Westover, a prestigious Eastern girls' boarding school, Mother had been sent to Rome for a year to study the history of Italian art and architecture. She had a glorious time there, visiting and in later years remembering and recalling in detail the things that made the Holy City the most fascinating place in the Western world. And here I can't resist adding an aside about what an odd education she and her sister Katharine were provided with. They were taught at home by tutors until at sixteen or so they were packed off to boarding schools in the East—her sister to Ethel Walker, I think. I don't believe Mother learned a thing of value at hers, but in maturity read so intensely in such a variety of areas, and remembered what she read in such minute detail, that she passed for a highly educated woman. But the fragile under-pinnings of it all were starkly revealed in her later years when one day she confesssed to me that she could not figure out her domestic employees' Social Security taxes because she had never been taught *long division.* I told her that was an extraordinary lack considering all the money that had been spent on her education—here I was getting back at comments she had made to *me* over the years—but that she was not to worry because the problem involved multiplica-tion, not division, and that I would buy her a small calculator that would solve all her mathematical problems with virtually no effort on her part. I gave her one the next day. She never even looked at it, let alone used it, but I was glad enough to have it as I insisted upon taking over the mathematical side of her affairs the following week.... When I was a schoolboy complaining about geometry or trigonometry, she told me that she couldn't imagine why mathematics was taught in school since all anybody had to know in real life was how to balance a checkbook. Which she did with minute accuracy, down to the last penny, often struggling for hours to resolve any discrepancies.

What with her household to run and the glories of Paris to explore, not to mention enjoying her little boy Brosie, she must have been a very happy woman indeed, though she saw little of her husband, engrossed in his demanding studies.

In the summer of 1919, Mary's parents decided to take advantage of Gracie's being established in the *ville lumière* to send over her fifteen-year-old sister to acquire a little continental polish before being enrolled at Foxcroft in Virginia. Grandmother had heard that Foxcroft was considered the chicest of the chic among girls' schools. In that connection, Unky, Mary's brother, used to say that, as the school was situated in foxhunting country and girls had to become proficient riders and jumpers, no girl was awarded a diploma until she had suffered at least one major concussion and a broken collarbone. If that was a requirement for graduation, it must have been the only one.

WELL, MY FATHER AND THE PRETTY YOUNG schoolgirl fell madly in love. I don't know any details. It was never the sort of thing anyone in the family volunteered to discuss, and it wasn't a matter I could very well question the principals about, even as I grew older. I don't know, for example, whether Mary was sent over to Paris again before the situation became known; it would seem very likely that the lovers would have wanted urgently to meet again. Mother, of course, was a dutiful guide, and I'm sure spent hours holding forth about the finer points of Notre Dame and the Sainte Chapelle, while Mary, who had even in full maturity the powers of concentration of a kindergartner, cared for nothing but the charming presence of her brother-in-law, being lectured to at the tiresome old Beaux-Arts. Still, he must have earned a summer vacation, and the lovebirds, with the stealth common to guilty lovers, surely found moments and places to be alone together, abetted by one of the servants whom Father had suborned.

What one is sure of is that Mother knew of the sorry business by at least the winter of 1922 and probably well before because I was conceived in late '21, and having a baby, as I mentioned at the beginning of this memoir, was her way of trying to hold the marriage together. Learning the truth must have been a hideous blow to Mother, whose nature was trusting and naive and who loved her husband, though she had discovered early in their marriage that he had a serious drinking problem. And not just to lose his love, but to lose it to a teenage sister! What could be more humiliating, more intolerable? And Father, with his Calvinist Presbyterian conscience—I'm sure he suffered. And drank. And went on loving little Mary Meeker, his sister-in-law.

Which of those involved told the senior Meekers I don't know, but when they learned of it, of course they were hopping mad—chiefly, I am sure, at my father. Mary was forbidden to see her brother-in-law again. That was that. In the fall of 1922 I was born (an *annus mirabilis* not so likely to be remembered by Parisians for that reason as for the fact that Joyce's *Ulysses* was born there and Marcel Proust died there, all in the same year). Nine tense months after my birth, Mother gave up hope of salvaging the ruined marriage and set sail for home. Which brings us back to this book's first page.

Not so long after that, Father brought his architectural studies to a close and, since Mother had established herself in a new life in Santa Barbara, felt free to head back to Chicago, where Mary awaited him in spite of parental prohibitions. Over the next year or two they often met secretly, and in time her parents gave up the vain struggle of trying to make Mary forget him. Instead they forbade them to marry until Gracie herself should marry again; and if they did marry, they were never to have any children (an odd though I suppose understandable prohibition, and sweet music to Father's ears, I am sure).

And out in California, Mother and Frank Lloyd fell in love and were married in the garden of La Villetta in 1927, I think, leaving the way blessedly clear for Father and Mary, the latter now about twenty-three and Father some twelve years older, to marry soon after. I find to my astonishment that I have absolutely no idea of where or when their wedding took place. It must have been a hole-and-corner sort of thing because many, perhaps most, of the relatives on both sides disapproved of the whole affair and would not have wanted to give it their blessing. Grandfather Cramer, for one, who was said to be very fond of Mother, took it hard and held it against his son until he died. But the newlyweds brazened their way as best they could back into the social world of Chicago that they had grown up in.

One may well ask why they didn't move to another city and start a new life together. The answer is an economic one, with two sides to it. Father and his sister Siddy had been brought up to consider themselves the heirs of their two Skinner "aunties," who lived together and shared a fortune of several million dollars bequeathed them by their father, Judge Skinner. With this happy prospect, Father had devoted himself to the study of architecture without any thought that he would have to support himself or anyone else by the practice of it; he saw it rather as an attractive and challenging hobby that would give him an interest and purpose in life. He would design palatial residences of exquisite balance and proportion for those rich friends that he considered worthy of his talents.

Meanwhile, his sister Siddy had moved with her delightful Lake Forest husband, Jim McClure, to live on a gentleman's farm in the country outside of Asheville, North Carolina. There the latter started a cooperative movement dedicated to improving the lives of the bitterly poor farm folk in the region and became an almost saintly figure to them. By nature an irrepressible enthusiast, he got caught up in the boosterism of the heady '20s and, deciding as he looked about that there were fortunes to be made out of the lovely land that surrounded him, persuaded the old ladies to invest their fortune in North Carolina real estate. For a while there was a boom—and then a swift, cataclysmic bust that wiped out their investment. And there went the moneys that were supposed to insulate Father from the buffetings of the world. That was bad enough, but by now he was committed to the practice of very expensive architecture, the only sort he knew anything about. But now it had to support him, and Mary, and those darned boys. And soon after he had stepped out from under the sheltering wing of his master,

David Adler, and had proudly hung out his own architect's shingle, the stock market crashed—the second intolerable blow. What a time to be the sort of architect he had been trained to be—the designer of what today would be multimillion-dollar houses for plutocrats who had lost their all or at best were having to retrench severely in every aspect of their lives! His only chance for architectural commissions was to hang on in Chicago where he and his young bride and their respective parents were widely known among the dwindling group of people who might be counted on to build large, formal houses no matter what the economic climate.

The '30s, which should have been the prime of his architectural career, turned out to be the very worst decade in the entire century for the practice of his profession. He had a terrible time keeping his office force together. One year he would make a lot of money, but the next year there might be no commissions at all, yet the relentless office overhead would continue. One year he was so hard up that he and his wife moved in with the Meekers, where in the evening he would retreat to their bedroom to work on his "stamp collection" (he hated stamps) just to escape from his in-laws. During the decade, he designed houses in Lake Forest and other Chicago suburbs, in Kentucky and Virginia, and of course Constantia in Montecito; he also designed a factory in Chicago. Because he was an eclectic architect, each of his houses was different in appearance, but what they shared were a warm elegance and a marvelous feeling for balance and proportion and grace, as well as a love for detail and an insistence that everything about the house should "work."

In this connection, he had great antipathy to Frank Lloyd Wright, both the man and his work. I remember how pleased he was by his first visit around 1948 to the recently built Taliesin West outside of Scottsdale, where Father and Mary spent their winters after his retirement. The pleasure was stimulated not by the beauty of the structure, but by the fact that it had just been subjected to its first heavy desert cloudburst, and the exotic edifice, supposed to be teeming with young interns bent over their drafting boards, was instead six inches deep in water, with the interns disconsolately formed into bucket brigades. Father fairly danced with delight.... Another time in Scottsdale he was accosted by two young men with long hair while he sat in a parking place downtown at the wheel of his expensive new convertible, his white hair blowing in the sunny breeze; one of them asked, his voice trembling with the emotion of the hero-worshipper, "You're Frank Lloyd Wright, aren't you, sir?" He admitted that he was indeed the very same, and told them to climb aboard if they wanted a ride. Soon they were gushing out their devout appreciation of his *oeuvre*. Then, when he had heard all the fulsome praise that he could endure, he said, or at least he *said* he said, "Boys, I'm going to tell you something I've never told anyone else. But you must promise to keep it to yourselves.... My whole career is a gigantic hoax that I have perpetrated on the American public. I wanted to see if they would fall for it, and bless them, they've gone for it hook, line, and sinker.... Now what do you think of that?" What indeed? Not another word was spoken until he dropped them off, stunned, at their street corner.... I must add that after the great man's death, Father and Mary developed a warm friendship with his widow, Olgivanna, a majestically authoritarian Montenegrin, and with the architects in charge at Taliesin.

IN THE SUMMER OF 1934, when I was eleven, Mother announced one day that Joanie Gray and I were to travel by train together to Chicago to stay with Daddy and Aunt Mary for two weeks. The Chicago World's Fair, "A Century of Progress," was in its second year, and I would love it (even if I didn't love my host and hostess was perhaps implied). Heaven knows who concocted this plan; my guess would be Aunt Mary, perhaps thinking it was time to make a gesture to the little unwanted boy (not knowing that that glorious present from a few years back, the model sailboat, which he had often sailed in the Santa Barbara harbor from a following rowboat, had made a sufficiently fine impression to last a lifetime), and deciding to include sister Katharine's daughter partly to stay in the former's good graces but chiefly, I think, to relieve the pressure of entertaining a single child. It was smart thinking. Certainly it was a comfort, beginning with the exotic, multi-night train ride, to have Joanie along, and fun throughout the stay to share experiences and reactions with her.

I don't remember the meeting at the Chicago station; one would think that it would have remained as a vivid impression, the beginning, after all, of glorious new relationships in my life. Perhaps the reason I don't remember it is that there were so many similar meetings over the following years, in Chicago, in Boston, in New York, in Washington, D.C., in Asheville, North Carolina, in Portland, Maine, and the stations of other cities, each of them marking the start of a new adventure with the "other" set of parents. But Daddy and Aunt Mary don't come to life at all till we are at Peanut Cottage, the charming white two-storey house with a screened porch around the ground floor that the Cramers were renting in Lake Forest, an hour's drive from Chicago. Daddy was of course the man who had taken me to get the sailboat; enough said. But what of Aunt Mary, Mother's young sister married, most oddly, to Daddy? But it wasn't really odd at all, since I had never—at least knowingly—seen Mother and Daddy together. Mother belonged with, perhaps even belonged *to,* Pop.

I fell in love with Aunt Mary the first day. Why, she wasn't an aunt at all; she was my big sister, the sister of any small boy's dreams. Full of fun and laughter, utterly spontaneous and childlike, and so young, so huggably pretty! So enthusiastic, and so quick to laugh appreciatively at anything amusing I might say or do! She was adorable. One of Daddy's pet names for her was Maria, pronounced with a long *i* as in Black Maria, the paddy wagon; that instantly became my name for her and remained so till after my Father's death many years later, after which time she became to me simply Mary, as she was called by almost all who knew her.

And Father, now that I had a chance to get to know him, turned out to be a huge delight as well. When he greeted one, when he smiled, he seemed to exist only to radiate happiness and joy over one's presence. Perhaps he felt he had a good deal to make up for. But if so, he was totally successful. I adored him even as I did Maria. His gusts of playful charm were matchless, even if unsustainable. Luckily for him, he had his office duties to escape to while Maria bore the daily burden of finding things for Joanie and me to do.

Lake Forest was steamily hot, and of course nothing was air-conditioned in those days, but that was a new experience that wasn't going to last forever, so I didn't mind. We played a lot of tennis at country clubs and slipped and slid on *en-tout-cas* courts, an unpleasant novelty. I had thought all Western courts were cement and all Eastern, grass. Now why would anybody want slippery courts? We went for a day cruise on Lake Michigan on the boat of a man named Hammond, said to be the inventor of the Hammond electric organ. We must have been taken to visit Amama at Rathmore, and Aunt Isabelle Ryerson, her daughter and Daddy's beloved stepsister, widowed untimely by her husband's suicide after mental derangement. I say we must have because I have no clear memories of any family visits dating from this stay; they seem all to have blended with memories of subsequent visits to Lake Forest over the years. (The Meekers of course, it being summertime, were in their new house in Montecito.) One almost unbearably exciting day I was sent off with a pleasant middle-aged woman, a Cramer cousin who was known to be if not passionate about baseball, at least interested in it. The trouble was, the White Sox were my team, not the fashionable Cubs, and no well-brought-up Chicagoan ever ventured into Sox territory over on the forbidden South Side. But Margaret Farwell was game, and I had a marvelous time. The experience was everything I expected of major-league baseball, thrilling beyond measure. (Many years later, when the Dodgers had moved to Los Angeles, baseball had ceased to mean anything to me. I've never been to Dodger Stadium in Chavez Ravine, I am ashamed to admit. Maybe if the Dodgers had been an American League team, or if there weren't those notorious traffic jams. Maybe.)

BUT THE REAL EXCITEMENT during our visit was the World's Fair. What a shrewd stroke on the part of my parents to have had our visit coincide with that intoxicating event! Its delights filled our days with either anticipation or its fulfilment. And yet I have few specific memories. The Midway, of course, which was the amusement park section, was my favorite; the little electric bumper cars that entitled one to bump viciously into strangers, including adults, were irresistible. Five years later, at San Francisco's fair, I remember watching with astonishment while my dignified and introverted uncle, Horace Gray, M.D., circled around in his little car, savagely sideswiping strangers with an expression of intense satisfaction on his face, often grinning from ear to ear. And a few months later during that same year, 1939, when I was sixteen, my happiest memory of New York's fair, filled as it was with thought-provoking visions of the future, was the little dodge-'em boats with rubber tires around them that allowed them to be used in the same way as the electric cars with the added advantage that skillful piloting could not only shake up the other pilot but soak him with a shrewdly placed wavelet.

Sally Rand, artfully manipulating fans to cover her nude front and rear, was the most highly publicized feature of the Fair, but I was not allowed to see her. Did anyone succeed in snatching those fans? Not likely; she was a shrewd showwoman. Oddly, I remember with great fondness the Czechoslovakian exhibit, in the picturesque foreign section, with its pink-cheeked women in their peasant dirndls and their men blowing glass into beautiful shapes while I watched entranced. And somewhere there was an exhibit of chimpanzees, who performed with such charm that I wanted desperately to take one back to California with me as a playmate. Somehow I found out that one could be had for fifty dollars, which seemed reasonable enough for a beguiling little brother that I could presumably boss around, and *begged* to be given one. But here my indulgent new parents put down their feet very firmly indeed, and I learned the sad lesson that no one, including newfound and apparently loving parents, is perfect.

By now I am sure that they had come to the same conclusion about me, though I think I was pretty well behaved on the whole. However, one evening I did vomit messily on the pavement outside the Midway; too much excitement was the diagnosis. There was no blame attached, but it cut short a long evening of fun. We drove back to Lake Forest in Daddy's beautiful and superbly elegant Chrysler phaeton with custom coachwork, which elevated him in my eyes because it was such an improvement over Pop's and Mother's lumbering Buicks. It seems to me now as I think back that I had a great many stomach problems of one sort or another when I was very young. I was forever being threatened with or actually subjected to enemas. Does anyone use them now? A fearsome red-rubber bag hung on a hook in my bathroom for years as a continuous threat, ready at a moment's notice to be filled with warm, soapy water and go about its nasty business. "Just hold back a few more moments, dear, and it'll all be over." Then whoosh, and "How do you spell relief?"

Two weeks raced by, and it was time to board the Chief at the station. Daddy had to drive very fast to get us there on time, the big Chrysler squealing rubber. He was invariably behind schedule, I was to find. As was said of Winston Churchill, he always gave a train a sporting chance to get away. In fact, never in his life did he catch or meet a train or arrive at an appointment comfortably on time. And Maria, a punctual Meeker, always had a fit. But we made it, then and on later occasions, but not without tension and drama and recriminations. (A propos Meeker punctuality: Mother was so obsessively punctual that when she was due to be picked up by a friend or relative and taken to a concert or party or whatever, after the appointed time had passed or even before, she would station herself, fuming and muttering, outside the front door or even out in the street, presumably to hasten the arrival by a second or two. And when the miscreant did finally arrive, her relief was so intense that she was all smiles and good cheer and never berated the wretch she had just been condemning to outer darkness a few moments before.)

Just before we boarded the train, Daddy spotted a middle-aged man with red hair on the verge of mounting the steps and murmured to me that he was a corrupt Chicago politician with whom I was under no circumstances to converse. I couldn't keep my eyes off the sleazy stranger the whole trip to Pasadena, and was dying for him to accost me. What would he have said? Perhaps "Vote the straight Democrat ticket, son. And remember, vote early and vote often." Why, I might have been tainted for life! Anyway, I have always liked machine politicians as long as they could deliver the Democratic vote. Wasn't it, after all, the Chicago Daley gang that won the 1960 election for JFK?... Daddy and Maria looked teary-eyed on the platform, and I was close to crying myself. It had been a wonderful introduction to my new parents, and I headed home with a glowing sense of enrichment.

Mother, dying of curiosity, of course wanted to know how things had gone, but I was enough of a politician at eleven to know that I shouldn't tell any more than I had to about these marvelous new people who had come into my life, so I limited myself to answering specific questions and filling in trivial details, but not giving myself away. And that's the way I handled the situation for the rest of Mother's long life. I never let her know how deeply attached I was to her "rivals." And of course I never mentioned Mother to Daddy and Maria except in the most casual way.

MY MEMORIES OF THE CRAMERS from that time on until after World War II are nearly all intertwined with trips we took together, i.e., vacation trips of theirs that they planned to coincide with my vacations from school and college; and these trips, individually and collectively, have for years provided me with some of my most delightful memories. An astonishing degree of harmony prevailed. Of course there were irritations on all sides, but only fleeting ones; no angers, no hot tempers, no hard things said and remembered and regurgitated later. Over the years we all remembered only the funny things, and some of these memories were retold and embellished so often that they attained an almost legendary status. There was nothing else in my growing-up years that gave me the same intense pleasure that these visits and these trips offered me. When I was with Daddy and Maria, there was no greater bliss that I could imagine, and I gave my entire attention to them. I was not the sort of boy who would rather be with his friends in his free time (to my mind, I had a bellyful of my friends during the interminable months at school) or chase girls (mysterious creatures that made me on the whole uncomfortable with their alien interests and attitudes); I wanted nothing so much as to travel with or simply be in the company of these two lovable people who made amusing things happen and who seemed greatly to appreciate my own qualities even as I appreciated theirs.

Over the years we traveled, just the three of us, through French Canada and Maine down to Boston; to Washington, D.C., and the James River plantations in Virginia; to visit our McClure relatives in North Carolina; to New York City with my brother and cousin Joanie Gray just before we caught our ship to Ireland in 1939. Just before the war they came to California to see Brosie and me when we were both living in the Los Angeles area, and invited us for glamorous weekend visits to fancy resorts where they were staying in southern California. When I got my discharge from the Army Air Force, I visited them in Georgetown, D.C., when Father's war-time service was winding down. (A close friend of Adlai Stevenson's, he sought his help in finding a job in wartime Washington, where Stevenson had gone to be assistant secretary of the Navy. Father served with great distinction, helping on one occasion to write a speech for President Roosevelt, and serving as a chief administrator for the Lend-Lease program that did so much to save the United Kingdom in its desperate struggle against the Germans.)

When Father left government service, he was in his mid-fifties and his wife twelve years younger. Maria wanted him to reopen his architectural office in Chicago, but he would have none of it. He was panting to retire. But where? For a couple of years he combed the Eastern seaboard, with me as his companion on one canvassing trip from Massachusetts down through Connecticut. His passion for sailing, held in check for so many years, was bursting its bonds.

I visited him one summer right after his retirement in a wonderful old hotel, the Wentworth-by-the-Sea on the shore in Portsmouth, New Hampshire, of the same period and flavor as the old Hotel del Coronado in San Diego. There he puttered about in the broad river in a very racy day-sailer which seemed a little too "tender," as yachtsmen put it, for his needs. I remember the hotel very happily because twice a week I played exhibition singles with the resident tennis pro while the audience watched and clapped from the hotel's huge veranda. Then he rented a house for the next summer on Marblehead Neck in Massachusetts, the yachting capital of New England, where I visited him with my fiancée. The humidity was so energy-sapping that Maria put her foot down, slammed shut her checkbook, and said if he wanted the coast, it would have to be Maine or nowhere.

Before we visit them in their home in Maine, where they summered joyfully from about 1947 till the end of their days, I want to write a few words about the Cramers' quite different characters and natures, as I came to apprehend them, then and later. Maria was easy to read because everything was on the surface. It seemed she was always in motion and always talking: all extrovert with no reflective tendency; full of herself, yet in a lighthearted, innocent, inoffensive way. Clearly a greatly indulged youngest child, she expected everyone to love her and find her delightful, and for the most part people did; but she could be easily manipulated by flattery, a quality that caused problems in her old age, if not before. But she was not taken in by her husband's flattery because it was often intended to atone for some misdeed committed while he was in his cups. In spite of a hectic quality, she was a good organizer and manager and surprisingly competent in anything she chose to take on; for example, she learned under Daddy's guidance to be the interior decorator in his practice, and she taught herself to be a gourmet cook. She took people at face value, and only rarely did they let her down. Endearingly, she treated servants and tradespeople exactly as she treated her friends; in many cases they *became* her friends. Though she was rarely witty herself, her lively sense of humor enabled her to appreciate wit in others and find rollicking pleasure in comical situations. We loved to make her laugh, Daddy and I.

HIS QUALITIES were those of a complicated and contradictory human being. At his best, he was more attractive than anyone else I have ever known. His interest in others, his irresistible enthusiasm, his quickness to see the humor in a situation and to express it with perfect felicity, his ability to appreciate and compliment others, his exquisite manners, his keen intelligence—these were the essence of his charm and appeal, qualities that almost never faded for me in the thirty-six years of a loving friendship that began with that first visit to Chicago in 1934 and ended only with his death in 1970 in his summer house in Maine at the age of 79. I adored him for as long as I knew him and overlooked his failings even as he seemed to overlook mine.

But he was flawed, more so than most. For one thing, he had a hopelessly addictive nature. If a thing was bad for him but made him feel good, then that thing was something he must have. Alcoholism was a problem that began in college and caused great difficulties for the rest of his life for him and for those who loved him, most especially Maria. In fact, over the years it watered down, if it did not quite kill, that love for him that had started at such an intense level. (Some of the scrapes he got into when drunk were so appalling as to be extremely funny, to Brosie and me at least. I hope I'll have the inclination to relate some of them later in the chapter. At this point I haven't made up my mind.) Early in his marriage to Mother, he had to be sent away to the then-famous establishment in Stockbridge, Massachusetts, of Dr. Austen Fox Riggs, where rich neurotics and addicts lived a simple life compounded, as far as I could tell, of equal parts of Dr. Riggs's wisdom and courses in basket-weaving. Though Daddy paid extravagant lip service to the former and raised only mild objections to the latter, every time he was discharged as cured, like Miniver Cheevy in E.A. Robinson's eponymous poem, he "went on drinking." Years later, in the latter part of his life, his wife sent him several times at ruinous cost to a comparable place in Connecticut called Silver Hill, "Silly Hill" to the irreverent. He enjoyed making friends with his fashionable or even famous fellow-residents, but bent his elbow harder than ever when he returned home to Maine. Maria toyed with putting him in a hard-nosed "institution" but lacked the grit to force it on him. Over the years she must have been sickened by the rustle of new leaves being turned over…and over…and over.

When I was a boy, he was the fiercest smoker I'd ever known. At fifty-six, he was stricken with a terrifying attack of breathlessness diagnosed as emphysema, which plagued him relentlessly and increasingly till his death many years later. He *had* to stop smoking (or stop breathing), but of course he found a nicotine-free life intolerable and persuaded his doctors to prescribe Miltown, one of the earliest of the tranquilizers. Another dependency. For years he hid bottles of Miltown all over his house and slurred his words even when he was swearing honestly he hadn't had a drop to drink. In time he did stop smoking, but alcoholic binges he clung to until, near the end of his life, his doctor painted such a grim picture for him that he was able at last to exorcise the demon.

Chicago is preeminently a city whose social pecking order is based on money. When the fortune he had counted on inheriting was squandered by others on Southern real estate, his hopes for leading the life of a dilettante architect-cum-gentleman esthete-cum-leisured socialite were blasted, leaving him with a good deal of bitterness in his heart. "Life is tough, son, life is tough," he would often say to me as I was growing up during what have been called the "Threadbare 'Thirties." Of course as a Montecito boy I knew better, but I nodded sympathetically.

Because of his background and history, he put far too great a stress on money to suit me. Though he treated everyone he knew with the same charming courtesy, he was far too impressed by people with big money, whether friends or acquaintances or unknowns. He greatly resented having to be supported after his retirement by his wife, though he did say to her in my hearing and with a twinkle in his eye, "I've been supporting you all these years; now it's time for you to take care of me." And she was well able to, since his retirement at the end of the war (from high-level government service in Washington) coincided with the death of her father, my Grandfather Meeker. When in later years I would visit them in their homes in Scottsdale or Camden, Maine, he never failed to identify scornfully those among his friends who were apparently rich men but were in fact supported by their wives. The trouble was, as I could plainly see, that most of those rich women allowed their husbands to behave as though the latter controlled the pursestrings, but Maria most emphatically did not. Having decided (correctly) that he was both self-indulgent and extravagant, she kept him on a tight financial leash. And of course this was a heaven-sent way to punish him for all the trouble his addictive nature had caused her. He confided to me once, when the two of us were on an outing in Arizona and he was an old man wheezing with emphysema, that if he had known as a young fellow just out of Yale that he would lose his inheritance, he would have become a bond salesman instead of an architect. A bond salesman! I drew back and changed the subject. What a concession to conformity, I thought (because, I told myself, that's probably what ninety percent of proper Chicago Yale graduates were doing in those days) and to putting money values first (I have to presume there was lots of money to be made in those days in that curious field). Still, what a way to fill one's precious, irreplaceable days on this earth! I thought none the worse of him for all his obvious sins and transgressions, but *here* my admiration faltered.... I never brought it up. I pretended to myself he never said it, but I had to face the fact that because of the ethos of the world in which he was brought up, he was irremediably conventional at heart. This was a great disappointment to me, but it in no way diminished my love for him.

By way of contrast, as a Montecito youth I felt very little pressure to conform. Of course my horizon was limited and of course Montecito was no microcosm of the big world, but there was within it a marvelously rich variety of human types and occupations and opposing lifestyles to be observed or even copied if one was so inclined. And I soon apprehended that there was no need to have more than a modicum of money to participate fully in that milieu. Manner, intelligence, charm—if one had these, or two of them, or *one* of them, then a person could find a place at the table. Father (as I came to call him when I was old enough to think about responsibilities and goals and the dreary like) was all for what has come to be known as the Protestant work ethic; I was not. Would he have been pro-work if he hadn't been gypped out of his inheritance? Interesting question. I had no real goals when I went to college or when I left it, except that I wanted to be a writer without having to write. My brother had a goal: to become rich. I wanted to be left alone to be myself (whatever that might turn out to mean), and I wanted to have nothing to do with competition or money-making. The idea of having a job, any job, was repulsive. Poor Father; when as a college boy I would pass through Chicago on the way back to California for summer vacation, he would give me a pep talk about the need to find a summer job, stressing the notion that Santa Barbara was a lotus land that would taint me forever if I didn't get cracking and accept my responsibilities. What responsibilities, I wondered? Besides, I didn't know a soul my age who worked in the summer. I would have been profoundly humiliated to have a real honest-to-god paycheck kind of job. In that sense I suppose I was a conformist, but of the rather special Montecito variety. Could one not raise shiftlessness and love of pleasure to an art form? Each summer, I told Father I'd see what could be done (note the sly use of the passive) about getting a job and then swiftly changed the subject. "Life is tough, son." Why should it be? Life is what you make it, I thought. A much nicer cliché.

Only once did I succumb to Father's goading. I had heard that there were jobs for college-boy messengers in the Hollywood studios. I asked my good friend and former Cate classmate Richard de Mille if he thought his father, Cecil B., could get me one (provided there wasn't much work to do and I wouldn't have to give up my tailor-made J. Press coats and flannels for a messenger's—as I envisioned it—whipcord breeches and cap). In due time Richard gave me a sealed envelope from the great man, which I took apprehensively to Paramount. I handed it in and was told politely by a secretary to go back whence I had come. I didn't call them; they didn't call me; and so we both came out winners. Probably Mr. de Mille's letter said something like "Don't touch this slacker. He's just a friend of my son's."

"Well, Father, I tried.... I guess there really aren't any worthwhile jobs in my part of the country." Or anywhere else, I might have added.

IT WAS MARIA who picked out their retirement community in 1947. Together they found a magnificent piece of shore property in Rockport, Maine, next to the larger and better-known town of Camden. The twenty-five acres they bought overlooked a fjord-like harbor, a deep indentation in the highly irregular coast of Maine, with small yachts and lobster boats moored between forested hillsides dotted with just enough cottages and houses to provide visual interest and with the little village of Rockport visible at the upper end of the harbor. The property rose steeply from the rocky shore (though it had its own beach of fine white sand, a great rarity in those parts) to a noble site well above on which there was a large, comfortable Maine farmhouse that would serve to house a caretaker and his family. The slope provided a commanding view up and down the harbor and was the obvious site for their dream house. Strange to say, Father in his late fifties and Mary in her mid-forties, though married twenty years, had never before owned a house of their own except for a weekend cottage in Illinois.

In the nearby village of Rockport, they found an unpretentious but attractive Greek Revival house dating from about 1840, with a central section and two parallel side wings set slightly back, and had it moved a mile or so to the clearing on their new acreage. There Father proceeded to work his architectural magic upon the simple building, improving it to such an extent that it became a noted showplace of the area. The upstairs, nothing but a large attic, he turned into multiple bedrooms with gracefully proportioned dormer windows on both the facade and the harbor-facing rear. They furnished it with antiques, chiefly French and English, that they had collected over many years, and covered the walls with handsome papers, notably a very rare eighteenth-century hand-painted nautical French paper of museum quality that they positioned between the many windows in the dining room. (In a story on the Camden-Rockport area in the July 1991 issue of *Town and Country,* there is a handsome two-page spread of Mary, by then a white-haired *grande dame,* in her elegant dining room, the picture doing full justice to both Mary and the wallpaper.) In all the dozens and dozens of times I entered the gate to 1 Sea Street and crossed the wooden bridge just inside, I never failed to catch my breath when I rounded the bend and looked down the sloping drive to the house, outlined against the harbor and the opposite shore: a vision of prim but mellow New England beauty, with its soft-yellow clapboards, clean white trim, and dark-green shutters, its two gable ends punctuated by tall, slender chimneys of weathered old brick, and the whole placed amid acres of green lawn that set it off to perfection.

From the beginning they involved themselves with Camden-Rockport. Father really didn't know how to relax, except on vacation trips or on the water in a boat. He seemed to me to be a driven man, so different was he from me with my own languid ways. Was he afraid of his inmost thoughts, ridden by guilt? But his lust for activity made him a good citizen. As board vice-president, he worked hard for the improvement of the local hospital that served a wide area, and he did important work for the Searsport Marine Museum. But he became testy with advancing age (though I saw no signs of this; in fact, it seemed to me that the years had mellowed him, at least within the family) and on occasion, primed with alcohol, he would berate his fellow board members for sundry errors or omissions in a way that was not to their liking. The hospital board retaliated by locking him out of his office at the hospital, effectively ending that involvement. Something, too, went very wrong at the Searsport museum. And Brosie, who has summered with his wife at Camden for many years, told me recently that in the local yacht club there hangs a plaque commemorating the service of all the commodores in the club's long history: he observed that every commodore *but one* had served for two consecutive terms. We both are dying to know what misdeed shortened his tenure there, but I suspect that it was a combination of cocktails and ill-chosen words while speechifying at a banquet, for that was the usual ignominious pattern. (When he was being given a farewell dinner in Washington by his colleagues in Lend-Lease, he rose to acknowledge their encomia but unfortunately began to deliver his address facing the bank of mirrors *behind* the lectern. Maria gave him a vicious 180-degree twirl, but tongues must have done a good deal of wagging.) I suppose public speaking made him nervous, and he thought he needed "just a little nip" to steady himself. Woe!

But there was occasional civic testiness even without alcohol. Mary told me after his death that at a Rockport meeting someone's aggressively expressed opinion so outraged him that he had shouted to the fellow, "You should be horsewhipped!" Mary was told about the outburst and gave him hell. Far from chastened, in fact fairly purring with pleasure, he answered, "When you get to be my age, you can say anything you want!" He was about seventy-five at the time. I am nearly seventy-three as I write these words, and I've already started to jump the gun. It's a lovely feeling. I haven't yet threatened fellow board members with horsewhippings, but I do know what he meant, and I reserve the right.

Far and away his most important accomplishment during his thirty-odd Maine summers was his establishment of a process to document in detail and then print in book form records and photographs of all the buildings in the state that were of architectural or historic significance. Maine, a remarkably casual, as well as a very poor, state, had paid little attention to these jewels, and for this reason the task he undertook and ably directed took up much of his time and energy for a long while. He made endless trips to the state capitol, where he became almost a fixture as he strode down the halls waylaying legislators and officials on behalf of his project. And during his Arizona winters he spent half his time writing letters back to Maine to further the cause. Twenty years after his death, I attended a ceremony in Rockport with his widow that celebrated the opening of a park named after Ambrose and Mary

Cramer in honor of their many benefactions to the community, and the chief speaker of the day referred to Father as "a man who did more for the state of Maine than any other person who was not native-born." A singular tribute, and one he would have relished, as he loved praise more than most.

And next to praise, perhaps, he loved yachting. Shortly after they moved into their house in the late 1940s, he was able to buy with what little money he had left a fifty-seven-foot black-hulled John Alden schooner (sailors will know what that means) that became his special joy and delight till the money he needed to maintain her ran out. There is no more beautiful place for sailing, whether cruising or just out for the day, than island-studded Penobscot Bay, and even I, dedicated landlubber that I am, loved every moment aboard *Voyager*. Father was the most genial of skippers, always smiling, infinitely tolerant of ignorance or clumsiness unlike that other skipper whose harsh barking I remembered so well from childhood sails in the Santa Barbara Channel. *Voyager* required the services of a two-man professional crew, and that was more than his slender resources could manage; I suppose he hoped to hang on till his wife one day, equally infatuated with the vessel, might open up her purse. That day never came. "I told you you couldn't afford a boat like that," she said.

One day when I was aboard and we had put in at *Voyager's* mooring in Camden Harbor after a lovely sail to Eggemoggin Reach, the paid captain and the dour little mate, sitting in a skiff tied up alongside, tilted their heads upward to address their employer. "Amos and me's gettin' pretteh shaht o' moneh," the captain boomed out so that people on nearby craft could hear, and Father flushed scarlet. It wasn't long before the schooner was sold to a man from Massachusetts and never seen again in those waters. Father must have made a profit, because ever after he had boats ("stinkpots" as he grew old, but ones with real character) and always a paid hand aboard, for there were things, mechanical things in particular, that no gentleman should concern himself with.

Maria loved Maine, and most especially Camden/Rockport, even more than did her husband. She developed a keen interest in the history of the area and almost single-handedly fanned the embers of the local historical society into a crackling blaze with her passionate interest and generosity. She bought a very old cottage and made it, along with the Mary Meeker Cramer Museum that she built next to it, the focal point of an historical complex next to Route 1 that attracted multitudes of tourists who swarmed there in the summer months for a vision of New England life in olden times. Overseeing the work of the society (and performing a good deal of it herself) was her preoccupation during the forty-five or so summers that she spent in Maine, but with her gregarious nature she also led a very active social life, natural enough because in summer the community pullulated with convivial activities involving the summer residents who migrated there from all over the country to enjoy the natural beauty and the coolest summer climate in the East. In July and August for weeks on end there were at least two or three cocktail parties every day, and there was no question of Maria's missing any of them.

It must have been hard for Father to control himself. "Ambrose, drink your tomato juice. You know how fond you are of it," she would call out to him as he was standing in a nearby group of fellow-guests. Sometimes he heeded her call; sometimes he didn't; but she dragged him along to all the parties because she wanted to keep an eye on him, no matter how great the risk. Who knew what he might be up to if she left him home alone?

He enjoyed her popularity among their social contemporaries (though he did name her "Titania" because, he claimed, she was queen of the fairies) and admired her ability to be on easy terms with the natives, a thing he could never quite manage. Once she rashly accepted an invitation to dinner at the lakeside lodge of the local grocer, who had grown fat and sassy from trading with the summer folk, but the evening did not go well because Father—predictably—couldn't seem to fit in and ended up on a sofa by himself pretending to be engrossed in their hosts' fly-specked old photograph album.

MAINE'S CLIMATE, brutal except in the summer months, required that they spend the rest of the year somewhere else, and after years of brief, joyless winter vacations in Florida during Father's working years, they tried Arizona, spending a few retirement winters in the Camelback Inn in Scottsdale before buying a pleasant house with a pool set in ten acres of suburban desert under Mummy Mountain in Paradise Valley, next to but less urban than Scottsdale. Father breathed better there than anywhere else and kept up his Maine involvements with a stupendous daily correspondence, while Maria greatly enjoyed horseback riding in the desert (after Father's death, she bought or bred a half-dozen or so American Saddle-bred show horses, complete with trainer, and loved the competitive thrill of horse shows in Arizona and California; expensive hobby though it was, it was probably far less expensive than Father had been). They led an active social life with fellow sunseekers ("snowbirds," as they were called locally) from the East and Chicago.

And of course they had houseguests. One of them was Maria's widowed elder sister, Katharine Gray (there must have been an important conference in Phoenix for Planned Parenthood or Hospice or both, for Aunt K. would never have bothered with the desert on its own merits). Mary was very fond of Aunt Katharine in spite of the fact that the latter, ten years her elder, bossed her unremittingly. Father resented having his wife treated like an irresponsible and even naughty child, while Aunt Katharine nursed her own resentment of my father for the devastation he had caused with his abandonment of one sister for another. It was amusing to see them together, each trying, but not very hard, to mask a strong dislike for the other. Aunt K., in her effort to be cheerily friendly to her brother-in-law, came across as arch and coy and hostile, all at the same time. Father was offended and irritated by her manner and used to refer to her with deep satisfaction as "your Aunt Sappy" when he was with Brosie or me. But not long before he died, they had a mellow and altogether delightful lunch together without Maria in one of Scottsdale's smart restaurants. Father returned home to his wife smiling broadly and announced, "You know, your sister is really a very attractive woman.... I think I'll marry her, and then I'll have had all three of you!"

AND SO LIFE WENT ON for the most part very agreeably, as they rotated households according to the season. Then early one morning in November of 1970, Mary telephoned from Maine to say that Father had died in the night, soon after his seventy-ninth birthday, just as they were readying themselves for the long drive to Arizona (Father got claustrophobia on planes). He had been feeling weak lately, and a few nights before his death she had come upon him in his pyjamas, kneeling in prayer beside his bed.

On a tight schedule, Brosie and I flew on together a week or two later from Santa Barbara, arriving at the house in Rockport just as the family party was leaving for the funeral. The countless Episcopal funeral services I have attended over the years have fused together in my mind with the result that Father's made no distinct impression on me, even though the church, at least, was an unfamiliar one. I was a pallbearer, and I remember the tears trickling down my cheeks as I looked straight ahead past all the faces while we carried the heavy coffin through the doors to a hearse, bound for a graveyard burial in the rustic Camden cemetery a mile or so away.

There was a gathering at the house of Cramer relatives who had arrived from Chicago and North Carolina, attractive people we hadn't seen for years. The atmosphere was more convivial than sorrowful, perhaps because Father had so obviously been living on borrowed time as his emphysema worsened, dragging down his overall condition and making his days a burden to him. Still, he had given much pleasure, joy even, to the members of his extended family, and all of those present expressed feelings of loss.

I see Mary, dressed in black and teary-eyed, sitting upright on the sofa in the library, poring over letters of condolence that have recently arrived. I take it that the ones read earlier were conventional in their expressions of regret, but among a batch of new arrivals is one from a Chicago cousin of hers, and she thrusts it forward. "Look at this, Nevie. I think it's just dreadful! It's from Cousin Eleanor. She says, 'But of course you and I, Mary, were aware of the dark side of Ambrose's character.' What on earth does she mean? And what a thing to say now, anyway, even if it were true, which it isn't!"

After a lively dinner party at Mary's house to entertain the out-of-town people, Brosie and I drove to the place where we were staying, thinking this was no time to burden Mary with houseguests. Looking out on Camden harbor was an attractive bookshop that we had patronized in past years but that had now turned its two upper floors into delightful harbor-facing bedrooms for travellers. Well oiled from Mary's dinner party, we had each brought along from her pantry two partial bottles of whatever we drank in those days, probably bourbon for him and vodka for me, to tide us over till sleep time. We began to reminisce about this and that, laughing helplessly and of course drinking as we laughed. The bourbon bottle before long was exhausted; it must have had a lower level to start with than my vodka. What to do? No Cramer can stop drinking until he is fully unwound, and Brosie was in no mood to quit. The state-run liquor store had closed hours before.... Aha! There was a light showing under the door of the proprietor, who like us slept on the premises. Brosie knocked boldly at the door, which was eventually opened by the poor pyjama-clad man with rumpled hair and a dazed look. Yes, he did have a bottle of bourbon, and yes, he would be more than willing to let his guest have it. Bubbling with satisfaction, Brosie returned to our room, and we picked up where we had left off, boozing and laughing (but at least not wenching) far into the night.

The next morning we each guiltily bought books from the "enabling" proprietor, and Brosie presented him with a fifth of premium bourbon he had procured the moment the liquor store opened. Our accounts squared, we could face the world, at least after slipping on dark glasses.

I don't remember exactly how the day passed, but I think we took Mary out to lunch at a favorite restaurant of hers, and I had a chance for the first time to savor the dry air and lovely crystalline light of Maine in October, so different from the softer, blurred air of summertime. We dined again at Mary's to say goodbye to the relatives who had flown in for the funeral. On our way out, because it was late, I snitched another partial bottle of vodka while Brosie knew he was returning to the comforting remains of the bottle he had borrowed from our host at the bookstore inn. Once there, we began again to reminisce; not so strange, really, since we almost never ran into each other in Montecito because of the different patterns of our lives. And we began again to laugh and of course to fill and refill our toothbrush glasses. Suddenly Brosie's bottle was empty again. What to do *now?* Well, said our befuddled brains, same problem, same solution. At eleven o'clock Brosie knocked at the poor wretch's door again. "Gee, I know this is terrible, but could I borrow that bottle of bourbon back?" He could and he did, and it was nearly dawn before we turned off the lights. I don't think we have ever had such a good time together, before or since. It wasn't till years later that I dared to tell Mary about it because I thought the whole thing was so absurdly amusing; and fortunately she agreed, pleased that Father's death had brought us together so happily, yet not seeing that it was Father's genes that had brought us together in just that particular way.

FOUR YEARS LATER, in 1974, my wife Pat and I are visiting my daughter, Kendal Bazemore, and her husband in San Anselmo in Marin County. We've had a very merry night on the town, and for some reason we are staying with Kendal and David rather than at the motel where we usually put up. They have charitably given us their bedroom while they doss down in their living room on a convertible sofa I had bought for them a day or two before; perhaps the reason we are staying with them is to see them break it in, not to mention saving $100 a night at the motel. As we undress, they call out from the living room that the sofa is a success, it makes a fine bed. I close the door for privacy and climb contentedly into our borrowed bed. I close my eyes…and suddenly I am assailed by a vision of my father a week before he died as described to me by Mary when she first told me of his death: he is in his pyjamas, hauntingly frail, with his white head bowed and his neat small hands folded in prayer like a child's…. What is he thinking, the supplicant? Does he know how close death is? Is he satisfied with what he has done with his life? With his Presbyterian conscience, he must feel he has much to atone for. Does he remember at that moment that the cornerstone of the Christian faith is forgiveness? Suddenly what I see as the pathos of his life overwhelms me, and I begin to sob uncontrollably, harder than I have ever cried. I feel as though I will never stop, that there is an undiminishable well of tears inside me.

I knew how much he had loved me; but did he know how

much I loved him?... I have written this chapter for him. It would embarrass him frightfully to read it, but he would enjoy it all the same because it speaks of my love for him. And his sense of humor, thank God, was even stronger than his sense of propriety. Mine, too, thanks to him; for how else could I have written this book?